"The volume [is] an original contribution to scholarship, especially at a time when Ethiopia is increasingly of interest to international audiences."
— ***Jan Erk***, *Leiden University, Netherlands*

"[T]his book is very timely and capable of informing the [political] debates currently taking place in Ethiopia."
— ***Zemelak Ayele***, *Addis Ababa University, Ethiopia*

Eurasian Empires as Blueprints for Ethiopia

This book is a contribution to the global history of the transfer of political ideas, as exemplified by the case of modern Ethiopia.

Like many non-European nation-states, Ethiopia adopted a Western model of statehood – that is, the nation-state. Unlike the postcolonial polities that have retained the mode of statehood imposed on them by their colonial powers, Ethiopia was never successfully colonized, leaving its ruling elite free to select a model of 'modern' (Western) statehood. In 1931, via Japan, it adopted the model of unitary, ethnolinguistically homogenous nation-state, in turn copied by Tokyo in 1889 from the German Empire (founded in 1871). Following the Ethiopian Revolution (1974) that overthrew the imperial system, the new revolutionary elite promised to address the 'nationality question' through the marxist-leninist model. The Soviet model of ethnolinguistic federalism (originally derived from Austria-Hungary) was introduced in Ethiopia, first in 1992 and officially with the 1995 Constitution. To this day the politics of modern Ethiopia is marked by the tension between these two opposed models of the essentially Central European type of statehood. The late 19th-century 'German-German' quarrel on the 'proper' model of national statehood for Germany – or more broadly, modern Central Europe – remains the quarrel of Ethiopian politics nowadays.

The book will be useful for scholars of Ethiopian and African history and politics, and also offers a case in comparative studies on the subject of different models of national statehood elsewhere.

Asnake Kefale is an associate professor of political science and international relations at Addis Ababa University, Addis Ababa, Ethiopia.

Tomasz Kamusella is a reader (*professor extraordinarius*) in modern history at the University of St Andrews, Scotland, UK.

Christophe Van der Beken is an associate professor of constitutional law, federalism and human rights at Addis Ababa University, Addis Ababa, Ethiopia.

Routledge Studies in Modern History

Nietzsche, Heidegger and Colonialism
Occupying South East Asia
R.B.E. Price

Atlantic Crossroads
Webs of Migration, Culture and Politics between Europe, Africa, and the Americas, 1800-2020
José Moya

Food History
A Feast of the Senses in Europe, 1750 to the Present
Edited by Sylvie Vabre, Martin Bruegel and Peter J. Atkins

Engaging with Historical Traumas
Experiential Learning and Pedagogies of Resilience
Edited by Nena Močnik, Ger Duijzings, Hanna Meretoja, and Bonface Njeresa Beti

Chinese Theatre Troupes in Southeast Asia
Touring Diaspora 1900s —1970s
Zhang Beiyu

Eurasian Empires as Blueprints for Ethiopia
From Ethnolinguistic Nation-State to Multiethnic Federation
Asnake Kefale, Tomasz Kamusella and Christophe Van der Beken

For more information about this series, please visit:
https://www.routledge.com/history/series/MODHIST

Eurasian Empires as Blueprints for Ethiopia
From Ethnolinguistic Nation-State to Multiethnic Federation

Asnake Kefale, Tomasz Kamusella and Christophe Van der Beken

LONDON AND NEW YORK

First published 2021
by Routledge
2 Park Square, Milton Park, Abingdon, Oxon OX14 4RN

and by Routledge
52 Vanderbilt Avenue, New York, NY 10017

Routledge is an imprint of the Taylor & Francis Group, an informa business

© 2021 Asnake Kefale, Tomasz Kamusella and Christophe Van der Beken

The right of Asnake Kefale, Tomasz Kamusella and Christophe Van der Beken to be identified as authors of this work has been asserted by them in accordance with sections 77 and 78 of the Copyright, Designs and Patents Act 1988.

All rights reserved. No part of this book may be reprinted or reproduced or utilised in any form or by any electronic, mechanical, or other means, now known or hereafter invented, including photocopying and recording, or in any information storage or retrieval system, without permission in writing from the publishers.

Trademark notice: Product or corporate names may be trademarks or registered trademarks, and are used only for identification and explanation without intent to infringe.

British Library Cataloguing-in-Publication Data
A catalogue record for this book is available from the British Library

Library of Congress Cataloging-in-Publication Data
Names: Asnake Kefale, 1970– author. | Kamusella, Tomasz, author. | Beken, Christophe van der, author.
Title: Eurasian empires as blueprints for Ethiopia : from ethnolinguistic nation-state to multiethnic federation / Asnake Kefale, Tomasz Kamusella and Christophe Van der Beken.
Description: Abingdon, Oxon ; New York, NY : Routledge, 2021. | Series: Routledge studies in modern history | Includes bibliographical references and index.
Identifiers: LCCN 2020057614 (print) | LCCN 2020057615 (ebook) |
Subjects: LCSH: Ethiopia—Politics and government—20th century. | Ethiopia—Politics and government—1991– | Ethiopia—Foreign relations—20th century. | Ethiopia—History—20th century.
Classification: LCC DT386 .K44 2021 (print) | LCC DT386 (ebook) | DDC 963/.05—dc23
LC record available at https://lccn.loc.gov/2020057614
LC ebook record available at https://lccn.loc.gov/2020057615

ISBN: 978-0-367-74479-3 (hbk)
ISBN: 978-1-003-15809-7 (ebk)

Typeset in Times New Roman
by Apex CoVantage, LLC

Contents

List of contributors	ix
List of figures	xi
List of tables	xii
List of acronyms	xiii
Preface	xvii
Acknowledgments	xx

Introduction   1
Modern Ethiopia: the beginnings 1
Transfer of ideas: from Central Europe to Ethiopia 7
Antecedents and terminology 12

The 1931 Constitution: the importation of Western concepts via Japan   23
Nation building and assimilation: the 1955 Revised Constitution and the 1974 Draft Constitution 28

From the Soviet Union to Ethiopia's ethnoterritorial federalism   35
Contesting ethnolinguistic homogenization: the Soviet Union as an inspiration 35
Comparing Soviet and Ethiopian constitutional approaches to ethnicity 38
The 'ownership' of ethnoterritorial units 44
Extensive rights but limited autonomy 48
The incessant rise of ethnic demands 50

Conclusion 56

Sociopolitical timeline of modern Ethiopia 80

Bibliography 110
Index 132

Contributors

Asnake Kefale is an associate professor of political science and international relations at Addis Ababa University, Addis Ababa, Ethiopia. His research interests include federalism and conflict management, political economy, migration and regional politics in the Horn of Africa. His recent publications include 'Federalism and Regional Politics in Africa' in *Oxford Research Encyclopedia* (2019) and 'Shopping for Ideas to Unlock Africa's Economic Potential' in the *Africa Review of Books* (2018). He coauthored *Remittance and Household Socio-economic Well-Being: The Case of Ethiopian Labour Migrants to the Republic of South Africa and the Middle East* (2018), and his 2013 monograph *Federalism and Ethnic Conflict in Ethiopia: A Comparative Regional Study* was reissued in 2019.

Tomasz Kamusella is a reader (*professor extraordinarius*) in modern history at the University of St Andrews, Scotland, United Kingdom. He specializes in the interdisciplinary study of language politics and nationalism in modern Central Europe. His recent English-language publications include the monographs *Ethnic Cleansing During the Cold War: The Forgotten 1989 Expulsion of Turks from Communist Bulgaria* (2018), *The Un-Polish Poland, 1989 and the Illusion of Regained Historical Continuity* (2017) and *Creating Languages in Central Europe During the Last Millennium* (2014). He also initiated and coedited the following volumes: *The Social and Political History of Southern Africa's Languages* (2018), *The Palgrave Handbook of Slavic Languages, Identities and Borders* (2016) and *Creating Nationality in Central Europe, 1880–1950: Modernity, Violence and (Be) Longing in Upper Silesia* (2016). In 2019, a bilingual – that is, English-Silesian – edition of his stories, *Styknie/Limits*, came off the press.

Christophe Van der Beken is an associate professor of constitutional law, federalism and human rights at Addis Ababa University, Addis Ababa,

Ethiopia. His areas of expertise and research interests include comparative constitutional law, federalism, minority rights, local government and good governance. His recent publications include 'Balancing between Empowerment and Inclusion: Multi-national Federalism and Citizenship Rights in Ethiopia' in the *African Journal of International and Comparative Law* (2019), 'Subnational Constitutional Autonomy, Local Government, and Constitutionalism in Ethiopia' in C. M. Fombad and N. Steytler's edited volume *Decentralization and Constitutionalism in Africa* (2019), alongside his own monograph *Completing the Constitutional Architecture: A Comparative Analysis of Sub-national Constitutions in Ethiopia* (2017).

NB: The authors' names are given in alphabetic order, though it may not be obvious at first glance. Personal names tend to be binomial both in Ethiopia and in Europe. However, in the latter case, they consist of a given (first) name and a surname (family name, last name). On the other hand, in Ethiopia a person's name consists of two or more given names. Usually the second (or last) given name is that of a person's father (or another parent), while the third of a grandfather (grandparent). Hence, this name is a kind of 'patronymic' – that is, a given name in the function of a patronymic (Fikru Helebo 2007). In Europe, when personal names are listed, they are given in the alphabetic order of the surnames. On the other hand, in Ethiopia, the alphabetic order is applied to the initial name of the person's entire binomial (multinomial) name (Gupta 1992). That is the case of Asnake Kefale, which is an Ethiopian name. Tomasz Kamusella is a typical European binomial name. Furthermore, in Europe, some surnames are composite, as in the case of Christophe Van der Beken. In such a case, the alphabetic order may be applied either to the nominal element of the surname (for instance, 'Beken') or to the initial preposition (e.g., 'Van'). The choice is dictated either by the legislation of a given country or by personal choice.

Figures

0.1	Ethiopia in the mid-19th century	2
0.2	Ottoman Egypt's empire in 1880	3
0.3	Menelik's campaigns, 1889–1896	5
0.4	Menelik's campaigns, 1897–1904	6
1.1	People's Democratic Republic of Ethiopia, 1987–1991	32
2.1	Administrative regions and zones of Ethiopia in 2000	53

Tables

0.1	Terminology of ethnolinguistic nationalism across languages	16
0.2	Pyramids of autonomous national (ethnolinguistically defined) territories	19
3.1	Transfer of the two models of statehood from Central Europe to Ethiopia	67
3.2	Officially recognized ethnic groups in Ethiopia	68
3.3	National autonomous territorial entities in federal Ethiopia (in early 2019)	69

List of acronyms

NB: Many acronyms – though derived from organizations' names in Amharic (or some other of Ethiopia's languages) – are actually based on the English translations of these organizations' names. For practical reasons, English has been the most important foreign language. To this day, in Ethiopia, English is the sole medium of university-level education and a language of instruction in secondary schools.

ADP, or the Amhara Democratic Party; in Amharic, አማራ ዴሞክራሲያዊ ፓርቲ *āmara dēmokirasīyawī paritī*.

ANDP, or the Afar National Democratic Party; in Amharic, የአፋር ብሔራዊ ዴሞክራሲያዊ ፓርቲ *ye'āfar biḫērawī dēmokirasīyawī paritī*.

BDP, or the Benishangul-Gumuz Democratic Party; in Amharic, ቤኒሻንጉል ጉሙዝ ሀዝቦች ዴሞክራሲያዊ ፓርቲ *bēnīshanigul gumuz hiziboch dēmokirasīyawī paritī*.

CPSU, or the Communist Party of the Soviet Union; in Russian, Коммунистическая партия Советского Союза *Kommunisticheskaia partiia Sovetskogo Soiuza* – that is, የሶቭየት ህብረት ኮሚኒስት ፓርቲ *yesoviyet hibiret komīnīsit paritī* in Amharic.

Derg, *see* **Soviet-Derg**

EC, or the Ethiopian calendar; in Amharic, የኢትዮጵያ ዘመን አቆጣጠር *ye'ītiyop'iya zemen āk'ot'at'er*[1] (Fritsch 1999). It is seven to eight years 'behind' the Western (Gregorian) calendar. Hence, 2019 is 2011 EC from January to September, or 2012 EC from September to December (cf Current 2019; Ethiopian Calendar 2019).

EPLF, or the Eritrean People's Liberation Front; in Tigrinya, ህዝባዊ ግንባር ሃርነት ኤርትራ, *hizibawī ginbar harinet ēritira*, and in Arabic, الجبهة الشعبية لتحرير إريتريا *aljabhat alshaebiat litahrir 'iiritria*.

EPRDF, or the Ethiopian People's Revolutionary Democratic Front; in Amharic, የኢትዮጵያ ሕዝቦች አብዮታዊ ዴሞክራሲያዊ ግንባር *ye'ītiyop'iya ḥiziboch ābiyotawī dīmokirasīyawī ginibar*. The EPRDF is composed of the ADP, ODP, TPLF and SEPDM. In late 2019, the EPRDF was transformed into the Prosperity Party, but the TPLF decided to stay away.

EPRP, or the Ethiopian People's Revolutionary Party, known in Amharic as the የኢትዮጵያ ሕዝባዊ አብዮታዊ ፓርቲ *Yethiopia Hizbawi Abyotawi Pariti*, hence also abbreviated as ኢሕአፓ *īḥi'āpa*; founded in 1972 in West Berlin, West Germany.

ESM, or the Ethiopian Student Movement; in Amharic, የኢትዮጵያ ተማሪዎች ንቅናቄ *ye'ītiyop'iya temarīwoch nik'inak'ē*. Importantly, the term ESM does not refer to any specific organization but rather to the spontaneous grassroots university and secondary school student opposition movement against the Haile Selassie government, which emerged at the turn of the 1970s.

GPDM, or the Gambela People's Democratic Movement; in Amharic, የጋምቤላ ሕዝቦች ዴሞክራሲያዊ ንቅናቄ *yegamibēla hiziboch dēmokirasīyawī nik'inak'ē*.

HNL, or the Harari National League; in Amharic, የሐረሪ ብሔራዊ ሊግ *yeharerī biḫērawī līg*, in Harari, ዚሐረሪ መሐዲያ ሊግ *zīḫārerī mehādīya līgi*.

LN, or the League of Nations – that is, የመንግሥታቱ ማህብር *yemenigišitatu mahibir* in Amharic.

MEISON, or the All-Ethiopia Socialist Movement. This acronym (መኢሶን *me'īson*) is derived from the organization's Amharic-language name መላ ኢትዮጵያ ሶሻሊስት ንቅናቄ *mela ītiyop'iya soshalīsiti nik'inak'ē*, founded by members of the Ethiopian Student Movement (ESM) in 1968 in Hamburg, West Germany.

NDRE, or the program of the National Democratic Revolution of Ethiopia (1976); in Amharic, የኢትዮጵያ ብሔራዊ ዲሞክራሲያዊ አብዮት ፕሮግራም *ye'ītiyop'iya biḫērawī dīmokirasīyawī ābiyot pirogram*. In other English-language publications, it is also referred to as the Program for the National Democratic Revolution (PNDR)

OAU, or the Organization of African Unity; in Amharic, የአፍሪቃ አንድነት ድርጅት *ye'āfirīk'a ānidinet dirijit*. The OAU was established in 1963 in Addis Ababa.

ODP, or the Oromo Democratic Party; in Oromo, *Paartiin Dimokraatawa Oromoo*.

PDRE, or the People's Democratic Republic of Ethiopia (1987–1991); in Amharic, የኢትዮጵያ ሕዝባዊ ዲሞክራሲያዊ ሪፐብሊክ *ye'ītiyop'iya ḥizibawī dīmokirasīyawī rīpebilīk*. The name followed the pattern of the official names of the Soviet bloc's member states, or 'people's democracies' (The People's 1981) – for instance, the Polish People's Republic (in Polish, *Polska Rzeczpospolita Ludowa*), the Romanian People's Republic (in Romanian, *Republica Populară Romînă*) or the People's Republic of Bulgaria (in Bulgarian, Народна Република България *Narodna Republika Bılgariia*).

PP, or the Prosperity Party; in Amharic, ብልጽግና ፓርቲ *bilits'igina paritī*, and in Oromo, *Paartii Badhaadhiinaa*. The PP was founded in 2019 on the basis of the EPRDF, but without the TPLF. The following parties joined the PP: the ADP, the ANDP, the BDP, the GPDM, the HNL, the ODP, the SEPDM and the SPDP.

SEPDM, or the Southern Ethiopian People's Democratic Movement; in Amharic, ደቡብ ኢትዮጵያ ህዝቦች ዴሞክራሲያዊ ንቅናቄ *debubi ītiyop'iya hiziboch dēmokirasīyawī nik'inak'ē*.

Soviet-Derg, or council. In Amharic, the term ደርግ *derg* 'committee or council' is the translation of the Russian term совет *sovet* 'council,' usually rendered as 'Soviet' in English. (In the context of the late First World War, the Russian term *soviet* was borrowed from the German *Rat* 'council,' then employed in their names by numerous councils ['soviets'] of soldiers, workers and peasants founded from Alsace to Galicia and from Finland to Greece.) In literature, the term *Derg* was established for referring to the Soviet ('communist', 'socialist') regime of Ethiopia. Between 1974 and 1987, it was the preferred shorthand name for Soviet Ethiopia, officially known as the Provisional Military Government of Socialist Ethiopia – that is, the የሕብረተሰብአዊት ኢትዮጵያ ጊዜያዊ ወታደራዊ መንግሥት *yeḥibiretesebi'āwīt ītiyop'iya gīzēyawī wetaderawī menigišit*. However, using this Amharic translation of the term 'Soviet' – or Derg – instead of the anglicized Russian term 'Soviet' makes one oblivious to the fact that Derg Ethiopia was a member of the Soviet bloc. Hence, in this study, we emphasize this unduly often-forgotten connection by using the combined adjective 'Soviet-Derg,' instead of 'Derg' alone, for referring to communist (Soviet, socialist, communist) Ethiopia. In 1987, the official name of Soviet-Derg Ethiopia was changed to **PDRE**. The adopted novel usage 'Soviet-Derg' should not make readers and researchers oblivious to the fact that it took about a year and a half before the Soviet-Derg managed to establish a working alliance with the Soviet Union (SU). Furthermore, instead of using the simplistic catch-all term 'communism' (or ኮሚኒዝም *komīnīzim* in Amharic) for characterizing the SU and the Soviet Bloc's countries, these polities themselves, including Ethiopia, in their own documents and publications, claimed that they were introducing the sociopolitical and economic system of 'socialism' (or ሶሻሊዝም *soshalīzim* in Amharic). This kind of Soviet socialism de facto meant the Soviet-style system of 'really existing socialism' (Benner 1995), steeped in the SU's ideology of marxism-leninism (or ማርክሲዝም-ሌኒኒዝም *marikisīzim-lēnīnīzim* in Amharic).

SNNPR, or the Southern Nations, Nationalities and Peoples' Region; in Amharic, የደቡብ ብሔር ብሔረሰቦችና ህዝቦች ክልል *yedebub biḫēr biḫēresebochina hiziboch kilil.*

SPDP, or the Somali People's Democratic Party; in Somali, *Xisbiga Dimuqraadiga Shacbiga Soomaalida.*

TPLF, or the Tigray People's Liberation Front; in Tigrinya, ሕዝባዊ ወያነ ሓርነት ትግራይ *həzbawi wäyanä harənnät təgray*, literally 'Popular Struggle for the Freedom of Tigray,' commonly abbreviated as ወያነ *wäyanä* 'Struggle.'

UN, or the United Nations (Organization) – that is, የተባበሩት መንግሥታት ድርጅት *yetebaberut menigišitat dirijit* in Amharic.

WPE, or the Workers' Party of Ethiopia; in Amharic, የኢትዮጵያ ሠራተኞች ፓርቲ *ye'ītiyop'iya šeratenyoch parit*ī, abbreviated as ኢሠፓ *īšepa.*

Preface

The origins of this study go back the 24th Annual Conference of the Centre for Russian, Soviet, Central and East European Studies, cohosted with the Institute for Transnational and Spatial History, at the University of St Andrews in Scotland. This conference, held on 29 May 2015, was titled 'Between Federalism, Autonomy and Centralism: Central and Eastern Europe in the 20th and 21st Centuries.' It was organized by Tomasz Kamusella with the assistance of Tadek (Tadeusz) Wojtych (now at Cambridge University). This event featured nine speakers, including a specialist on Roma history, Elena Marushiakova-Popova (Bulgarian Academy of Sciences); a historian of the British Union, Colin Kidd (St Andrews University); and a renowned journalist with a long-standing focus on Scotland and Central Europe, Neil Ascherson (Lawson and Wojtych 2015). The follow-up discussion brought about the topic of the transfer of ideologies and of models of statehood across the world in the process of 'globalized modernization' during the past two centuries. Michael Talbot's (Greenwich University, London) lecture tackled this issue directly by delving into how, under the Western influence, the non-national Ottoman category of *millet* ملت (or non-territorial autonomy for an ethnoreligious group) was made into the present-day Turkish-language term for the word 'nation,' defined in the Central European manner, as all the speakers (or speech community) of Turkish.

Meanwhile, thanks to the good offices of Fernand de Varennes (at present serving in the capacity of United Nations Special Rapporteur on Minority Issues), with whom Tomasz Kamusella had met at the European Center of Minority Issues (ECMI) in Flensburg, Germany, the latter had an opportunity to establish cooperation with a specialist in African law, Christophe Van der Beken, then based in the Ethiopian Civil Service University in Addis Ababa (cf Van der Beken 2012). In 1991, Tomasz had chanced, in a book on Coptic art, upon a picture of a rock church, Lalibela (ላሊበላ) (Bourguet 1991: 268), and since that moment, he has wanted to visit Ethiopia. Another inspiration and an Ethiopian connection with Central Europe was the tantalizing piece of information that Tomasz learned in 1998: the silver Maria Theresia thaler, first minted in Vienna in 1741, used to be the preferred form of currency in Ethiopia between the mid-18th century and shortly after World War II (Semple 2005; Tschoegl 2001). What is more, during the work on this study, Tomasz chanced upon an excellent Ukrainian-language novel on the Soviet involvement in Ethiopia, written by a former army translator, then from Soviet Ukraine (Synhaivskii 2016).

On Christophe's invitation, in early 2016, Tomasz delivered two lectures at the Ethiopian Civil Service University: 'The Difficult Marriage of Diversity and Democracy in Central and Eastern Europe After 1989' and 'Is Federalism Conducive for Furthering Diversity and Protecting Minorities? A View from Central and Eastern Europe.' In the ensuing discussion, it turned out that the 20th-century Ethiopian tension between the ethnolinguistically homogenous and centralized nation-state and ethnolinguistic (ethnoterritorial) federalism is eerily reminiscent of the discussion on the 'appropriate' form of national statehood, as had been conducted in Central Europe since the 19th century. In their subsequent email correspondence, Christophe and Tomasz talked about the possibility of idea transfer in this regard, namely from Central Europe to Ethiopia.

Another inspiration for the discussion stemmed from Tomasz's interest in how Japan borrowed the model of the ethnolinguistic nation-state from the German Empire in the late 19th century. Drawing on this well-documented transfer of state-building and (ethnolinguistic) nation-building expertise, he proposed that during the interwar period such a model of ethnolinguistic national statehood might spread further afield – that is, from Japan to Southeast Asia. On 5 September 2014, Tomasz presented on this hypothesis during the MEXT Funded Research Project Second Symposium: Standard Norms in Written Languages – Historical and Comparative Studies Between East and West, held in the Institute of Mongolian Studies at the University of Inner Mongolia in Hohhot, China (Hohhot 2014). Two years later, his talk, titled 'Are Central Europe, and East and Southeast Asia Alike? The Normative Isomorphism of Language, Nation and State,' was published in the conference's proceedings (Kamusella 2016) in English and also in Japanese and Chinese translations.

Finally, after Christophe's move to Addis Ababa University, he decided to pool his own expertise with Tomasz's for the sake of probing into the history and potential paths of the transfer of 20th-century Ethiopia's two opposed models of national statehood from Central Europe to this country. Serendipitously, Christophe's colleague Asnake Kefale (Addis Ababa University), who has an in-depth knowledge of the history and legal practices of Ethiopian federalism and imperial state centralism (cf Kefale 2013), expressed an interest in joining the project. Apart from their own fields of research, these three scholars brought to the project their knowledge of different languages written in a variety of scripts, through which ideas were channeled from Central Europe via Asia to Ethiopia. All too often – and quite regrettably for that matter – the history and politics of Ethiopia, alongside the country's links with the rest of the world, are analyzed and presented almost exclusively through sources and publications written in English with the use of the Latin (Roman) alphabet. This myopic approach obfuscates both the aforementioned channels of idea transfers and the multiethnic, polyglot and multiscriptal character of Ethiopia. Hopefully this study can serve as a modest corrective in this regard.

This brief book is the fruit of Asnake, Christophe and Tomasz's collaboration on the history and practices of the transfer of models of national statehood from Central Europe to Ethiopia during the 20th century. They began researching these issues and writing the study in late 2018, despite their having to shoulder heavy teaching loads and administrative duties at their respective universities.

This kind of near-instantaneous intercontinental cooperation and comparative reflection on a global scale would have been much more difficult to attain and carry out two decades ago, when the internet and email were not available. This possibility is a hallmark of 'late modernity.' On the other hand, the 'first globalization' of the turn of the 20th century allowed for the worldwide circulation of ideas, courtesy of stable and regular maritime, train, road and air transportation routes that continue to span the continents. Obviously, we should not forget about the dark side of this process, which was enabled by Western imperialism, or the European (Western) colonization of or military and economic domination over the rest of the world. Hopefully, at present, in a more multipolar global reality, the discussion can be conducted on equitable footing and with a clearer understanding of the painful past.

Addis Ababa and St Andrews
January 2020

Acknowledgments

The project and book would have been impossible without the initial inspiration of Michael Talbot's 2015 talk on the transfer of Western ideas to the late Ottoman Empire and early republican Turkey, delivered in 2015 at the University of St Andrews. Interestingly, some of these ideas arrived to Istanbul by way of Japan, which defeated the Russian Empire in 1905. Meanwhile, Hara Kiyoshi kindly encouraged Tomasz Kamusella to delve into the potential channels of idea transfers from (Central) Europe to (Southeast) Asia. Tadek (Tadeusz) Wojtych and Tomasz discussed many of these ideas when they organized a conference in 2015. We thank Fernand de Varennes, who put Christophe van der Beken and Tomasz in touch. Subsequently, Christophe invited his colleague Asnake Kefale to join the project. Konrad Lawson kindly helped with Japanese terms and their transliterations.[1] We also thank the two anonymous reviewers whose advice and suggestions let us improve the argument. Last but not least, we thank Catherine Gibson, who read and commented on the entire manuscript. Any remaining infelicities are the sole responsibility of the authors.

Note

1 In transliterations (romanization) from Amharic, Arabic or Tigrinya, no capital letters are employed, because capital letters do not occur in these languages' writing systems.

Introduction

The short book is an attempt at sketching the routes along which different ideas of 'modern' (i.e. Western) statehood reached Ethiopia in the 20th century, as consciously (or not) adopted by the elite intent on modernizing (i.e. Westernizing) the country. The preliminary assumption, based on the available literature, is that such a transfer of these ideas took place from (Central) Europe to Ethiopia by way of Eurasia (mainly Japan, the Soviet Union and China). Ethiopian thinkers and politicians appear not to be aware of the Central European origin of the two models of statehood implemented in their country. Instead, they consciously borrowed these Central European models of statehood as employed in Japan and the Soviet Union. The volume's authors check this hypothesis with the use of relevant literature and, most importantly, by looking at Ethiopian sources. The material and sources indispensable for researching and writing this book are in numerous languages (Amharic, English, Chinese, German, Japanese, Polish or Russian) and stem from a variety of sociopolitical, historical and geographical contexts. Not a single scholar can be reasonably expected to master all these languages and gain in-depth knowledge of all these contexts and their history. Therefore, an endeavor of this type needs to be collaborative in its approach for the sake of doing justice to such a highly 'transnational' subject matter (cf Manifesto 2018).

Modern Ethiopia: the beginnings

In the mid-19th century, Ethiopia[1] was a landlocked, decentralized ('federal' or 'fragmented'), predominantly Christian (Coptic, Oriental Orthodox – i.e. Miaphysitic) polity located in the northern half of the Ethiopian Highlands with Lake Tana at its center. This polity was composed of the historical regions of Begemider (በጌምድር *begēmidir*), Gojjam (ጎጃም *gojam*), southern Tigray (ትግራይ *tigiray*), western Wello (ወሎ *welo*) and Shewa (ሸዋ *shewa*), meaning that its territory overlapped with the northern quarter of

2 Introduction

today's Ethiopia, or the present-day regional states (provinces) of Amhara and Tigray. The Semitic-speaking ethnic group of Amharas constituted the majority of the population. The kindred Semitic ethnic group of Tigrayans were united with the Amharas through faith and the liturgical and official Semitic language of Ge'ez (ግዕዝ *gə'əz*). Since the early Middle Ages, Ethiopia had been gradually surrounded by Muslim polities in the wake of the early expansion of Islam across the Arabian Peninsula and North Africa (Sluglett and Currie 2014: 69).

The rule of Emperor Tewodros II (ዳግማዊ ዓፄ ቴዎድሮስ *dagimawī 'ats'ē tēwodiros*, reigned 1855–1868) marked the beginning of modern Ethiopia. He subdued the regional princes and centralized power in the country, especially by bringing the southern historical region of Shewa under his control. Later, in 1886, in the center of Shewa, the present-day Ethiopian capital of Addis Ababa was founded. During Tewodros's reign, the

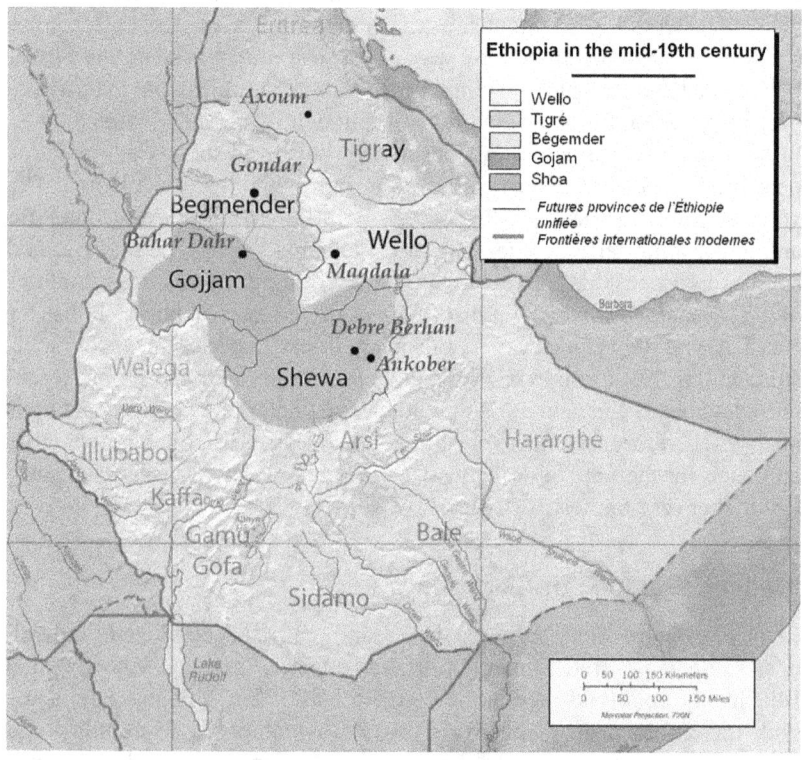

Figure 0.1 Ethiopia in the mid-19th century (Ethiopia around 2010)

imperial and state administration decisively shifted from the antiquated liturgical language of Ge'ez to vernacular Amharic, thus linguistically signaling the growing separation of state from church (Shinn and Ofcansky 2013: 7). The 1868 British invasion defeated the Ethiopian forces and plunged the polity into a brief period of internal strife, from which Emperor Yohannes IV (ዓፄ ዮሐንስ ፬ኛ *'ats'ē yoḥānis āratenya*, reigned 1872–1889) emerged successful as the country's ruler. In 1875–1876, in the north, he defeated the encroaching armies of the de facto independent Ottoman Egypt, which by 1880 had extended its rule to Eritrea; northern

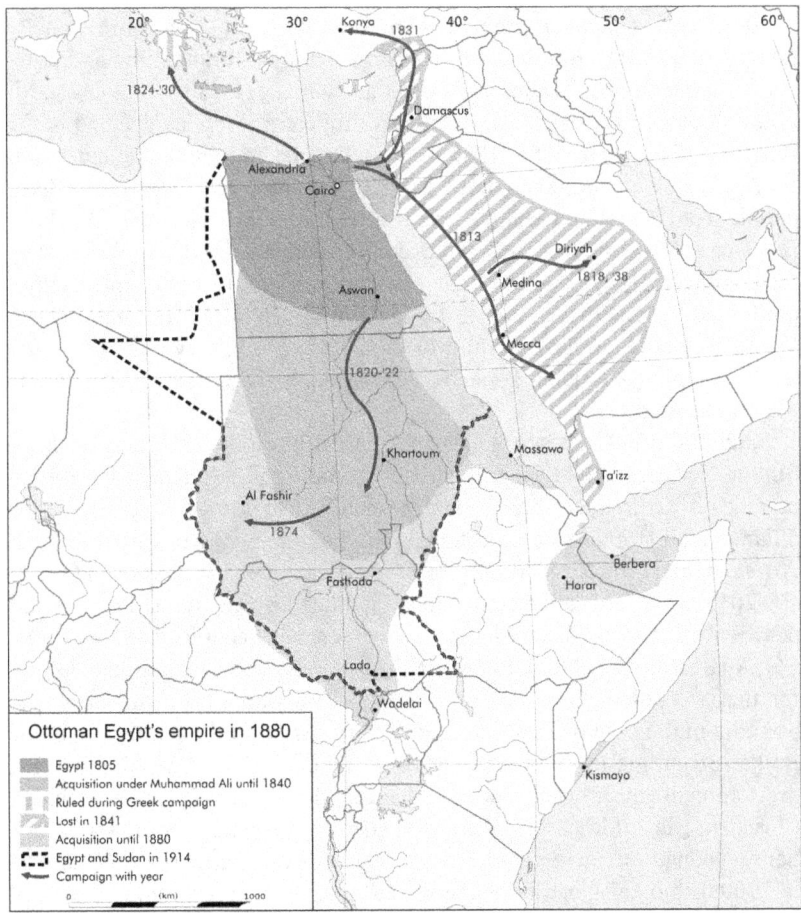

Figure 0.2 Ottoman Egypt's empire in 1880 (Don-kun and Gaba 2011)

and southern Somalia; and Harar in the east and today's northwestern Uganda in the west. From the Egyptian perspective, Christian Ethiopia sat between these new possessions, preventing their territorial integration (Gaba 2011). Subsequently, the Mahdist War (1881–1899) in Sudan frustrated Egypt's imperial designs but also endangered northern Ethiopia (Shinn and Ofcansky 2013: 233).

Emperor Menelik II (ዳግማዊ ዓፄ ምኒልክ *dagimawī 'ats'ē minīlik*, reigned 1889–1913) continued with the policy of centralizing the country and embarked on numerous campaigns of conquest in the west, east and south. By 1904, these conquests had extended Ethiopia's borders to where they remain now, in 2020 (Marcus 1975; Plaut 2018; Zheim 2010a, 2010b, 2010c). In this manner, from a relatively ethnically and confessionally homogenous polity Ethiopia was transformed into a multiethnic and polyconfessional empire (Levine 1974). In the context of the then ongoing partition ('scramble') of Africa among the European powers as decided at the Berlin Conference of 1884–1885, Ethiopia managed to retain its independence, alongside Liberia (founded in 1822 for freed and free-born 'Black' people from the United States). Italy, in quest for an empire in the Mediterranean and the Horn of Africa, attacked Ethiopia, but the Italian forces were resoundingly defeated at the Battle of Adwa in 1896. In this manner, Ethiopia joined the exclusive club of the few non-Western polities that escaped Western colonization. At the turn of the 20th century, they numbered only five: Ethiopia (Abyssinia[2]), Japan, Persia (Iran), the Ottoman Empire and Siam (Thailand).

Landlocked and fully surrounded by the British colonies of Anglo-Egyptian Sudan, British East Africa and British Somaliland, alongside the Italian colonies of Eritrea and Somaliland, Menelik II in 1894 forged a tentative alliance with Britain's fierce colonial opponent that enjoyed no foothold in Africa, namely the Russian Empire (Podeszwa 2000: 17; Shinn and Ofcansky 2013: 357). This alliance was also facilitated by the mutually perceived confessional ('Orthodox') closeness between both countries (Eribo 2001: 56). Apart from the external Western European powers, the ultimate 'Other' for the two allied 'Orthodox' empires was Muslims, be it in Sudan and Somalia in the case of Ethiopia or in Central Asia, the Caucasus and in the Balkans from the Russian perspective. Another similarity was the fact that the dominant ethnic group – be it Amharas and Tigrayans (Semitic-speaking Christians) in Ethiopia or (Great) Russians (Slavophone Orthodox Christians) – constituted a mere plurality in the respective imperial populations. In 1900, Ethiopia's population amounted to 12 million (Ethiopia: Historical 2019; Kibruyisfa Achamyeleh 1997), while the Amharas and the Tigrayans together accounted for a third of the inhabitants. Should the Amharas be

Introduction 5

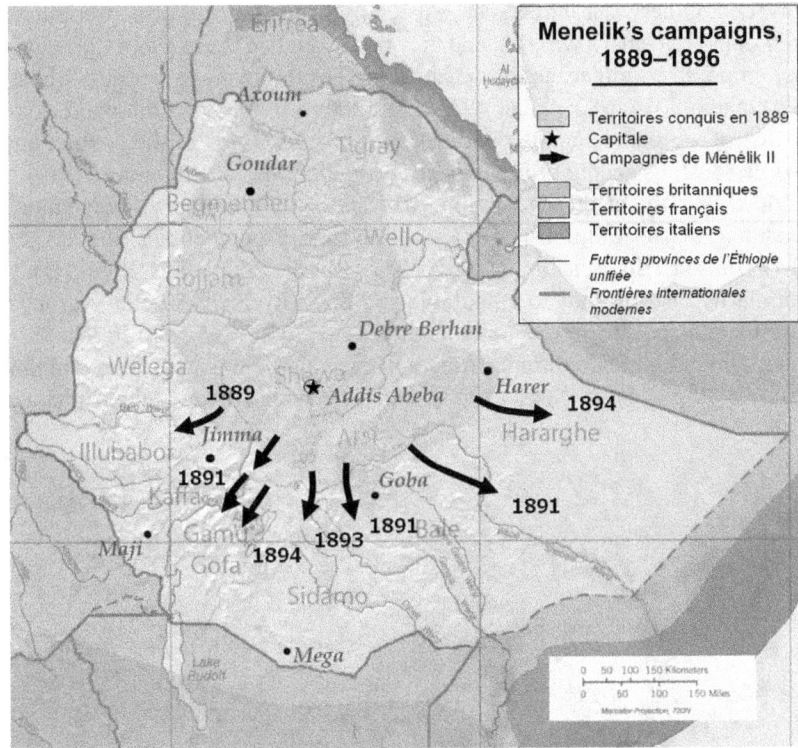

Figure 0.3 Menelik's campaigns, 1889–1896 (Zheim 2010a)

considered separately, their number would amount to a mere quarter of the Ethiopian populace (Demographics of Ethiopia 2019).

With its 125 million inhabitants in 1897, Imperial Russia's population was then ten times that of Ethiopia's. Ethnic Russians accounted for 44 percent of the inhabitants (Russian Empire Census 2019). However, from the vantage of confessional statistics, Orthodox Christians accounted for almost 70 percent among the Russian population, while Muslims amounted to no more than 12 percent (Russian Empire Census 2019). The situation was quite different in the Ethiopian Empire,[3] which because of its sudden territorial expansion during the second half of the 19th century lost its previous confessionally homogenous character. Hence, Miaphysitic Christians, Muslims and adherents of nonscriptural (local, 'traditional') religions each roughly accounted for one-third of the inhabitants. As a result, cooperation

6 *Introduction*

with Muslims was a must, especially when foreign or colonial powers invaded. Otherwise, intolerance, especially of the faithful of nonscriptural religions ('pagans'), was rife, and they had no choice but to adopt Christianity, imposed by either the Ethiopian Church or foreign missionaries (Abbas H. Gnamo 2014: 180; Caulk 1972; Ford 2009). In today's Ethiopia, Christians (of various denominations) account for two-thirds of the population, while Muslims account for one-third (Demographics of Ethiopia 2019).

Interestingly, at present (i.e. in 2019 and 2020), Ethiopia's population, standing at 109 million, is quite close to that of post–Soviet Russia's, at 144 million (Ethiopia Population 2019; Russia Population 2019).[4] This similarity also extends to ethnolinguistic diversity: over 80 ethnic groups are recognized in Ethiopia, and as many as 160 are recorded in the Russian Federation. The difference is, however, that ethnic Russians amount to over 80 percent of Russia's inhabitants, while in Ethiopia, the Amharas,

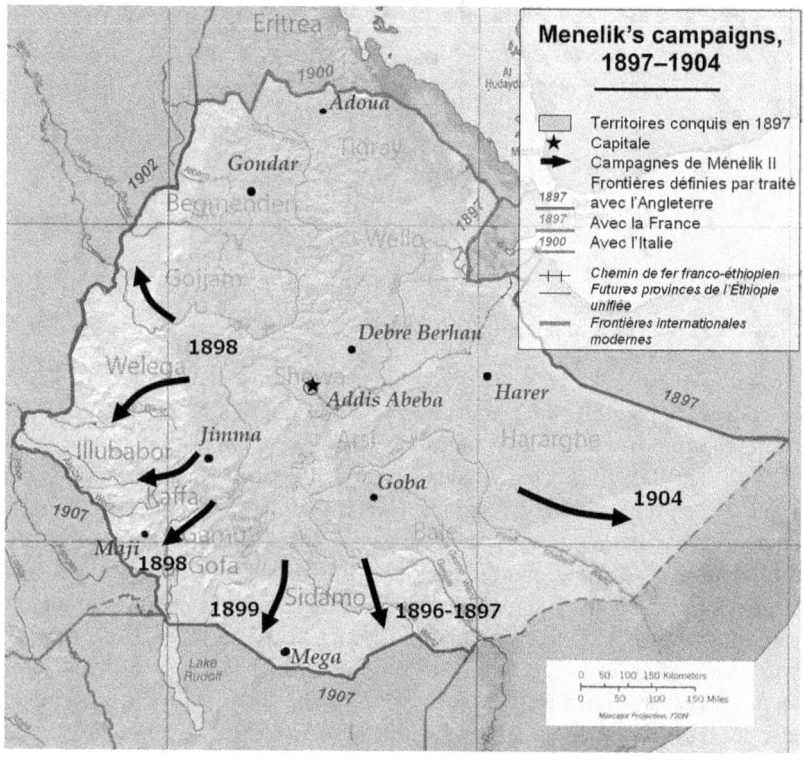

Figure 0.4 Menelik's campaigns, 1897–1904 (Zheim 2010c)

Introduction 7

at 27 percent, have been unseated as the plurality of the country's population by the Oromos, who make up 35 percent. From this angle, present-day Ethiopia's ethnolinguistic diversity is comparable more to that of the Russian Empire and the Soviet Union (Demographics of Ethiopia 2019; Demographics of Russia 2019).

The making of Ethiopia into a fully recognized member of the world's West-dominated international system of nation-states is connected to the person of *Ras*[5] (Duke) Tafari Makonnen (ተፈሪ መኮንን *teferī mekonin*). He embarked on a swathe of ambitious modernizing reforms, first as Empress Zewditu's (ንግሥት ዘውዲቱ *nigišit zewidītu*, reigned 1916–1930) regent and later in his own right as Emperor Haile Selassie (ንጉሠ ነገሥት ቀዳማዊ ኃይለ ሥላሴ *niguše negešit k'edamawī ḫayile šilasē*, reigned 1930–1974). Hence, his effective rule lasted for 58 years. The first international success came in 1923, when Makonnen secured for Ethiopia membership in the League of Nations (LN) (Vestal 2011: 21). The following year, he led the Ethiopian delegation, which for four and a half months toured Europe (Britain, Belgium, France, Greece, Italy, Sweden and Switzerland) and the Middle East (Britain's Protectorate of Egypt and Mandatory Palestine) (Vestal 2011: 21–22). To a degree, this effort to observe and learn the ways of Western modernity was modeled on the Japanese governmental delegation to Europe and the United States in 1871–1873 (Tsuzuki and Young 2009). In turn, the Japanese emulated Russian ruler Peter the Great's 1697–1698 diplomatic and fact-finding delegation to the West (England, the Holy Roman Empire, the Netherlands and Poland-Lithuania) (Nish 2008: 130). It would be interesting to check whether Makonnen's retinue might have been aware of the 1890 Ottoman embassy to Japan and the Ottoman Sultan's efforts to modernize his empire by copying western solutions adopted in Imperial Japan (Selçuk 2011: 132; Worringer 2014). Hopefully, a scholar will take up this research challenge.[6]

Transfer of ideas: from Central Europe to Ethiopia

Japan had been an inspiration to the Ethiopian Emperor since his youth, first of all thanks to Tokyo's then-shocking victory over the Russian Empire in 1905 (Russell 2009: 102). Second, Japan became the most successful non-Western country, which modernized without giving up its tradition and culture. This proved that modernization without Westernization was a clear possibility (Clarke 2011: 12–13). In Haile Selassie's second year on the Ethiopian imperial throne, he granted his realm a constitution (ሕገ መንግሥት *hige menigišit*, literally 'the law of the government, kingdom, state') in 1931 (1923 EC). His then Minister of Finance, Tekle Hawariat Tekle Mariyam (ተክለ ሐዋርያት ተክለ ማርያም *tekile ḫāwari'at tekile mariyam*, 1884–1977), who drafted this document, closely modeled the first Ethiopian Constitution on the Japanese Imperial Constitution of 1889 (Shinn and Ofcansky 2013: 100). In turn, Meiji Japan had borrowed its own first constitution from the German Empire's Constitution, promulgated in 1871 (Kazuhiro 2014: 48–51). In this way, the Western (or rather Central European) model of centralized ethnolinguistic nation-state became the initial model of 'modern' (Western) statehood that was adopted for Ethiopia through the intermediary of the aforementioned Japanese Constitution. The ethnolinguistic nation-state, as implemented in Ethiopia, came together with the slowly coalescing policy of Amharization – that is, the ethnolinguistic homogenization and assimilation (or cooption) of the elites of the country's other ethnic groups (Baxter 1983; Girma Awgichew Demeke 2014: 16–21; Levine 1974: 148–152, 117–119; Triulzi 1983: 118–125). Amharic was promoted as the country's sole national and official language, and a de facto ban was imposed on the development of other languages. This policy became official when the Revised Constitution was promulgated in 1955 (1948 EC). Article 125 proclaimed that '[t]he official language of the Empire is Amharic' (Cooper 1976a: 188). The goal was elusive 'national integration' (አንድ ሕዝብ *ānid hāzib* 'one people, nation'), despite the fact that the Amharas accounted only for one-third of the population, while Miaphysitic[7] Christians at best just for over half of the inhabitants (Levine 1965; Levine 1974: 148–152; MacLeod 2014: 41–42; Triulzi 1983: 118–119). Germany's ethnolinguistic nationalism and the entailed ideal of the ethnolinguistic homogeneity ('purity') of the nation-state (cf Sundhaußen 1973; Welch 2004) were part and parcel of the ideological package of this Western model of statehood adopted in late imperial Ethiopia.

Unsurprisingly, the Soviet-Derg (ደርግ *derg* 'committee or council' is the translation of the Russian term совет *sovet* 'council,' usually rendered as 'Soviet' in English),[8] which overthrew the monarchy and seized power in 1974, built its popularity on the promise to end the aforementioned policy of ethnolinguistic homogenization (Amharization, Amhara domination), among other things.[9] To this end, the revolutionaries included in their 1976 program of the National Democratic Revolution of Ethiopia (NDRE) (የኢትዮጵያ ብሔራዊ ዲሞክራሲያዊ አብዮት ፕሮግራም *ye'ītiyop'iya biḥērawī dīmokirasīyawī ābiyot pirogram*) the right to self-determination for Ethiopia's numerous ethnic groups, speaking a wide variety of languages (Praeg 2006: 70). The Soviet-Derg regime was increasingly supported by Moscow as an element of the Soviet Union's global ideological and military struggle against the United States and the West (Patman 1990: 150–202). In return, following the Kremlin's official ideology of marxism-leninism, Addis Ababa borrowed the principles of Soviet nationality policy[10] and adopted, at least in principle, the practice of ethnoterritorial autonomy for recognized nationalities (ethnic groups). This form of 'national self-determination' came in a limited form of ethnicity-based decentralization and a few regional ethnic autonomies, as practiced in communist China (that had also emulated the Soviet Union), and actually in the postwar USSR (Keller 1985: 15; Semahagn Gashu Abebe 2014: 118). In reality, even though the Soviet-Derg regime paid lip service to the nationalities question (like the postwar Soviet government), it actually retained and even fortified the centralization of Ethiopia. The use of Ethiopian languages other than Amharic was allowed only for the sake of literacy campaigns[11] (Getachew Anteneh and Derib Ado 2006: 48), but exclusively in the Ethiopic (Amharic, Ge'ez) script (cf Baxter 1983: 137). However, for instance, in neighboring Somalia, Latin letters had been intensively employed for writing and publishing in the Somali language since 1972 (Adam 1983: 33). The establishment of the Workers' Party of Ethiopia (WPE) (የኢትዮጵያ ሠራተኞች ፓርቲ [ኢሠፓ] ye'ītiyop'iya šeratenyoch paritī [īšepa] in Amharic) in 1984 was considered to be an important instrument for consolidating the power of the Soviet-Derg 'socialist state' under the leadership of Mengistu Haile Mariam.

In 1987, 13 years after the overthrow of the Emperor, the Soviet-Derg regime adopted a new constitution, which, in line with the Soviet bloc's model, renamed the country as the People's Democratic Republic of Ethiopia (PDRE, የኢትዮጵያ ሕዝባዊ ዲሞክራሲያዊ ሪፐብሊክ ye'ītiyop'iya ḥizibawī dīmokirasīyawī rīpebilīk in Amharic). This constitution provided a new administrative structure of socialist Ethiopia. Accordingly, 24 regular (i.e. non-autonomous) regions (አስተዳደር አካባቢ āsitedader ākababī 'administrative regions') and five autonomous regions (የራስ ገዝ አካባቢዎች yeras gez ākababīwoch 'autonomous areas') were established. Autonomy was given to the restive regions of Eritrea, Tigray and Ogaden. In addition, two autonomous regions, Assab (for Afars) and Dire Dawa (for Somalis), were formed. The autonomous regions were based on ethnicity only in part, because the de facto objective was to restore the government's control over the areas hotly contested by anti-Soviet-Derg forces recruited from among these regions' dominant ethnic groups. For instance, the two separate autonomous regions for Somalis were intended to divide the growing Somali ethnic (national, separatist) movement in Ethiopia in the wake of the Ogaden War (1977–1978), when Somalia – with communist China's support (Thrall 2015: 5; Lyons 1978) – attacked Ethiopia, seeking a unification of Ogaden with the rest of the Somali nation-state (Semahagn Gashu Abebe 2014: 118–119). In sum, the PDRE Constitution allowed only for the establishment of the aforementioned five autonomous regions. Moreover, this document affirmed that Amharic would remain the sole working language of government at all administrative levels. The actual pressing on with the policy of Amharization, though with a (never actually realized) promise of some ethnolinguistic autonomy in five of socialist (communist) Ethiopia's regions was similar to the model developed in communist China. Over the course of the Chinese Revolution, the communists promised a federalization of the country on the ethnolinguistic principle in emulation of the Soviet Union. After the communist victory, they limited this program to five autonomous regions among communist China's 27 regions. Nevertheless, communist China remained a centralist unitary state (Hao 2016: 98–100).

In 1991 the leftist (marxist) coalition of ethnic (ethnolinguistic) liberation movements called the Ethiopian People's Revolutionary Democratic Front (EPRDF, የኢትዮጵያ ሕዝቦች አብዮታዊ ዲሞክራሲያዊ ግንባር *ye'ītiyop'iya ḥiziboch ābiyotawī dīmokirasīyawī ginibar* in Amharic) unseated the military regime, thus ending the Ethiopian Civil War that had lasted since 1974 (Henze 2007: 286–298). The EPRDF was spearheaded by the Tigray People's Liberation Front (TPLF, ሕዝባዊ ወያነ ሓርነት ትግራይ *ḥəzbawi wäyanä ḥarənnät təgray* in Tigrinya), which, along with the Eritrean People's Liberation Front (EPLF, ህዝባዊ ግንባር ሃርነት ኤርትራ *hizibawī ginibar Harnet Eritrea* in Tigrinya and الجبهة الشعبية لتحرير إريتريا *aljabhat alshaebiat litahrir 'iiritria* in Arabic), had been fighting in northern Ethiopia against the Soviet-Derg regime since the late 1970s. Both TPLF and EPLF were ethnically Tigrayan in their membership, though the latter organization also included some members from other ethnic groups (alongside Christians), thanks to its state-centered (non-ethnic) pan-Eritrean ideology. The Eritrean Liberation Front (ELF), which was established in 1960, was dominated by Muslims.[12]

This former Italian colony of Eritrea, under British administration since 1941, was passed to Ethiopia in 1952. In this way, the imperial administration at Addis Ababa obtained long-desired access to the sea, while the fears of Eritreans were calmed by the UN-sanctioned federal arrangement in which Eritrea was given wide-ranging autonomy, including its own constitution and a multiparty system. The Federation of Ethiopia and Eritrea was, however, abolished by the Haile Selassie government in 1962 (Tekeste 1997). The abrogation of the Ethiopian-Eritrea federation was followed by a civil war between different Eritrean separatist movements (e.g. the ELF and the EPLF) and the successive Ethiopian regimes. The provision of an autonomous status to Eritrea in the 1987 Constitution of Soviet-Derg Ethiopia was too little too late (Bereket Habte Selassie 1989). In 1991, following the defeat of the Soviet-Derg regime by the combined efforts of the EPLF and the EPRDF, Eritrea became de facto independent. Two years later, after the independence referendum (1993), it became a de jure independent nation-state (Eritrea 1993). The two governments in Asmara and Addis Ababa maintained cordial relations from 1991 to 1998. However, in 1998, due to disputes over territory and other strategic issues, a devastating war broke out between the two countries. This war ended in 2000, after the signing of the Algiers peace treaty. However, both countries maintained a no-war-and-no-peace style of relations until the signing of a peace treaty in 2018 (Busari and Elwazer 2018).

The EPRDF government promised a genuine federalization of Ethiopia and respect for the post-imperial country's ethnolinguistic diversity. The July 1991 Peace and Democracy Conference, convened by the ERPDF, brought together 25 political organizations. This conference adopted a transitional charter (የኢትዮጵያ የሽግግር ወቅት ቻርተር *ye'ītiyop'iya yeshigigir wek'it chariter*) and legalized EPRDF's consent to Eritrea's secession. This charter incorporated in Ethiopian legislation the 1948 United Nations Declaration on Human Rights (UDHR) and promised multiparty democracy, alongside the freedom of association and speech in Ethiopia. What is more, this document also legalized the right to national (ethnic) self-determination, up to and including secession. In 1992, Ethiopia's administrative division underwent restructuring with the creation of 14 regions along ethnolinguistic lines. In 1995, Ethiopia became a federation with the establishment of the Federal Democratic Republic of Ethiopia (የኢትዮጵያ ፌዴራላዊ ዲሞክራሲያዊ ሪፐብሊክ *ye'ītiyop'iya fēdēralawī dīmokirasīyawī rīpebilīk* in Amharic). The 1995 Constitution recognized nine ethnolinguistically defined states (regions): Afar for the Afars; Amhara for the Amharas; Benishangul-Gumuz for five ethnic groups; Gambela; Harari (ostensibly for the historically dominant Semitic and Muslim Hararis, though ethnic non-Hararis constitute the majority of the region's population); Oromia for the Oromos, who constitute the plurality of Ethiopia's inhabitants; Somali for the Somalis; Southern Nations, Nationalities and Peoples for more than 50 ethnic groups in the southwest; and Tigray for the Tigrayans. In addition, the Constitution recognized Addis Ababa as the seat of the federal government with an autonomous status. Dire Dawa, which is a multiethnic city contested by the regions of Oromia and Somali, was put under the federal government's control and given a charted status through a proclamation in 2004 (የድሬዳዋ አስተዳደር ቻርተር አዋጅ *yedirēdewa āsitedader chariter āwaj* 'Charter of the Administration of Dire Dawa'). Hence, although the Soviet-Derg regime promised a Soviet-style ethnic decentralization in Ethiopia, the EPDRF actually introduced and broadened it to full-fledged ethnic federalization, as practiced in the interwar Soviet Union (Asnake Kefale 2013: 31–37; Van der Beken 2017).

Nevertheless, the Ethiopian Federation is still a work in progress. For example, to this day, no official map of the country's regions has been released, for the fear that such a cartographic document might incite ethnic conflicts if the still vaguely sketched administrative boundaries were to be officially confirmed. In 2014 and 2015, many Oromo students protested against alleged changes in the administrative boundaries of Addis Ababa at the expense of Oromia, leading to mass imprisonment, suppression and numerous casualties. In 2016, a wave of generalized protests on different issues, but mainly against the increasingly authoritarian character of the EPRDF government, cost hundreds of demonstrators their lives. More protests followed until 2018, when political prisoners were freed and the first ethnic Oromo, Abiy Ahmed, was nominated to the post of Ethiopian Prime Minister. He embarked on a raft of democratizing and developmental reforms, which lessened the tensions and secured much-needed rapprochement with Eritrea (Burke 2018; Endalk Chala 2015; Sandner 2016). For these achievements, in 2019, Abiy Ahmed received a Nobel peace prize (Burke and Henley 2019).

Antecedents and terminology

Nationalism is a Western ideology, which proposes that each nation should reside in its own polity – that is, nation-state, or in other words the state for one nation only. In revolutionary France, the country's people were declared to be citizens. In turn, the thus created citizenry was defined as the French nation, understood as the ultimate font of legitimacy for the French statehood and government. In this way, the previously divine legitimation of monarchical rule was replaced with a secular (national) one (Declaration 1789). The French Revolutionary War and Napoleonic War (1792–1815) spread the model of nation-state across Europe and the Middle East (especially in Ottoman Egypt). Faced with the unprecedented effectiveness of France's national army, defeated polities strove to copy the model of the French nation-state. Self-proclaimed anti-French German nationalists faced the stumbling block of the lack of any pre-existing polity which they would have agreed to transform into a German nation-state and its population into a German nation. The Holy Roman Empire might have served this purpose had it not been dissolved in 1806 under Napoleon's pressure. After much discussion, German poet Ernst Moritz Arndt provided a reply to this German national dilemma in his 1813 patriotic song. In this song, he proposed to equate the German nation with all the speakers of the German language and their desired nation-state with the territory compactly inhabited by this language's speakers (Arndt 1813). This is the succinct definition of ethnolinguistic nationalism. In the case of French (civic) nationalism, state equals nation, while in this German case of ethnic (ethnolinguistic) nationalism, language equals nation, which equals state. In the former case, state is primary, while in the latter, language is primary, and state is of a merely tertiary importance. Subsequently, ethnolinguistic nationalism spread across Central and Eastern Europe (Sundhaußen 1973), before becoming the norm of statehood creation, legitimation and maintenance in this region after the Great War (Kamusella 2018).

The re-establishment of the monarchical order in Central Europe at the Congress of Vienna in 1815 hindered the rise of nation-states in this corner of Europe (though with Western European and Russian help, they kept springing up in the Balkans at the expense of the Ottoman Empire). A semblance of the Holy Roman Empire was put back on the political map of Europe in the form of the German Confederation. The Austrian Empire dominated this confederation, but half of this empire's lands (i.e. the Kingdom of Hungary) were located outside the confederation. The same situation was observed in the case of Prussia, with half of this kingdom's lands located in the confederation and the other half outside. The economically burgeoning Prussia pressed for including all the German-speaking polities in a future German nation-state. This *Großdeutsche* ('Greater Germany') solution would have sundered the Austrian Empire apart, three-quarters of its inhabitants *not* being German speakers. Faced with Austria's understandable opposition, after the 1866 Austro-Prussian War, victorious Prussia pressed on with the *Kleindeutschland* ('Little Germany') solution, or the unification of Prussia with all the confederation's polities located outside the Austrian Empire. The German Empire, founded in 1871, produced a '*Little*' German nation-state – that is, *without* the German speakers of Austria-Hungary. This German Empire was a territorial (*not* ethnic) federation (literally, *Bundesstaat*, or 'federal state') composed of 26 constitutive polities (i.e. kingdoms, duchies, principalities, free cities and an imperial territory), created for the *single* (unitary) German nation (*Volk*) that on the ideological plane of ethnolinguistic nationalism also encompassed Austria-Hungary's German speakers (Die Verfassung 1871: 64). Subsequently, the German Empire was increasingly made into a unitary state, on the model of France, until any semblance of federalism had vanished by the mid 1930s under Adolf Hitler's national socialist (nazi) rule. In 1938, Germany annexed Austria, and in this way, practically all Germans (commonly identified as German speakers) found themselves in a single and unitary nation-state of their own, in wartime Germany. Amid World War II (1943), this nation-building success was marked by the change of the state's name to Greater German Empire, which proved short-lived (Schulze 2010).

14 Introduction

The German term *Volk* has two meanings: 'a people' and '[ethnolinguistic] nation.' The originally French or Latinate term *Nation* ('[civic] nation') also exists in German but is not used in the German or Central European political tradition for building or legitimating the nation, which in the German or Austrian context has been invariably referred to as *Volk* during the past two centuries. German-speaking scholars delineate this distinction between the political concept of *Volk* typical for Central Europe and that of *nation* predominating in Western Europe (and nowadays also outside Eurasia) by referring to them in academese as *Kulturnation* and *Staatnation*, respectively. In the former case, language (identified with culture, or *Kultur* in German) constitutes the 'normal' basis for forming a nation, while in the latter, a pre-existing state (*Staat*) does (Lemberg 1967–1968).

As mentioned earlier, in the late 1870s, Meiji Japan borrowed the German model of ethnolinguistically homogenous and unitary nation-state from the German Empire (Tsuzuki and Young 2009). The Japanese Imperial Constitution, promulgated in 1890, translated the German term *Volk* into the neologism 民族 *minzoku*, composed of two characters, namely 民 *min* 'a people' and 族 *zoku* 'family' (Dainihonteikokukenpō 1889; Die Japanische 1940). Subsequently, many Japanese students and officials entered German universities and visited Germany. In this way, they learned about the ethnolinguistic model of the German nation (*Volk*) and transplanted it wholesale to Japan. The German concept of *Muttersprache* (literally 'mother tongue'), employed as the ideologized synonym for German in the meaning of the national language of the German Empire, yielded the Japanese neologism 国語 *kokugo*, constructed from the characters 国 *kuni* 'country' and 語 *go* 'word, language' (Heinrich 2012: 60–66). This German ideological package came complete with the policy of the ethnolinguistic (and partly, ethnoconfessional) homogenization of the nation-state, meaning the ban or suppression of the use of any other languages, so that every inhabitant would employ only the *Muttersprache*, thus proving their membership in the *Volk* (cf Fitzpatrick 2015). The Japanese readily emulated this policy of Germanization with their own policy of Japanization for the growing Japanese Empire (Yeounsuk 2010: 160–169). In the early 20th century, these two examples of the economically and militarily highly successful nation-states of Germany and Japan convinced the Ethiopian elite to adopt this model. It appeared that building a nation through the policy of the ethnolinguistic homogenization of the nation-state was the 'most progressive' way of modern politics outside Europe, should a non-European polity seek to escape colonization by a Western power.

In the Western ideology of colonialism, a 'civilizing mission' in the form of a military-assisted seizure of non-Western territories and polities was considered legitimate as long as the non-European polity in question had not 'modernized' (i.e. Europeanized) itself yet (Chinweizu 1987: 211). In the case of Ethiopia, such hallmarks of Europeanization, before the adoption of the model of ethnolinguistic nation-state, were Christianity as the state religion and the rapid acquisition of firearms from Europe (Teshale Tibebu 1995: 51). What is more, Ethiopia's 1896 victory over Italy, as an aspiring imperial power, bolstered the international status of Ethiopia as an independent country. This victory of a non-Western country over a Western colonial power became an early inspiration for anticolonial movements, before Japan defeated the Russian Empire in 1905 (cf Phạm and Shilliam 2016: 7).

The legitimacy of the Habsburg Monarchy was seriously shaken by the 1866 defeat at Prussian hands. As a result, in 1867, the Austrian Empire was transformed into the Dual Monarchy of Austria-Hungary. This new state remained a *non*-national polity but at the price of concessions to ethnolinguistic national movements at the substate level. First of all, the eastern half of the Dual Monarchy, or the Kingdom of Hungary, was made into an ethnolinguistically defined Hungarian nation-state. The 'Austrian half' was officially known as the Kingdoms and Lands Represented in the Imperial Council (*Die im Reichsrat vertretenen Königreiche und Länder*). Gradually, besides the imperial language of German, also Czech (Czech and Moravian), Italian, Polish, Romanian, Serbo-Croatian (Bosnian, Croatian and Serbian), Slovak, Slovenian and Ruthenian (Ukrainian) were recognized as official or co-official languages in some crownlands (regions). Ethnic groups speaking different languages were identified in accordance with the tenets of ethnolinguistic nationalism, but in legislation, they were referred to as 'nationalities' (*Volkstämme*, literally 'tribes'), *not* nations (*Völker*) (Judson 2017; Wandruszka and Urbanitsch 1980). In light of the Austro-Hungarian legislation, nationalities had the right to territorial autonomy, but *not* to independence. Article 19 of the Austrian half's 1867 Basic Law on the General Rights of Citizens distinguished between *Volkstamm* (nationality, literally 'people-tribe,' i.e. ethnic group) and *Nationalität* (literally 'nationality'), meaning the essential qualities and features of a *Volkstamm* and the fact of one's membership in such a *Volksstamm* (*Staatsgrundgesetz* 1867). In the Austro-Hungarian public discourse and press, this distinction soon became blurred, because *Nationalität* and *Volksstamm* began to be used as synonyms for 'ethnic group.' Hence, at present, the preferred English translation of *Volksstamm* is 'nationality.'[13]

The Soviet model of ethnolinguistic (ethnoterritorial) federation was borrowed from Austria-Hungary. Vladimir Lenin was surprised, contrary to Karl Marx's prediction, that workers – instead of flocking to communist

Table 0.1 Terminology of ethnolinguistic nationalism across languages

English	German	Japanese	Russian	Chinese	Amharic
a people	Volk	民 min	народ narod	人民 rén mín	ሕዝብ hizib
state	Staat	国家 kokka (literally, country + house)	государство gosudarstvo	國 guó	ኣገር ማሃተ āger gizat (literally, country + polity)
civic nation	Nation = Staatnation	国民 kokumin (literally, country + people)	NA	国民 guó mín (literally, country + people)	ኣገር āger
ethnolinguistic nation	Volk = Kulturnation	民族 minzoku (literally, people + tribe)	нация natsiia = народ narod	國族 guó zú (literally, country + family)	ብሔር biḥēr ብሔረሰብ biḥēreseb
nationality = membership in an ethnolinguistic nation	Nationalität	国籍 kokuseki (literally, country + family register)	национальность natsional'nost' = народность narodnost'	国籍 guó jí (literally, country + membership)	?
nationality = ethnic group with the right to autonomy	Volkstamm = Nationalität	民族 minzoku (literally, people + tribe)	национальность natsional'nost' = народность narodnost'	民族 minzú (literally, people + family)	ብሔረሰብ biḥēreseb ብሔር biḥēr
backward nationality	NA	NA	народность narodnost'	NA	nationalities at [a] lower level of development (በዝቅተኛ የዕድገት ደረጃ ላይ የሚገኙ ብሔረሰቦች bezikețegna dereja lay yemigegnu biḥereseboch) (Art. 2.3, 1987 Constitution)

(socialist) parties on the basis of their class interest – predominantly threw their lot with their co-ethnics of different (social and economic) classes. When in 1912 his pupil Joseph Stalin visited Lenin in Cracow (then in Austria-Hungary), the latter decided to send Stalin on a fact-finding mission to Vienna. The idea was to learn how the non-national polity of Austria-Hungary contained the sociopolitical force of ethnolinguistic national movements. At that time, the issue was intensively discussed and analyzed by the Dual Monarchy's social democrats (marxists), including Otto Bauer (1907) and Karl Kautsky (1908). Stalin gathered his reflections on this subject in his 1913 essay *Marxism and the National Question* (Stalin 1954).[14] After 1922, it became *the* blueprint for the Soviet Union's federal structure, composed of ethnolinguistically defined union republics (Blank 1994). Stalin defined the nation as 'a historically constituted, stable community of people, formed on the basis of a common language, territory, economic life, and psychological make-up manifested in a common culture' (Stalin in Hao 2016: 311).

However, the adoption of the German-language terminology into the Soviet Union's Russian nomenclature was anything but straightforward. The Russian term народ *narod* 'people' or 'a people' was preferred to нация *natsiia* 'nation.' In reality, the term *narod* often doubles as 'nation' in Russian; hence, the term советский народ *sovetskii narod* for all the Soviet Union's inhabitants was variously translated into English as 'Soviet people' or 'Soviet nation.' In the discussion on the Soviet Union's ethnolinguistic diversity, the term народность *narodnost'* 'nationality' was employed as the preferred translation of the German term *Nationalität/Volksstamm*. However, at times, *narodnost'* was used interchangeably with the term национальность *natsional'nost'* 'nationality.' In the interwar Soviet Union, the administrative and ideological distinction between these two variants was at times maintained: *natsional'nost'* used for referring to 'developed nationalities' and *narodnost'* for 'culturally backward nationalities.' The litmus test was whether a nationality had already enjoyed its own written language, alongside a publishing industry and educational system in the medium of this language. In the latter case, such a written language, alongside a publishing industry and educational system in its medium, were to be created for such a 'backward nationality' (*narodnost'*), which would thus be transformed into a 'developed nationality' (*natsional'nost'*). The process of such mass creation of languages for the sake of 'socialist development' during the interwar period was known in the Soviet Union as the policy of коренизация *korenizatsiia* (literally 'rooting in') – that is, 'nativization' or 'indigenization.' Part and parcel of this process was endowing each nationality or its fragment with an ethnolinguistically defined autonomous territory (Martin 2001). Over 17,000 such autonomous territories were created at different administrative levels, from union republics to autonomous villages and autonomous kolkhozes (Martin 2001: 413). However, in 1938, the policy was rolled back to around 51 ethnolinguistically defined union republics and autonomous republics and districts (Martin 2001: 446).

After World War II, the Soviet model of ethnolinguistic federation was introduced, with some local variations: in communist Yugoslavia (Blagojević 1974), India (Brass 1990; Modak 2006; Schwartzberg 2009) and communist China (Mullaney 2012). Perhaps the non-Western examples of India and China, alongside Soviet support for the revolution, convinced communist (Soviet-Derg) Ethiopia to adopt ethnolinguistic decentralization (Klinger 1992: 46; Yordanov 2017: 134–135). In this attempt, Addis Ababa mostly emulated the Chinese model, as an appropriate model of statehood for Ethiopia. Article 1 of the 1987 Constitution refers to Ethiopia's population as 'a people' (ሕዝብ *hizib*) (rather than 'nation,' አገር *āger*). In Article 2 the country's various ethnic groups are recognized as 'nationalities' (ብሔረሰቦች *bihēreseboch*) defined through their languages (ቋንቋዎች *k'wanik'wawoch*) (The Constitution of the People's Democratic Republic of Ethiopia 1987). These usages are immediately reminiscent of the Soviet terms *narod* and *narodnost'*. This is unsurprising given that they were thoroughly codified in Amharic and introduced into sociopolitical practice through the extensive 580-page *yemarikisīzim lēnīnīzimi mezigebe k'alat* የማርክሲዝም ሌኒኒዝም መዝገበ ቃላት (The Dictionary of Marxism-Leninism) (*yemarikisīzim* 1978 EC [1986]), published in 1986. These usages closely followed the tenets of the Soviet Union's state ideology of marxism-leninism.

The 1995 postcommunist Constitution of the Ethiopian Federation implicitly ranked the country's ethnic groups into 'nations' (ብሔር *bihēr*), 'nationalities' (ብሔረሰብ *bihēreseb*) and 'peoples' (ሕዝብ *hizib*) (Ethiopia – Constitution 1994). However, in light of Article 39.5, from the purely legal standpoint, the three terms are synonymous and provide the identical right to national self-determination. Hence, these three terms are often used interchangeably in federal and regional legislation for the sake of referring to Ethiopia's recognized ethnic (ethnolinguistic) groups.

The administrative organization of the federation, however, suggests a hierarchy of ethnic groups. Indeed, Ethiopia pursued a multitiered approach to territorial autonomy, in which apparently 'bigger' ethnic groups ('nations') such as the Tigrayans, Amharas, Oromos and Somalis were given their own 'titular' and eponymous regions – or rather regional states (ክልል *kilil*) – in which they constitute the majority of the population. In contrast, several dozen (around 80) smaller ethnic groups ('nationalities, nations and peoples') were put together to create 'multiethnic' regions – for instance, the SNNPR, Gambela and Benishangul-Gumuz regions. In turn, within such multiethnic regions, numerous ethnic groups are given their own 'titular' and often-eponymous subregional administrative entities, namely 'zones' (ዞን *zone*), 'woredas' (ወረዳ *wereda*, literally 'district, region'), or 'special woredas' (ልዩ ወረዳ *liyu wereda*) and kebeles (ቀበሌ *k'ebelē*, literally 'neighborhood') at the level of small towns (municipalities) and villages (Subdivisions 2019).

This system closely emulates the Soviet model of ethnically defined union republics (союзныя республика *soiuznyia respublika*), autonomous republics (автономная республика *avtonomnaia respublika*), autonomous oblasts (автономная область *avtonomnaia oblast'*, literally 'region') and autonomous okrugs (автономный округ *avtonomnyi okrug*, literally 'district'). After World War II, communist China borrowed the Soviet system of multitiered autonomous regions – that is, autonomous regions (自治区

Table 0.2 Pyramids of autonomous national (ethnolinguistically defined) territories

Austria-Hungary	interwar Soviet Union	postwar Soviet Union	Russian Federation	communist China	federal Ethiopia
Kingdom of Hungary	union republic	union republic	NA	NA	regional state
autonomous crownland condominium (Bosnia)	autonomous republic	autonomous republic	autonomous republic	autonomous region	(special) zone
NA	autonomous oblast	autonomous oblast	autonomous oblast	autonomous prefecture	(special) woreda
NA	autonomous okrug	autonomous okrug	autonomous okrug	NA	NA
county	national district	NA	NA	autonomous county	NA
corpus separatum (City of Fiume and its District) free city (Trieste)	NA	NA	(federal city)	ethnic township	(chartered city)
Gemeinde (commune, municipality)	NA	NA	NA	ethnic city district	nationality kebele
	national village	NA	NA	ethnic village	NA
NA	national kolkhoz	NA	NA	NA	NA

zìzhìqū), autonomous prefectures (自治州 *zìzhìzhōu*) and autonomous counties (自治县 *zìzhìxiàn*). In China, there are also ethnic townships (民族乡 *mínzú xiāng*) and ethnic villages (民族村 *mínzú cūn*) (Autonomous Administrative 2019). These were borrowed from the interwar Soviet Union, where national districts (национальный район *natsional'nyi raion*), national villages (национальный сельсовет *natsional'nyi sel'sovet*, literally 'village council') and national kolkhozes (национальный колхоз *natsional'nyi kolkhoz*, literally 'collective farm') existed until 1938 (Martin 2001: 413). It appears that at present, Addis Ababa does not intend to implement similar autonomous entities at the level of a single kebele (commune), as a matter of course. But constitutionally, it is possible, and two such nationality kebeles (ብሔረሰብ ቀበሌ *bihēreseb k'ebelē*) were founded in Gambela.

Notes

1 The name Ethiopia is derived from the Greek name for this country, namely Αἰθιοπία Aithiopía, which was probably formed from αἴθω *aitho* 'I burn' and ὤψ *ops* 'face,' meaning either 'burnt-face' or 'red-brown.' In turn this name was borrowed to Amharic as ኢትዮጵያ *ītiyop'iya* (Mojdl 2005: 19, 111).
2 Abyssinia used to be the widespread name of Ethiopia in Europe and the West. This usage was mediated by way of the Ottoman Empire from the Arabic name of Ethiopia, namely الحبشة *al-habsha* (rendered as ሐበሻ *ḥabesha* in Ge'ez). Nowadays the term 'Habesha,' of unclear etymology, refers to all the Semitic- and Cushitic-speaking ethnic groups in Ethiopia and Eritrea (Messay Kebede 2003a: 5–6, 13; Shinn and Ofcansky 2013: 4). Hence, the name Ethiopia is more inclusive, because it encompasses *all* the country's ethnic groups. On the other hand, in popular discourse across Ethiopia, the ethnonym Habesha is employed to draw a racialized line of stereotypical division between 'better, paler, more European-like' Ethiopians and 'lower, darker, more negroid-like' non-Habesha Ethiopians (Fikru Helebo and Ephrem Madebo 2009; Nyang 2009; Osmond 2012: 193).
3 In the official language of Amharic, the name of the Ethiopian Empire was rendered as follows: መንግሥተ ኢትዮጵያ *menigišite ītiyop'iya*. The Amharic word መንግሥት *menigišite* also means 'kingdom' or 'government,' though in the latter case, the word is usually spelled a bit differently, namely መንግስት *menigisiti*.
4 The number of Russia's inhabitants slowly decreases, while the Ethiopian population continues to grow dramatically. Both countries are estimated to have equal populations in 2030: 143 million in Russia and 145 million in Ethiopia. Afterward, Ethiopia is estimated to overtake Russia in demographic terms. By 2050, the former country's population is estimated to reach 205 million, while the latter country's is to decline further to 135 million (Ethiopia Population 2019; Russia Population 2019). Should the predictions turn out to be right, in 2050 the number of Ethiopia's inhabitants will be actually equal to that of the Soviet Union's populace in 1957. And thirty-five years later, in 2085, at 290 million, Ethiopia's population is bound to be equal to that of the Soviet Union at the time of its demise in 1991 (Ethiopia Population 2019; File:Population of Former USSR 2014). Likewise, given both countries' highly multiethnic character,

which was made into the basis of their political organization, Ethiopia will face many similar challenges that used to plague the Soviet Union.

5 The ducal title *Ras* is the Ge'ez word ራስ 'head,' derived from, or similar to, Arabic *Rais* رئيس 'chief, leader' (Ethiopian Aristocratic 2019).

6 One of our anonymous reviewers rightly pointed out that some elements of the Ethiopian Empire could be usefully compared with their counterparts in the Ottoman Empire –, for instance, the core imperial populations of the Amharas in the former and the Turks in the latter. In the imperial period, the Turks were overwhelmingly contained to Anatolia, while the Amharas to the Ethiopian Plateau. These 'imperial cores' interacted – through succession conflicts, the appointment of regional governors, economic impositions or military expeditions – with the non-Turkic or non-Amharic peripheries that in terms of space and demography were more extensive than were the aforementioned imperial cores. A similar situation was observed in Austria-Hungary or the Soviet Union (though *not* in Germany or in Japan). Yet the focus of our book on the vagaries of the transfer of models of statehood from Central Europe to Ethiopia does not allow us to tackle this challenge. On top of that, the three authors do not have a knowledge of Osmanlıca or Turkish, indispensable for accessing necessary material. We decided to include a footnote on this highly interesting comparative subject for further research within the scope of imperial studies, hoping that a scholar will probe into it in the near future.

7 Miaphysitism (from the Greek expression μία φύσις *mía fýsis* 'one nature') – the Christian theological doctrine, which maintains that in the person of Jesus Christ divine nature and human nature are united in a compound nature, the two being united without separation, without mixture, without confusion and without alteration (Hunt in Parry 1999: 88). In relation to the Ethiopian Church the anglicized form of the theological Ge'ez term 'Tewahedo' (ተዋሕዶ *tewaḥido*) is used to indicate the Miaphysitic character of this church.

8 In literature, the term 'Derg' was established for referring to the Soviet ('revolutionary, communist, socialist') regime of Ethiopia. However, using this Amharic translation of the term 'Soviet' instead of the anglicized Russian term 'Soviet' makes one oblivious to the fact that Derg Ethiopia was a member or client of the Soviet bloc. Hence, in this study, we emphasize this often-forgotten connection by using the combined adjective 'Soviet-Derg,' instead of 'Derg' alone, for referring to communist Ethiopia.

9 During the 1920s, Vladimir Lenin and Joseph Stalin issued a similar promise in order to attract ethnic non-Russians to the Soviet cause. The former liked to refer this policy as a struggle against 'great power chauvinism' (великодержавный шовинизм *velikoderzhavnyi shovinizm*) and the latter as against 'Great Russian chauvinism' (великорусский шовинизм *velikorusskii shovinizm*) (Chakrabarty 1979: 139, 148; Martin 2001: 8, 126, 156–159).

10 The Soviet term *nationality policy* is sometimes rendered into English as *nationalities policy* or *national policy*, but all these translations stem from the same Russian collocation национальная политика *natsionalnaia politika* (cf Karpov 2017).

11 To move beyond the official lip service to the idea of territorial ethnolinguistic autonomy, at the turn of the 1980s, the Soviet-Derg authorities considered an ethnolinguistically defined autonomous region for the small ethnic group of Kunamas (at that time numbering 20,000) on the then administrative border between Tigray and Eritrea. This idea was never realized (Lewis 1983: 20).

12 The name Eritrea is derived from the Greek name Ἐρυθρὰ Θάλασσα *Erythra Thalassa* for the Red Sea (Connell and Killion 2011: 7).
13 We thank Rok Stergar for drawing our attention to this important terminological issue.
14 Interestingly, it was Ioseb Besarionis dze Jughashvili's (იოსებ ბესარიონის ჯუღაშვილი in Georgian) first publication where he employed his nom-de-plume 'Stalin' (literally 'man of steel,' Сталин in Russian; სტალინი *st'alini* in Georgian).

The 1931 Constitution
The importation of Western concepts via Japan

Emperor Haile Selassie ascended to the throne in November 1930. With renewed vigor and tenacity, he followed his predecessors' then-well-established twin policies of centralization and modernization. In 1931, as a clear sign of his commitment to Western-style modernization, Haile Selassie adopted the first written constitution for Ethiopia. Earlier, the three medieval 'sacred laws' (law codes) had constituted the legal basis of this country since the mid-13th century. These three law codes were titled as follows: the Fetha Negast (ፍትሃ ነገሥት *fitiha negešit* 'Law of the Kings'), the Kebra Negast (ክብረ ነገሥት *kibire negešit* 'Glory of the Kings') and the Serate Mengist (ሥርዓተ መንግሥት *širi'ate menigišit* 'Rules of Governance'). The law codes had been used to regulate all religious life, state administration and civil matters in imperial Ethiopia until 1931 (Corazza 2002: 351).

The adoption of the Constitution in 1931 followed the long power struggle between the reformists (including the young Emperor) and the traditionalist nobility. The reformists, led by Haile Selassie, sought to modernize the Ethiopian system of government in line with the political practices employed in European (Western) nation-states. As noted in Bahru Zewde's monograph *Pioneers of Change*, the first two European-style (secular) generations of Ethiopian intellectuals preoccupied themselves with the 'urgent' need to bring about a Western-style modernization to their country (Bahru Zewde 2002).

During the early years of his reign, the Emperor created an alliance with the aforementioned reformist intellectuals. They provided crucial support for his reform efforts. On the other hand, Haile Selassie emerged as the chief benefactor of the intellectuals in question. The Emperor supported the expansion of modern (Western-style) education – that is, independent of traditional religious (Christian or Muslim) models and under the state's control (Haile Gebriel Dagne 2007: 316, 326–328). In 1925, when he served as regent, under his orders, the eponymous Teferi Mekonnen secondary school was founded. It was the second public (government) secondary school in Ethiopia. By 1935, about 20 public (secular, government) schools had been founded across the country. They provided education for about 8,000 students (Amdissa 2008). In 1925, the Emperor also established a weekly newspaper, titled in Amharic as ብርሃንና ሠላም (*birihanina šelam* 'Light and Peace') (Shimelis Bonsa 2000: 8). This newspaper served as an important outlet for the aforementioned intellectuals to discuss their ideas of modernization. One of the recurrent themes, which they debated at that time, was the need to modernize Ethiopia by learning from the experiences of European nation-states (Shimelis Bonsa 2000: 8).

In the wake of the Japanese victory over the Russian Empire in 1905, Ethiopian intellectuals and the Emperor himself began to pay more attention to Japan. A revelation to Ethiopian intellectuals was that, in the span of three decades, Japan had been able to undergo a successful transformation from a feudal polity to a major industrial power, following the Meiji Restoration in 1868. This success of a *non*-Western country at *Western*-style modernization generated a strong motivation to learn from the Japanese experience (Clarke 2011: 7). The infatuation of the Ethiopian intellectuals with the Japanese experience was such that two renowned Ethiopian authors wrote in Amharic about Japan. In their books, they highlighted what Ethiopia should learn from this country. The first of these two books, namely ማኅደረ ብርሃን – ሀገረ ጃፓን (*maḥidere birihan – hāgere japan* 'Japan: The Source of Light'), came off the press in 1932. Heruy Welde Sellase (ኅሩይ ወልደ ሥላሴ *ḥiruy welide šilasē* 1878–1939), who authored this work, was a renowned writer but also served his country as a politician. Heruy held high posts in Haile Selassie's governments, such as that of Foreign Minister. Upon his return from Japan, which he had visited in 1931 (Clarke 2011), he published this book. The other book, ጃፓን እንዴት ሰለጠነች? (*japan inidēt selet'enech* 'How Did Japan Modernize Itself?'), written by Kebede Mikael (ከበደ ሚካኤል *kebede mīka'ēl* 1916–1998), was published in 1955. Kebede was also a writer of literature in his own right and served as a high-ranking official in Haile Selassie's administration. Both books highlighted similarities between the two countries and emphasized the importance of learning from Japan for the sake of implementing a Western-style modernization of Ethiopia, which would be customized to the African state's specific history and culture (Levine 2007; Clarke 2011).

The influence of Japan on Ethiopian intellectuals was such that the country's reformists of the early 20th century even came to be referred to as 'Japanizers' by later commentators. These reformists were convinced that the Japanese model of state centralization, by which the power of Japanese Emperor Meiji was consolidated and the influence of feudal lords curbed, could provide an important lesson for Ethiopia. Addis Hiwet, who in 1975 coined the term 'Japanizers' in his English-language monograph on this subject, observed that these intellectuals (i.e. the Japanizers) supported the Emperor and the pro-modernization nobility against the conservatives (traditionalists) (Addis Hiwet 1975: 77; Clarke 2011: 169). The strong influence of the Japanese experience on Ethiopia was clearly demonstrated by the country's first written Constitution, promulgated in 1931. The drafting of this Constitution was entrusted to the Minister of Finance, Tekle Hawariat Tekle Mariam (ተክለ ሐዋርያት ተክለ ማርያም *tekile ḥāwari'at tekile mariyam* 1884–1977), who had been educated in the pre-revolutionary Russian Empire (Augustyniak 2012: 111; Clapham 2006; Tsegaye Beru and Junker 2018). In drafting the Constitution, Tekle Hawariat drew on the Imperial Japanese Constitution of 1889, which is often referred as the Meiji Constitution.[1]

We claim that it is important here to briefly mention the main features of the 1889 Meiji Constitution. First of all, this Japanese Constitution emulated the model of the 1850 Prussian Constitution[2] (Pałasz-Rutkowska 2017 [1996]: 116). Historians of Japan generally divide the history of their country into two major periods: the period before 1868 (also known as the pre-Meiji period) and the period thereafter (O'Regan and Khosala 2014: 301). Before the Meiji Restoration, power in Japan was under the control of the feudal lords, where the Shogun[3] (military dictator) was at the top. One of the main achievements of the Meiji reforms (or revolution) was the consolidation of the power in the hands of the Emperor[4] by undermining the powers of the feudal nobility (Pałasz-Rutkowska 2017 [1996]; Horie 1952: 23). With an eye to consolidating the power of the Emperor, the Meiji Constitution declared the nature of the Emperor to be 'sacred and inviolable' (Berlin 1998: 388).

The strong influence of the Meiji Constitution on the Ethiopian Constitution of 1931 came from two sources. First, there was a feeling in the Ethiopian court, particularly among the reformist intellectuals who were then allied with the Emperor, that Japan 'was the closest in its political position to Ethiopia' (Augustyniak 2012:112). The second and most profound source was the gradual emergence of a widening 'movement' among educated and pro-reform Ethiopians, who promoted the idea of borrowing political models and institutions from the 'more developed' countries of the world (Augustyniak 2012: 112).

The 1931 Constitution was adopted on 16 July 1931. It was divided into seven chapters, which in turn comprised 55 articles. This Constitution provided for the establishment of a bicameral Parliament, consisting of the Chamber of the Senate (የሕግ መወሰኛ ምክር ቤት *yeḥig mewesinya mikir bēt*) and the Chamber of Deputies (የሕግ መምሪያ ምክር ቤት *yeḥig memirīya mikiri bēt*) (Ethiopian Constitution 1931). The members of the Senate were personally appointed by the Emperor, while the members of the lower Chamber of Deputies were appointed by provincial chiefs and the nobility. Both chambers of the Parliament did not have any legislative powers but rather served as a discussion forum on matters that would be of interest to the Emperor (Markakis and Asmelash 1967: 199). This Constitution guaranteed several rights for the Ethiopian subjects – for instance, the right of movement, due process of law, property rights and the secrecy of correspondence (Ethiopian Constitution 1931: Chapter 3, Art. 18–29).

The significant ideas from the Meiji Constitution adopted in the Ethiopian Constitution of 1931, included the consolidation of power in the Emperor's hands, alongside the introduction of the Western ideas of nation-state, a people and law. Tekle Hawariat Tekle Mariam, who drafted this Constitution, recollected in his autobiography that he was motivated to work on the Constitution, in spite of his strained relationship with the Emperor, because of two issues that he strongly believed were crucial for the country and its future. The first one was the need to maintain the power of the monarchy (የንጉሥነት ሥልጣን *yenigušinet šilit'an* 'royal authority'). This, according to Tekle Hawariat, was necessary to prevent the disintegration of Ethiopian unity in the event of succession problems. In this respect, the 1931 Constitution heavily borrowed ideas about the sacred and inviolable nature of the Emperor from the Meiji Constitution (cf The Constitution 1889: Art. 3; Ethiopian Constitution 1931: Art. 5). The other issue was the necessity to furnish the Ethiopian people (ሕዝብ *ḥizib*) with an instrument that would help protect their rights as individuals. Only on such a legally enshrined basis would the subjects be able to advance in a Western manner by receiving secular education as the foundational prerequisite for their increasing participation in public life and politics. Over the course of this process, the subjects would hopefully be allowed to become citizens, who could saliently contribute to the future political shape of Ethiopia (Tekle Hawariat Tekle Mariam 2006: 401–402).

Similarly, in a speech that Haile Selassie gave after the signing of the 1931 Constitution, he outlined the major rationales for his eagerness to promulgate this document (Mahteme Selassie Wolde Meskel 1970: 724–726). These included, first, the need to strengthen the unity (አንድነት *ānidinet*) of the people of Ethiopia (የኢትዮጵያ ሕዝብ *ye'ītiyop'iya ḥizib*). Haile Selassie likened them to a single family, who should be able to live peacefully and cooperate without any discord in the single and indivisible empire. Second, the Emperor emphasized the necessity of allowing the public (i.e. the subjects) to share the burden of governing the country. Third, the male primogeniture in the imperial linage was reconfirmed with an eye to preventing a political crisis and possible bloodshed in the event of any succession problems.

The key objectives of the 1931 Constitution were succinctly summarized by Tekle Hawariat in his speech on the occasion of the celebrations of the first anniversary of this constitution in 1932 (1924EC). He identified the foundations of the Ethiopian Constitution in the following four terms, namely monarchy (ንጉስ *nigus*, literally 'king'), people (ሕዝብ *hizib*), nation (ሀገር *hāger*, literally 'country') and law (ሕግ *hig*) (Mahteme Selassie Wolde Meskel 1970: 815). In this respect, Chapter 1 of the Constitution, composed of five articles, provided the rules for governing 'the Ethiopian Empire and succession to the throne.' Accordingly, 'throne and the crown of the empire shall be transmitted to the descendants of the Emperor' (Ethiopian Constitution 1931: Art. 4). Moreover, the Constitution provided that the Emperor was 'sacred, his dignity is inviolable and his power indisputable' (Ethiopian Constitution 1931: Art. 5). Obviously, this article was borrowed directly from the Meiji Constitution, which provided that the 'Emperor is sacred and inviolable' (The Constitution 1889: Art. 3).

The 1931 Constitution mentioned 'a people' (ሕዝብ *hizib*) in several articles. Article 1 provided that

> the territory of Ethiopia, in its entirety, is, from one end to the other, subject to the government of His Majesty the Emperor. All the natives of Ethiopia [are] subjects of the empire, [and] form together the Ethiopian People (ሕዝብ *hizib*).
>
> (Ethiopian Constitution 1931)

In addition, Chapter 3 of the Constitution outlined the rights and duties of the people (Ethiopian Constitution 1931). The Constitution also employed the concept of nation-state (ሀገር *hāger*, literally 'country'). However, this document, confusingly, used the same Amharic concept of ሕዝብ (*hizib* 'a people') when it referred to either 'the people of the country' or 'the country (i.e. nation-state)' itself. This is evident in the English version of the Constitution, where both the term *people* and the term *nation* are used interchangeably to refer to the country's population (Imperial Government 1969 [1955]). Similarly, this constitution in several articles mentioned the term *law*, because this document's central purpose was to legitimize the rule of the Emperor by borrowing Western ideas, as mediated through the Meiji Constitution.

In spite of the similarities that prevailed between the Meiji Constitution and the Ethiopian Constitution of 1931, these two documents also contain differences. One major difference worth mentioning is the provision for the elections of the members of the House of Representatives of the Japanese Diet by the people of Japan in the Meiji Constitution (The Constitution 1889). In the Ethiopian case, Article 32 of the 1931 Constitution provides that 'as a temporary measure until the people are capable of electing them themselves, the members of the Chamber of Deputies shall be chosen by the dignitaries and the local chiefs' (Ethiopian Constitution 1931). In sum, both the Meiji Constitution and the Ethiopian Constitution of 1931 were preoccupied with the consolidation and centralization of imperial power by introducing Western constitutional principles and institutions to both Japan and Ethiopia. The main goal was to curb the power of the regions and their traditional noble elites (Vlastos 1997; Smith 2013). In the Japanese case, the contribution of the Meiji Constitution to limiting the powers of the nobility was much more effective than it was in Ethiopia. For instance, the Meiji reforms led to the abolition of feudal ownership of land (Vlastos 1997). In Ethiopia, such a sweeping land reform took place only after the Soviet-Derg Revolution of 1974.

Nation building and assimilation: the 1955 Revised Constitution and the 1974 Draft Constitution

In 1955, the imperial government issued a Revised Constitution. In comparison to the 1931 Constitution, the revised document was more elaborate. It contained eight chapters with 131 articles (Imperial Government 1969 [1955]). Several reasons necessitated the revision of the 1931 Constitution. First of all, the 1930s modernizing reforms, the Italian occupation and the wartime and postwar aid extended by the United Kingdom and the United States introduced numerous social, political and economic changes in Ethiopia. Furthermore, under the supervision of the United Nations (UN), in 1952 Eritrea was incorporated, which importantly overhauled Ethiopia into a federation (Fasil 1997: 25). Under this arrangement, Eritrea was to receive its own constitution. Unlike the case of the Ethiopian Constitution of 1931, the Eritrean Constitution was prepared by the UN and adopted by the Eritrean Assembly in July 1952. The Eritrean Constitution contained several provisions on human rights, such as the freedoms of assembly, press and association (Fasil 1997). The document also provided for a democratic system of government. The Eritrea-Ethiopia Federation Act was drafted by the UN too. Emperor Haile Selassie ratified this Federation Act in September 1952, which formally completed the formation of the Federation of Ethiopia and Eritrea. The Federal Act was modeled on the UN's Universal Declaration of Human Rights (UDHR) (Fasil 1997: 25).

Hence, one of the main objectives of the 1955 revision of the Ethiopian Constitution was to narrow the gap between the Federal Act and the Eritrean Constitution on the one hand and the Ethiopian Constitution of 1931 on the other hand. Accordingly, Chapter 3 of the Ethiopian Constitution of 1955 contained a long list of rights, including equality before the law, the freedom of religious worship and the freedom of speech (Revised 1955). However, the 1955 Constitution did not provide for multiparty politics. Yet this document introduced the elections of members to the Parliament's lower Chamber of Deputies directly by the people of Ethiopia. In this manner, universal suffrage was at long last introduced to Ethiopia.

The quest for building a centralized 'nation-state' under the Emperor's absolutist power was also demonstrated by the 1955 Constitution. In this new document, the status and the role of the monarchy were defined in a more elaborate fashion than they were in the 1931 Constitution. Accordingly, Chapters 1 and 2 of the 1955 Constitution dealt, respectively, with succession and the Emperor's powers and prerogatives. The principle that the person of the Emperor is sacred, as included in the 1931 Constitution, was also maintained in the Revised Constitution of Ethiopia of 1955. Article 4 of the 1955 Constitution provided that 'by virtue of His Imperial Blood, as well as by the anointing which He has received, the person of the Emperor is sacred, His dignity is inviolable and His power indisputable' (Revised 1955). In spite of the law-making function with which the Ethiopian Parliament was entrusted, the 1955 Constitution reconfirmed the absolute power of the Emperor in all areas of state power.

In addition to consolidating the power of the Emperor, the 1955 Constitution aimed at building a nation-state by fortifying the national unity of Ethiopia. In this respect, Article 2 provided that all Ethiopian subjects, living within the empire and abroad, constituted the 'united people of Ethiopia' (በአንድነት የኢትዮጵያ ሕዝብ ነው *be'ānidinet ye'ītiyop'iya ḥizib new*) (Imperial Government 1965EC/1972 [1955]). The Constitution also adopted the Ethiopian national flag (Art. 124), declared Amharic as the official language of the empire (Art. 125) and proclaimed the Ethiopian Orthodox Church as the 'Established Church of the Empire' (Art. 126) (Revised 1955). These provisions made explicit what was implicit in the 1931 Constitution, namely the ambition of the imperial government to consolidate the Ethiopian Empire as an ethnolinguistic nation-state through the policies of assimilation (i.e. Amharization) and centralization. Indeed, the chief instrument that the imperial government deployed for unifying Ethiopia's ethnically diverse peoples (ethnic groups) was the assimilation (Amharization) of the elites of the country's different ethnic (or regional) groups. In return for a variety of economic and political concessions and privileges, these elites were expected to adopt the culture and language of the politically dominant Amharas and function as intermediaries between the state and their respective ethnic groups (Clapham 1988: 195).

The state policy of assimilation (Amharization) reached new, unprecedented heights after the restoration of the Emperor, following the wartime occupation of the country by Italy from 1936 to 1941. The first law that the Emperor promulgated immediately after the liberation of Ethiopia was Decree 1 of 1942. This decree dramatically deepened the centralization of the state (Markakis 1974: 290; Perham 1969: 348). As part and parcel of the state policy of assimilation, since 1941, the Amharic language had been used as a leading medium of instruction in elementary schools. Obviously, Amharic also continued in its traditional function of the official language of the government, state administration and army (Markakis 2003: 12–13). What is more, the imperial government prohibited publishing in the languages of Oromo and Tigrinya (Markakis 2003; Tubiana 1983). It was a reaction to the Italian occupation administration's efforts to increase the use of Ethiopia's other languages (including Arabic), for the sake of downgrading Amharic (Bowen 1976: 322).

Haile Selassie's project of building a highly centralized state faced numerous challenges. The most daunting was posed by the political marginalization and economic exploitation of the highly multiethnic south, which had been conquered only half a century earlier. Other problems, up north in the old imperial core, ranged from peasant rebellions in Tigray, Bale and Gojam to students' protests (Andargachew 1993). In addition, the undoing of the Federation of Ethiopia and Eritrea in 1962 led to a secessionist war in Eritrea, to which Eritrean historians refer as the War of Eritrean Independence. Apart from these burning issues, the imperial government was faced with the increasingly militant opposition staged by university students (Bahru 1991: 220). Their concerted and increasingly more vocal protests and opposition activities earned them the sobriquet of the Ethiopian Student Movement (ESM, የኢትዮጵያ ተማሪዎች ንቅናቄ ye'ītiyop'iya temarīwoch nik'inak'ē). It was never formalized as an organization. Nevertheless, during the late imperial period, the ESM left a bigger imprint on Ethiopian politics and society than any parties or organizations of this time. The ESM passed through several stages of radicalization before it reached a climax in the late 1960s (Bahru 1991: 222; Balsvik 2005: 71–78).

During the initial stage of their activism, the students' concerns were parochial in character and focused largely on campus issues (Kiflu Tadesse 1993: 35). However, in the late 1950s, students became more assertive and began raising political issues. If the Emperor thought that like the Japanizers of the 1930s, the students would support his modernizing (i.e. Westernizing) policies, he was proven mistaken. For instance, the students demonstrated in support of the abortive coup d'état staged against the Emperor in December 1960. Soon afterward, the ESM vociferously criticized the massively inequitable distribution of land. In this respect, beginning in 1965, the students demonstrated under banners brandishing the Soviet-style (marxist-leninist) slogan 'land to the tiller.' Their main demand was to end the system of tenancy, which de facto reduced peasants to the status of serfs on their lords' fields (Kiflu Tadesse 1993: 39), especially in the southern and eastern territories conquered by Ethiopia at the turn of the 20th century (Triulzi 1983: 120).

The end of the 1960s was marked by the further radicalization of the ESM and the adoption of the leftist (Soviet-style) ideology of marxism-leninism among the students. Both the Emperor and the ESM stood for Western-style modernization but of different types, which the Cold War had made into presumably irreconcilable opposites. Indeed, during this period, marxism-leninism emerged as the uncontested guiding sociopolitical ideology among the students, while the imperial regime stuck to capitalism and paid lip service to democracy and liberalism, as practiced in Western Europe and North America. The problem was that with time, practically each sociopolitical grouping claiming to be progressive embraced marxism-leninism. In their eyes, this ideology provided a coherent conceptual framework and legitimation for activism, which promised to bring modernizing change and benefits to everyone in all nooks of the country. Marxism-leninism appeared to be an apt answer to late imperial Ethiopia's burning problems. Many saw this ideology as the 'diagnosis of the malaise of Ethiopian society and the prescription for its remedy' (Bahru Zewde 2003: 3).

The left-leaning and pro-Soviet radicalization of the students took on a new dimension at the turn of the 1970s, when they decided it was high time to pay more attention to the issue of ethnic relations in Ethiopia. In November 1969, Wallelign Mekonnen (ዋለልኝ መኮንን *walelign mekonin* 1945–1972) published the seminal article 'On the Question of Nationalities in Ethiopia' (የብሔሮች ጥያቄ በኢትዮጵያ *yebiḥēroch t'iyak'ē be'ītiyop'iya*) in the bilingual (English-Amharic) student magazine, *Struggle*/ታገል *tagel* (Balsvik 2007: 33–34). In his text, Wallelign Mekonnen challenged the idea of Ethiopian national unity: 'Ethiopia was not yet a nation but an Amhara-ruled collection of a dozen nationalities, each with their own language, ways of dressing, history, social organization and territorial entity' (Makonnen in Balsvik 2005: 276–277). He saw Ethiopia as a 'prison of nations'[5] – that is, of ethnolinguistically defined nations (Praeg 2006: 69) – and failed to consider the possibility of a civic (state-wide) Ethiopian nation (Yared Tibebu 2019). In the spirit of the then observed worldwide popularity of the

32 The 1931 Constitution

Soviet Union's ideology of marxism-leninism, Wallelign Mekonnen's piece was a rallying call for challenging 'Great Amharic chauvinism' and introducing the policy of 'indigenization' (*korenizatsiia*). In other words, it was to be a proactive policy of 'affirmative action' for Ethiopia's non-Amhara ethnic groups. The impetus of Wallelign Mekonnen's diagnosis and plan for changing Ethiopia's ethnic relations was so immense that the Soviet-Derg had no choice but to at least pay some lip service to it. But only the EPRDF, after 1991, was able to make Wallelign Mekonnen's ideas into the ideological and administrative basis of contemporary Ethiopia's statehood, which is thus steeped in ethnolinguistic (ethnoterritorial) federalism.

Figure 1.1 People's Democratic Republic of Ethiopia, 1987–1991 (Dörrbecker 2019)

Meanwhile, the Emperor's rule was threatened by the political opposition stemming from different groups, be they connected to leftist ideologies (predominantly marxism-leninism) or the country's non-Amhara ethnic groups (nationalities). For the sake of improving the deteriorating situation, in 1974, the imperial government attempted to undertake a constitutional reform. To this end, the Higher Constitutional Congress (ከፍተኛው ሕግ መንግሥታዊ ጉባዔ *kefitenyaw ḥige menigišitawī guba'ē*) presented a Draft Constitution. The Draft Constitution included many innovations. Above all, this document envisaged the establishment of a constitutional monarchy (Art. 60). In addition, the concept of (ethnic) nation (ብሔር *biḥēr*) was introduced to Ethiopian politics and legislation. To this end, in Article 1, the Draft Constitution named the country as the ብሔረ ኢትዮጵያ (*biḥēre ītiyop'iya* 'Ethiopian [ethnic] nation'). Article 4 provided that 'the official language of the Ethiopian government is Amharic' (የኢትዮጵያ መንግሥት መደበኛ ቋንቋ አማርኛ ነው *ye'ītiyop'iya menigišit medebenya k'wanik'wa āmarinya new*). But in a major departure from the 1955 Constitution, Article 45 stated that all Ethiopian ነገዶች *negedoch* (literally 'tribes,' i.e. 'ethnic groups'), which could be reasonably transformed into viable ጎሳዎ *gosawochi*,[6] (literally 'ethnic groups and clans,' i.e. 'nationalities') have the right to enjoy the state's protection, alongside the right to develop and cultivate their languages and cultures. In addition, Chapter 2 of the Draft Constitution listed a long list of other rights inspired by the United Nation's Universal Declaration of Human Rights of 1948 (Higher 1974 [1966EC]). The Draft Constitution of 1974 was never promulgated, because the imperial government was overthrown in the course of the Ethiopian Revolution in September 1974. Subsequently, the marxist-leninist (communist) junta seized power in the country. Later, it came to be known as the Soviet-Derg (ደርግ *derg*, literally 'committee') (cf Halliday and Molyneux 1981; Harsch 1978).

Notes

1 The term *Meiji* in such collocations as the Meiji Constitution or the Meiji Restoration is eponymous in its character, because it was the name of Emperor Meiji, whose political power was restored in 1868. Japan's first constitution, promulgated in 1889, is formally titled the Constitution of the Empire of Japan (大日本帝國憲法 *Dai-Nippon Teikoku Kenpō*) (The Constitution 1889).
2 Prussia's 1850 Constitution was formally titled the Constitution for the State of Prussia (*Verfassung für den Preußischen Staat*) (Preußische Verfassung 2019).
3 The Japanese term *shogun* is the conventional abbreviated form of the title *Sei-i Taishōgun* (征夷大将軍 'Commander-in-Chief of the Expeditionary Force Against the Barbarians') (Khan 1997: 86).
4 In Japanese, the term *emperor* is 天皇 *Ten'nō* 'Heavenly Sovereign.'

34 *The 1931 Constitution*

5 Originally, during the Great War, Entente press and information coordinators came up with the politically pejorative phrase 'prison (house) of nation' for the sake of employing it in propaganda aimed against Austria-Hungary (Johnson 2011: 170).
6 Nowadays, ጎሳ *gosa* ('clan') also means 'ethnicity' in Amharic; compare with the Austro-Hungarian term *Volksstamm*, which originally meant 'tribe' but which came to mean 'nationality.'

From the Soviet Union to Ethiopia's ethnoterritorial federalism

Contesting ethnolinguistic homogenization: the Soviet Union as an inspiration

As mentioned earlier, the imperial nation-state-building project in Ethiopia became particularly contested in the late 1960s, when the Ethiopian Student Movement (ESM), inspired by marxist-leninist ideas – or even 'scientific socialism' (Balsvik 2007: 38) – 'discovered' and vehemently debated the 'nationalities issue.' In essence, this 'issue' referred to the forced assimilation (i.e. Amharization) of dozens of ethnic groups in the country (Van der Beken 2012: 77). The debates within the ESM resembled the discussions on similar topics conducted among the Bolsheviks in the aftermath of the October Revolution in 1917. Whereas the ultimately victorious faction led by Vladimir Lenin and then Joseph Stalin emphasized the importance of recognizing the right to national self-determination for all the Soviet Union's nations (nationalities), including secession (Connor 1989: 27), others – the so-called internationalists – subordinated the issue of national self-determination to class struggle. They argued that a successful class struggle would make the question of national self-determination irrelevant (Martin 2001: 2). The debate in the ESM similarly revolved around whether the recognition of the right to national self-determination (including secession) was a prerequisite for a successful class struggle or whether national self-determination had to be made secondary to the struggle against feudalism and imperialism. In the latter case, self-determination would not be allowed to proceed beyond regional autonomy (Bahru 2014: 205–211). Eventually, the recognition of the right to national self-determination up to and including secession prevailed among the Ethiopian students. This conclusion was in agreement with the position originally taken by Lenin and Stalin in the wake of the Bolshevik Revolution.

The ESM encouraged the creation of a variety of marxist-leninist parties that later exerted a fundamental impact on Ethiopian politics and on the successive Ethiopian governments' approach to the processes of nation and state building in the following decades (Bahru 2014: 263). The first category of marxist-leninist parties (notably the EPRP and the MEISON) had multiethnic memberships and adopted Lenin and Stalin's views on ethnolinguistically defined nationalism as a transitory phenomenon to be phased out by the government once the developmental stage of socialism has been reached (Ghelawdewos 1995: 134; Leenco Lata 1999: 199; Young 1997: 59–60). Although Lenin and Stalin supported the constitutional acknowledgment and institutionalization of ethnicity in the Soviet Union (including the right to national self-determination up to secession), they perceived this as a temporary and tactical concession while they were working toward the creation of a homogeneous socialist (communist) Soviet people in a potentially worldwide state (Connor 1989: 31; Brubaker 1994: 49).

This explains why the Soviet-Derg, or the military government that removed and replaced the imperial regime in the course of the 1974 Revolution, continued with the imperial regime's policy of strong centralization. As recommended by the Soviet model, the Soviet-Derg sought to centralize all power in their hands only. To this end, the regime annihilated the EPRP (Ethiopian People's Revolutionary Party) and MEISON (All-Ethiopia Socialist Movement) in the immediate years after the revolution. The process was similar in pattern to the power struggle between the Bolshevik and Menshevik factions of the Russian Social-Democratic Labour Party, which the Bolsheviks won after the Bolshevik Revolution. The victorious Bolsheviks suppressed the Mensheviks, finally banning them in 1921. However, the Bolsheviks took over many ideological tenets and policies developed by the Mensheviks. Like in the case of Bolshevik (Soviet) Russia, in revolutionary Ethiopia, the victorious Soviet-Derg and its ideology seriously benefited from the EPRP's and MEISON's intellectual contributions. This explains, to a degree, the official espousal of the dichotomy, which was also characteristic of the Soviet Union in this regard, between the official rhetoric and the actual practice in socialist (communist) Ethiopia's approach to ethnicity. While the Soviet-Derg formally recognized the right to national self-determination for all Ethiopian nationalities (ethnic groups), this regime in practice instituted a highly centralized authoritarian administration. The term *nations* in plural was consciously avoided, due to the traditional Central European and Soviet ideological distinction between nations and nationalities. In the marxist-leninist take on the nationality issue, the former have the right to secession, while the latter do not. Nationalities have the right to national (cultural, linguistic, ethnic) territorial autonomy.

The aforementioned dichotomy between rhetoric and practice in this regard generated a strong sociopolitical tension in communist Ethiopia, leading to the creation of a number of ethnolinguistically defined liberation movements. The Tigray People's Liberation Front (TPLF) was the main one among these movements. It also originated from the revolutionary intellectual ferment in the ESM circles (Bahru 2014: 258). Unsurprisingly then, the TPLF adopted a type of marxist-leninist ideology and practices. However, the TPLF differed from the EPRP, the MEISON and the ruling Soviet-Derg in the ways this party approached the issue of ethnicity. For the TPLF, ethnicity was not simply a tactical or rhetorical issue but the major foundation for and focus of the party's struggle. For the TPLF, national or ethnic antagonisms were a primary concern, and this party presented itself as a movement fighting for the right to national self-determination of the Tigray people or nation (Leenco Lata 1999: 210; Vaughan 1994: 11; Young 1997: 154). In 1989, when communism collapsed across the Soviet bloc in Europe and Asia, the TPLF decided to broaden its objectives. Quite ambitiously, the party decided to strive for bringing about the complete downfall of the ruling Soviet-Derg regime. To this end, the TPLF established the Ethiopian Peoples' Revolutionary Democratic Front (EPRDF), which was a coalition of four ethnicity-based parties that fought for the national liberation of a variety of ethnolinguistically defined ethnic groups (nationalities, nations). Apart from the leading TPLF, the EPRDF was also joined by the Amhara Democratic Party (ADP),[1] the Oromo Democratic Party (ODP) and the Southern Ethiopian People's Democratic Movement (SEPDM).

In 1991, the EPRDF's military forces decisively defeated the Soviet-Derg, and thus the almost three-decade-long Ethiopian Civil War finally came to an end. Since that moment, the EPRDF ruled postcommunist Ethiopia until 2019. In late 2019, the EPRDF morphed into the Prosperity Party, but *without* the participation of the TPLF (The EPRDF 2019). The EPRDF, in cooperation with other ethnicity-based parties, granted extensive rights to Ethiopia's 'nations, nationalities and peoples'[2] and pressed on with the ethnolinguistically construed decentralization of the country's administrative structure that was implemented in 1992.[3] This new administrative structure of Ethiopia became the foundation for the introduction of full-fledged ethnoterritorial federalism three years later. This momentous change became possible thanks to the Constitution, which was approved in December 1994 and promulgated in the following year.

This chapter's following section focuses on present-day Ethiopia's constitutional terminology, as employed for referring to ethnicity. Furthermore, it discusses the most important constitutional provisions adopted for the sake of fulfilling the EPRDF's promise of national self-determination for Ethiopia's numerous ethnic groups (i.e. nations, nationalities and peoples). Obviously, most of these terms and many provisions of this kind stem from the marxist-leninist tradition and practices of the Soviet nationality policy (Semahagn Gashu Abebe 2014: 123–127). Yet the Ethiopian Constitution of 1995 embraced ethnic diversity more fully than did the postwar Soviet Union's corresponding constitutional provisions, as evidenced in the Constitution of the Soviet Union of 1977.

Comparing Soviet and Ethiopian constitutional approaches to ethnicity

The TPLF was the major political force behind the overhauling of postcommunist Ethiopia into an ethnic federation. This party was strongly inspired by marxism-leninism and by the Soviet model in general, especially in the field of nationality policy, or the administrative and political management of ethnic (ethnolinguistic) diversity (cf Yordanov 2017: 195). Yet because of its origin as an ethnic liberation movement, the TPLF truly espoused ethnicity, unlike Soviet leaders who accepted it tactically with an eye to the eventual phasing out of ethnicity on the way to ethnic-less and classless communism. That is why the TPLF did not consider the accommodation of ethnicity as a temporary concession. This party genuinely rejected the imperial and – to a degree – Soviet-Derg program of making Ethiopia into a centralized and ethnolinguistically homogenous nation-state. This acknowledgment and respect for ethnic difference is fully reflected in the 1995 Ethiopian Constitution. In its approach to ethnicity, this document was strongly inspired by the TPLF's views on this matter. Although both the 1977 Soviet Constitution and the 1995 Ethiopian Constitution established ethnoterritorial federations, the latter is conspicuous for its strong emphasis on ethnic diversity.

Initially, the Soviet Union similarly emphasized and embraced the importance of ethnic diversity during the interwar period. This approach resulted in the founding of over 17,000 ethnolinguistically defined autonomous territories in the country (Martin 2001: 10). However, after 1938, this policy was gradually abandoned in favor of lavishing more attention on the unity of the Soviet state as a whole. As a result, many remaining provisions for the Soviet nationalities were rolled back, and even a merger (слияние *slianie*) of them into a Soviet classless and ethnic-less *narod* (i.e. 'nation' or 'people') was postulated (*Fundamentals* 1963: 676–678). Indeed, the 1977 Soviet Constitution paid more attention to what united all the communist polity's nationalities and to strategies that would facilitate their stable merger (Shtromas 1978: 267).

With an eye to this goal, the Soviet Constitution evoked the traditional marxist-leninist view on ethnicity, as a societal feature that would gradually wither away, like statehood. In this view, ethnicity (nationalism) and capitalism (alongside its dominant class of bourgeoisie) belonged to the earlier ('capitalist-bourgeois') stage of human development. It was to be followed by the transitory stage of socialism with a centrally planned economy and some ethnic diversity remaining, before the acme of human development – that is, the stage of communism could be achieved. In communism, both statehood and ethnicity would already be things of the past, replaced by grassroots organic self-organization and a single united classless and ethnic-less communist people (*narod*),[4] which would embrace all humankind, or at least the entire Soviet population (*Fundamentals* 1963: 698–717). Hence, when in the 1930s the Soviet authorities attempted to hasten this 'inevitable progress' from the stage of capitalism to communism, they criminalized this form of economy and ethnicity and denigrated it in the Soviet ideological slurs of 'national-bourgeois deviation' (национально-буржуазный уклон *natsional'no-burzhuazynyi uklon*) and 'local bourgeois nationalism' (местный буржуазный национализм *mestnyi burzhuaznyi natsionalizm*) (Cherednichenko 1985; *Fundamentals* 1963: 626–630; Kulichenko 1972: 224).

Conversely, the currently obtaining constitutional provisions in the Federal Democratic Republic of Ethiopia give ethnicity the primary role in the process of state building. The situation is similar to the interwar Soviet authorities' positive approach to ethnicity. Ethnic diversity was made into the foundation for building and legitimating the administrative division of the Soviet Union during the 1920s and early 1930s. As the foregoing analysis reveals, the Ethiopian Constitution is based on the strong normative assumption that the unity of the state is served best by the full acknowledgment of ethnic diversity. Therefore, the 1995 Constitution made it into the legitimizing basis of the Ethiopian Federation's institutions and administrative division. This assumption implies that in present-day Ethiopia the accommodation of ethnic diversity is not considered to be a mere temporary expedient. This accepting approach to ethnicity is intended to be genuinely instrumental for achieving the paramount objective of societal and state unity in Ethiopia.

The key role given to ethnic diversity in today's Ethiopia is visible in the first sentence of the Preamble to the Ethiopian Constitution of 1995. It affirms that the Constitution emanates from the general will of none other than all the country's 'nations, nationalities and peoples.' Article 8 explicitly reconfirms that this Constitution is an expression of the sovereignty of Ethiopia's 'nations, nationalities and peoples' (Ethiopia – Constitution 1994). In contrast, Article 1 of the Soviet Constitution of 1977 designated the USSR as a state of the 'whole people,' while Article 2 provided that 'All power in the USSR belongs to the people' (Вся власть в СССР принадлежит народу *Vsia vlast' v SSSR prinadlezhit narodu*) in *singular* (Constitution

1977). However, in the Russian-language original Article 1 actually refers to 'all the country's nations and nationalities' (все нации и народности страны *vse natsii i narodnosti strany*). So in this respect, the similarity with the Ethiopian Constitution of 1995 is stronger than suggested by the English translation of the Soviet Constitution (Konstitutsiya 1977).

The Ethiopian Constitution of 1995 also contains references to unity – for instance, the Preamble refers to 'our [i.e. nations, nationalities and peoples'] common destiny' and to the necessity of maintaining 'one economic community' for the sake of the 'collective promotion of our interests' (Ethiopia – Constitution 1994). However, the document does not explicitly aim at homogenization, be it ethnic or social. The 1977 Soviet Constitution, on the other hand, in Article 19, proclaimed the objective of social and ethnic homogeneity would be achieved through, among other methods, the 'drawing together of all the nations and nationalities of the USSR' (сближение всех наций и народностей СССР *sblizhenie vsekh natsii i narodnostei SSSR*) (Constitution 1977; Konstitutsiya 1977), on the way to their merger (*sliianie*), which was then thought to be imminent.

The centripetal objectives of the Soviet Constitution of 1977 were also strongly evoked in Article 70. It designated the USSR an integral state (единое государство *edinoe gosudarstvo*) and furthermore stipulated that this polity embodies the state unity of all the Soviet people (олицетворяет государственное единство советского народа *olitsetvoriaet gosudarstvennoe edinstvo sovetskogo naroda*) (Constitution 1977; Konstitutsiya 1977). On the contrary, the concept of 'Ethiopian people' is noticeably absent from the 1995 Ethiopian Constitution. Another constitutional provision that appears to reflect the genuine commitment of the drafters of the Ethiopian Constitution[5] to ethnic diversity is the right to secession, as enshrined in Article 39 (Ethiopia – Constitution 1994). Although the right to secession for all the 15 union republics of the USSR also featured in the 1977 Soviet Constitution (Article 72: За каждой союзной республикой сохраняется право свободного выхода из СССР *Za kazhdoi soiuznoi respublikoi sokhraniaetsya pravo svobodnogo vykhoda iz SSSR* 'Each union republic retains the right and liberty of leaving [seceding from][6] the USSR') (Constitution 1977; Konstitutsiya 1977), it did not seem to be anything more than a mere ritualistic piece of marxist-leninist rhetoric, given the Constitution's strong emphasis on state and societal unity (Uibopuu 1979: 179, 180). In contrast, not only does the Ethiopian Constitution of 1995 grant the right to secession to all the country's nations, nationalities and peoples (Article 39.1), but it also provides the procedure for exercising this right (Article 39.4) (Ethiopia – Constitution 1994).

Both constitutions established ethnically (ethnolinguistically) defined federated units, be they 'union republics' in the Soviet Union or 'states' (regions) in the Ethiopian Federation. Article 71 of the Soviet Constitution of 1977 provided the list of this communist polity's 15 ethnically defined union republics (Constitution 1977), while Article 47.1 of the 1995 Ethiopian Constitution lists the country's nine ethnically based regional states:

1 The State of Tigray
2 The State of Afar
3 The State of Amhara
4 The State of Oromia
5 The State of Somali
6 The State of Benshangul/Gumuz
7 The State of the Southern Nations, Nationalities and Peoples
8 The State of the Gambela Peoples
9 The State of the Harari People (Ethiopia – Constitution 1994)[7]

However, once again, important differences can be observed between both constitutions, clearly showing that the Ethiopian Constitution displays a stronger commitment to protecting and institutionalizing ethnic diversity in the administrative structure of the state. Whereas the Soviet Constitution of 1977 limited the number of ethnoterritorial union republics to 15, the Ethiopian Constitution gave the right to establish a regional state (or a substate autonomous unit) to all the country's over 80 recognized nations, nationalities and peoples (the list is open-ended) (*Summary* 2008: 84–85). To this end, Article 47.2 provides that 'Nations, Nationalities and Peoples within the States enumerated in [Article 47.1] have the right to establish, at any time, their own States' (Ethiopia – Constitution 1994). The Soviet Constitution of 1977 accepted the then extant 20 autonomous soviet socialist republics (Article 85) and eight autonomous regions (автономная область *avtonomnaia oblast'*) (Article 87), but did *not* provide any mechanisms for creating new ones. However, a certain leeway was left in Article 88 on autonomous areas (автономный округ *avtonomnyi okrug*), because no definitive list of such territories was included in the Constitution (Constitution 1977; Konstitutsiya 1977). As many as ten autonomous okrugs (areas) existed in the late Soviet Union. On the other hand, the 1977 Soviet Constitution somewhat downgraded their status, by changing their designation from 'national okrug' (национальный округ *natsionalnyi okrug*) to a mere 'autonomous okrug.' In the case of federal Ethiopia, in actual practice, several factors may impede the right of this country's nations, nationalities and peoples to their own autonomous territories. Among others, these factors include the small population size of a given ethnic group, this group's insufficient socioeconomic development or a dearth of qualified personnel versed in this group's language. However, the Ethiopian Constitution does not simply pay lip service to the ethnolinguistically defined right of ethnic groups to their own autonomous territory, in that Article 47.3 provides the procedure for exercising this right (Ethiopia – Constitution 1994).

The 1977 Soviet Constitution was characterized by its strong focus on the unity of the state and its citizenry, which was reflected in the distribution of state powers between the federal government and the union republics (Article 73). Federal powers such as ensuring 'the uniformity of legislative norms throughout the USSR' (обеспечение единства законодательного регулирования на всей территории СССР *obespechenie edinstva zakonodatel'nogo regulirovaniia na vsei territorii SSSR*) and the 'establishment of the fundamentals of the legislation of the . . . Union Republics' (установление основ законодательства . . . союзных республик *ustanovlenie osnov zakonodatel'stva . . . soiuznykh respublik*) significantly reduced the empowerment of the nationalities (ethnic groups) for whom the aforesaid union republics had been established. This was even clearer in the federal government's constitutionally enshrined power to 'settle other matters of all-union importance' (решение других вопросов общесоюзного значения *reshenie drugikh voprosov obshchesoiuznogo znacheniia*) (Constitution 1977; Konstitutsiya 1977). This provision allowed the Kremlin to significantly usurp the prerogatives of union republics (Shtromas 1978: 270). Such open-ended provisions that would de facto subject states to the will of the federal government are nowhere to be found in the Ethiopian Constitution of 1995.

As said earlier, both the Soviet and Ethiopian Constitutions established ethnoterritorial federations, in the sense that the federated units are defined in ethnic (ethnolinguistic) terms. The names of all the USSR's 15 union republics referred to specific ethnic groups (nationalities), known in the literature as the 'titular nations' (nationalities) of these republics (Brubaker 1994: 52). The same is true for the names of six of Ethiopia's regional states – that is, Tigray, Afar, Amhara, Oromia, Somali and Harari. However, the names of the country's further two regional states refer to two or more ethnic groups, namely Benishangul-Gumuz and the State of the Southern Nations, Nationalities and Peoples. On the other hand, the name of State of the Gambela is a mere geographic indication. Yet even in the case of these three regions with no ethnicity-based names, they are also ethnoterritorial in their character. It is so because these three regions (states) were established to empower not all ethnic groups living within their boundaries but rather specific ethnic groups ('nations, nationalities and peoples') that are "indigenous" to their territories.

The main idea of ethnoterritorial federalism is that federated units are established for the sake of empowering specific (titular) ethnic groups (one, two or more). In turn, an ethnic group of this type is able to effectively protect its interests within its own ethnic territory (homeland), or 'motherland' in a more emotive language. In other words, federated units constitute a forum where the empowered nations, nationalities and peoples (ethnic groups) exercise different aspects of their right to national self-determination. However, as pointed out earlier, the Soviet Constitution of 1977 limited the number of the fully empowered Soviet ethnic groups (nationalities) to 15. Only these 15 Soviet titular nationalities were permitted to enjoy their ethnolinguistically defined union republics. The other 72 Soviet ethnic groups (nationalities) were given the waning right to autonomous units of increasingly lower administrative statuses, such as autonomous republics, autonomous regions or autonomous areas (okrugs) (cf Constitution 1977: Chapters 10 and 11). To wit, in 1989, 17 nationalities enjoyed their own autonomous republics, while one of these republics, Dagestan, was earmarked for the autonomous republic's nine indigenous nationalities. Hence, in a broader sense, 26 nationalities had their 'own' autonomous republics. What is more, eight nationalities enjoyed autonomous regions, and further eight autonomous areas (okrugs) – hence 16 nationalities in total. Seven recognized non-indigenous and 24 indigenous nationalities did not have any autonomous territories. The 1989 Soviet census covered 87 nationalities (Anderson and Silver 1989: 619–622).

The Ethiopian Constitution of 1995 lists the country's nine regional states. However, all the recognized ethnic groups ('nations, nationalities and peoples') are constitutionally entitled to claim an ethnically defined regional state of their own. A number of ethnic groups have claimed such regions. So far (2020), one new regional state has been formed in Ethiopia. Following the November 2019 referendum on regional status, the Sidamas formed a new state from Sidama Zone within the Southern Nations, Nationalities and Peoples' Region. Almost 99 percent of the voters cast their ballots in favor of a stand-alone Sidama region for the ethnic group of Sidamas. The founding of a State of Sidama may prove a game changer in Ethiopian politics, especially in the area of nationality policy (Ephream Sileshi 2019).

Like the Soviet Union, some of Ethiopia's ethnic groups are provided with subregional autonomous territorial units. For instance, in Amhara Region, whose name refers to the regionally dominant Amhara people, a few ethnically based autonomous territorial units were founded for minority ethnic groups in their traditional homelands. These include three nationality administrations (zones) (የብሔረሰብ አስተዳደር ዞን *yebiḫēreseb āsitedader zon*), namely Agew Awi Zone for the Agaws, Oromia Zone for the Oromos and Wag Hemra Zone for the Himra (Kamyr) subgroup of the Agaws

(Revised 2001: Art. 73). Furthermore, two special nationality woredas (ልዩ የብሔረሰብ ወረዳዎች *liyu yebiḫēreseb weredawoch*) were established for the Argobbas and the Kemants.[8]

Another interesting example is the State of the Southern Nations, Nationalities and Peoples, where ethnically based nationality zones were secured for several ethnic groups. For example, Dawro Zone was founded for the Dawros, Gamo-Gofa Zone for the Gamos and the Gofas, Halaba Zone for the Halabas, Kafa Zone for the Kafas (Kaffichos),[9] Konso Zone for the Konsos and Wolayita Zone for the Wolayitas. At the still-lower administrative level, some ethnic groups were granted with their own special (nationality) woredas.[10] For instance, Amaro Special Woreda was established for the Amaros, Basketo Special Woreda for the Basketos, Burji Special Woreda for the Burjis, Dirashe Special Woreda for the Dirashes, Konta Special Woreda for the Kontas and Yem Special Woreda for the Yems. The Ethiopian Constitution of 1995 guarantees the identical right to national self-determination for all the country's recognized ethnic groups (nations, nationalities and peoples). However, in practice, the ethnic groups enjoy different degrees of autonomy, depending on the demographic size and political influence of a given ethnic group. At times, the existence of educated cadres versed in a given ethnic language is also an important consideration. Running an administration and educational system for a given ethnic group in this group's language is difficult unless the language in question has already been standardized (at least to some degree) and some publications (especially school textbooks) are available in it.

The establishment of numerous ethnically (ethnolinguistically) defined autonomous territorial units in Ethiopia empowers the concerned ethnic groups, which in this manner have been made into the titular groups of their territories. On the other hand, this process has created new majorities and minorities within these autonomous (national) territories, which often opens fresh cleavages between the titular group and members of other ethnic groups ('minorities'); cleavages that did not exist beforehand. Any administrative and political solution devised and implemented for righting old wrongs tends to generate new types of tensions and divisions. No solution is ideal.

The 'ownership' of ethnoterritorial units

Ethnoterritorial units are usually created to provide recognized ethnic groups (nationalities) with administratively acknowledged ethnic (national, autonomous, substate) territories (homelands, regions) within a state. In such a way, ethnic groups can exercise a certain degree of (national, ethnic) self-rule for the sake of protecting their group rights and interests in a state dominated by a different ethnic (ethnolinguistic or ethnoconfessional) majority (nation, nationality, ethnic group). In the Soviet Union, the establishment of ethnoterritorial units took place mainly in the first decade after the founding of this communist polity, as corroborated by the Kremlin's policy of 'indigenization' or 'nativization' (коренизация *korenizatsiia*). This policy, first of all, entailed the promotion of the language of the eponymous ethnic group (nationality) as the official language of this ethnic group's ethnoterritorial unit. Next step was 'affirmative action,' or highly politicized programs of expedited training in regional administration and governance to promote members of a given ethnic group to positions of leadership. The idea was that the ethnic group's ethnoterritorial unit (republic) should be run by this group's members, who would constitute the unit's new communist elite. Owing their careers to the Kremlin, they would staff the autonomous (union) republic's political and administrative institutions and work loyally for the Soviet Union. On the other hand, their rise to these high posts would convince their co-ethnics at large that the Soviet rule was acting in their ethnic group's interest, thus ensuring 'loyalty of the masses' Brubaker 1994 : 58; McGarry 2018 : 538; Martin 2001 : 177; Roeder 1991 : 204; Slezkine 1994).

However, such territorial empowerment of an ethnic group inevitably affects the rights and interests of people belonging to other ethnic groups who happen to reside in the concerned territory (Roeder 1991: 208). For instance, this kind of ethnoterritorial empowerment often leads to the rise of the popular preconception that residents who do *not* belong to the titular ethnic group may be seen as mere 'guests.' In this unofficial view, the continued residence of 'ethnic guests' in the autonomous territory depends solely on the goodwill of this territory's titular ethnic group (nationality). At times, the sentiment prompts practices that would nowadays be characterized as a form of ethnic cleansing (Martin 2001: 65). The adverse impact of ethnic empowerment on communities and individuals not belonging to the titular ethnic group (nationality) is one of the main challenges that confronts all ethnoterritorial federations. There is not a single ethnoterritorial federation where a perfect overlap would have been achieved between ethnic (ethnolinguistic) and territorial boundaries – that is, between ethnic groups and the federation's administrative (autonomous) units. This incongruity was particularly evident in the Soviet Union, where many people used to live outside their ethnic territory (homeland, autonomous republic) established for their ethnic group (nationality). In several union and autonomous republics of the USSR, the titular group did not even constitute the majority of the republic's population (Connor 1989: 37; Brubaker 1994: 55).

A similar incongruity between the demographic sizes of the titular group and other inhabitants who do not belong to this group also characterizes the Ethiopian Federation. For instance, in Benishangul-Gumuz, the non-empowered or 'non-indigenous' (as the Benishangul-Gumuz Regional Constitution terms them)[11] ethnic groups account for almost half of the population. The same situation can be observed in a few other ethnically based territorial units in Ethiopia, such as in Anywaa and Majang Zones, located in Gambela Region. In Majang Zone, the Majangs are in fact a small numerical minority of this zone's population (Van der Beken 2015: 155, 156, 170).

In accordance with the Ethiopian Constitution's emphasis on ethnicity and the principle of national self-determination, the country's ruling party, EPRDF, adopted a strong indigenization policy. This policy underlies and legitimizes the political and administrative structure of present-day federal Ethiopia. As is clear from the discussion earlier, in many ways, this Ethiopian 'nationality policy' emulates goals and practices of the interwar Soviet Union's policy of *korenizatsiia*. What is more, the EPRDF's own structure followed present-day Ethiopia's statehood logic of ethnoterritorial federalism. The EPRDF was not a unitary party but a coalition of four ethnically defined political parties, a kind of supra-ethnic 'all-Ethiopian' party. These four ethnic political parties were the Tigray People's Liberation Front (TPLF), the Amhara Democratic Party (ADP), the Oromo Democratic Party (ODP) and the South Ethiopian Peoples' Democratic Movement (SEPDM). In some ways, this unique feature made the EPRDF distinct from the Communist Party of the Soviet Union (CPSU), which was organized as a single All-Soviet party with regional (republican) branches.[12]

However, a striking similarity of the EPRDF and the CPSU is that formally the latter party's republican branches were organized as 'fraternal but separate' communist parties in their own right, of this or that Soviet socialist republic. For instance, in Soviet Belarus it was the Communist Party of Belarus; in Estonia, the Communist Party of Estonia; in Moldavia, the Communist Party of Moldavia; and in Ukraine, the Communist Party of Ukraine. Interestingly, the Soviet Union's largest republic – that is, the Russian Soviet Federative Socialist Republic (coterminous with the present-day Russian Federation) – did not have any republican ('Russian') party of its own until 1990. The Communist Party of the Russian Soviet Federative Socialist Republic was founded just one year before the breakup of the Soviet Union, in 1991. Basically, the CPSU doubled as the communist party of both, the Soviet Union and the Russian Soviet Federative Socialist Republic. Only geographic in their character names of the Soviet republics were allowed in the names of these republican communist parties. Names of ethnic groups (nationalities) were *not* permitted. But the Soviet Union's republics were tied to specific titular nationalities (ethnic groups) with their own ethnic languages, which de facto ethnicized these republican parties, often much to the Kremlin's irritation. Hence, the small difference in this regard between the EPRDF and the CPSU is that the '*Ukrainian* Communist Party' was an ideological *impossibility*. It *had to* be the Communist Party of Ukraine. On the other hand, in Ethiopia, the ethnic name 'Oromo' was allowed in the name of the Oromo Democratic Party (ODP). But in some cases, geographical designations were preferred to ethnic names, such as in the name of the *South Ethiopian* Peoples' Democratic Movement (SEPDM).

The EPRDF's four constituent ethnic parties were set up for the corresponding ethnic groups empowered (or 'indigenous,' to use the Ethiopian constitutional jargon) in the regional states of Oromia, Amhara, Tigray and the State of the Southern Nations, Nationalities and Peoples. This implies that cadres who belong to these empowered (titular) ethnic groups dominated the EPRDF's four respective parties. As in the case of the CPSU (and its republican branches–cum–republican parties), which doubled as the Soviet Union's administration, the EPRDF's constituent parties de facto monopolized the aforementioned four states' regional governments and institutions. However, *unlike* the Soviet Union, in Ethiopia, this situation means that the empowered (titular) ethnic groups also dominated - and to this day dominate - these four states' regional governments and institutions. For instance, all members of the Regional Parliament of the State of the Southern Nations, Nationalities and Peoples display a 'required' indigenous identity (Beza 2018: 8). The governments and administrative institutions of Ethiopia's five other regional states were also monopolized by the parties established for these states' indigenous (titular) ethnic groups (Zemelak 2018: 283). The aforementioned parties were *not* members of the EPRDF but subscribed to and closely followed the EPRDF's policies, values and plans (Arriola and Lyons 2016: 77; Ishiyama 2007: 92). In the Soviet Union, the republican communist parties were required to be 'socialist [communist, Soviet] in content and national in form,' as Joseph Stalin pronounced in 1930 (Martin 2001: 247). Ethnicity was to be subjugated to the construction of socialism (communism) in the increasingly de-ethnicized Soviet Union, especially after the end of *korienizatsiia* at the turn of the 1930s.

On the other hand, the indigenization (nationality) policy, as adopted in federal Ethiopia, leads to the political, administrative and economic dominance of titular indigenous groups in their respective ethnic homelands-cum-states (regions). This phenomenon can be illustrated by the example of the regional state of Benishangul-Gumuz. Although almost half of this state's population is composed of 'non-indigenous residents,' only nine out of the 99 members of the state's regional parliament displayed a non-indigenous identity, according to the results of the 2015 elections. The region's executive body (government) is even more strongly dominated by the titular ethnic groups (nationalities), in that all the cabinet's 17 members were indigenous at the time of writing (2020). This form of administrative indigenous empowerment is in line with the political objective of setting up ethnically (ethnolinguistically) defined regions (states) and autonomous territories of lower administrative status across Ethiopia. But this process generates serious tensions and has significantly contributed to the emergence of interethnic violence in almost all regional states in Ethiopia. On the other hand, as the following section discusses, the constitutional and political empowerment of indigenous (titular) ethnic groups has secured for them only a limited autonomy from the federation's center. This paradox also characterized the Soviet Union, but the Kremlin's empowerment of ethnic groups (nationalities) was not a goal in itself but rather a tactical means to transcending ethnicity for the sake of building an ethnic-*less* and class*less* homogenous Soviet communist people (*narod*).

Extensive rights but limited autonomy

Although the Soviet Constitution of 1977 upheld the federal structure of the USSR, the autonomy of the federated units was in practice severely restrained by the Communist Party of the Soviet Union (CPSU). The CPSU, in accordance with the marxist-leninist principle of 'democratic centralism,' made all the important decisions and de facto governed the Soviet Union and its republics (McGarry and O'Leary 2009: 9; Brubaker 1994, 53). Decision-making was centralized in the politburo of this party, and the governmental institutions at the federal level and in the constituent union and autonomous republics merely rubber-stamped and implemented the CPSU's decisions (McGarry 2018: 536). This CPSU's centralized decision-making was facilitated by the 1977 Soviet Constitution, which allowed the federal government to usurp regional (republican) prerogatives to whatever degree the Kremlin would think it necessary. The CPSU's dominance and centralist modus operandi entailed that the federated units (union and autonomous republics) had to exercise their constitutional powers and responsibilities within the changing framework set and reset at will by the Communist Party of the Soviet Union. As a result, republican (regional) prerogatives hardly ever amounted to anything more than a mere verbal rhetoric – that is, the 'national form' in Stalin's 1930 formulation – which subjected all Soviet politics to the 'socialist content.'

The case of the right to secession is an apt illustration of this situation. The Soviet Constitution of 1977 explicitly guaranteed this right for all the USSR's union republics. Although the CPSU accepted the right to secession in theory, the Kremlin's ideologues conceived of this right, in a dialectic way, as an antidote to secession rather than as a genuine possibility, which any republic would ever dare to exercise (Connor 1989: 28). Lenin, for instance, proposed that the formal grant of the right to secession would in fact prevent any exercise of this right. His argument was that state unity emanates from the free will of the nationalities residing in a polity that they treat as their own. Hence, as long as these nationalities feel free to decide their fate, they have no need to consider secession. In the actual Soviet practice, the highly centralized Communist Party of the Soviet Union (as de facto identical with the state and administrative structures of the USSR) resisted any secessionist demands and, when needed, even forcibly suppressed movements of this kind. The most important means to strengthen unity of the state and prevent secessionism was the ever wider and more intensive employment of the 'all-Soviet progressive socialist language' of Russian at the expense of the republican languages (Connor 1989: 28; Kaiser 1994: 250–324; McGarry 2018: 537).

Until recently, a similar situation of a highly centralized ruling party dominating all the constituent units of the federation characterized Ethiopia. Although the EPRDF was a coalition of ethnically based parties, this has not led to more autonomous regional decision-making. For better or worse, the EPRDF operated in accordance with the marxist-leninist principle of democratic centralism, entailing that important decisions were made in the Ethiopian capital of Addis Ababa by the leaders of the EPRDF's four coalition parties, with their ethnic bases in Amhara; Oromia; the Southern Nations, Nationalities and Peoples' Region; and Tigray (Assefa 2015: 251; Bach 2011: 647). As mentioned earlier, the other five regions (states) – that is, Afar, Benishangul-Gumuz, Gambela, Harari and Somali – were administered by EPRDF-affiliated regional parties that supported and implemented the EPRDF's policies.[13] As in the Soviet Union, the constituent units of the Ethiopian Federation exercised their constitutionally guaranteed powers and responsibilities within legal and political confines, as determined by the ruling party. The EPRDF drafted and promulgated the Ethiopian Constitution, which emphasizes and espouses the country's ethnic diversity by granting extensive rights to the recognized ethnic groups (nations, nationalities and peoples). On the other hand, this ruling party strongly resisted and even suppressed the actual exercise of some of these rights.

In particular, the EPRDF hindered any exercise of the right to establish new ethnically based territorial units in the form of either regional states, nationality zones or nationality (special) woredas, let alone in the form of sovereign polities that would actually secede from Ethiopia. Because the EPRDF was in control of all administrative units in the country, it used party channels to prevent or discourage such ethnic demands. In this regard, the EPRDF seemed to share Lenin's view that the constitutional grant of territorial autonomy is a mechanism for preventing its exercise. Yet given the emphasis on ethnicity in the Ethiopian Constitution, this attitude and practice generated a profound gap between constitutional norm and substance. Until recently, the EPRDF had been able to bridge this gap because of its centralized modus operandi and strong party discipline (i.e. the observance of 'democratic centralism'). Yet during recent years and particularly after 2018, a serious weakening of party discipline was observed.

As a result, tensions engendered by this mismatch between constitutional theory and practice bubbled to the surface in the form of disturbances and demonstrations (Van der Beken 2018). Against this background, one can interpret the founding of the Prosperity Party (PP) in December 2019. The hope is that the PP will effectively unite the EPRDF's member and affiliated ethnic parties into a single, unified all-Ethiopian multiethnic (multinational) party. It is a clear attempt at de-emphasizing the focus of the country's legislation and politics on ethnicity, to prevent administrative or even political disintegration along ethnolinguistic lines. However, it is too early to say how these latest developments will influence the situation in Ethiopia. The developments may pit the PP, which is accused of being unitarist, against ethnically-based parties and movements. This is what has actually happened in the case of many Oromo groups, who do not trust the PP and accuse ethnically Oromo Prime Minister Abiy Ahmed of 'betrayal.' In 2020, this tension erupted in violent protests (including ethnically motivated attacks) that followed the assassination of renowned and charismatic Oromo singer, poet and civil rights activist Hachalu Hundessa (Hacaaluu Hundeessaa in Oromo) (Gardner 2020). Over 230 people lost their lives in the course of these protests and disturbances (Ethiopia Arrests 2020), which is a stark warning that more attention needs to be paid to whether the political system appropriately meets variegated needs of individuals and Ethiopia's ethnic groups.

The incessant rise of ethnic demands

At the turn of the 1990s, the weakening of the CPSU in the Soviet Union was accompanied by increasing ethnic demands and heated grassroots discussions about the relationship between the federal center and the federation's constituent units (republics) (Brubaker 1994: 61). Ethnoterritorial federalism was implemented in the interwar Soviet Union to accommodate pre-existing ethnic demands (McGarry 2018: 536). In effect, the previously fluid and negotiable identities of ethnic groups (nationalities) were acknowledged, legitimized, bureaucratically standardized and politically reinforced (Kaiser 1994: 191–249). Marxism-leninism predicted the withering of both state and ethnicity (nationalism) on the way to a classless and ethnic-less communist 'people.' But contrary to theoretical expectations, ethnoterritorial federalism did not create such a new, ideologically novel and homogeneous Soviet people (Kaiser 1994: 325–377), which was also impatiently anticipated by the 1977 Soviet Constitution (Suny 1989: 507). As long as the CPSU was in full control, the party was able to mitigate and manage ethnic demands and tensions through intraparty procedures and heavy-handed impositions from above. Yet the withering away of centralized party control at the turn of the 1990s revealed that ethnic divisions were deepened by the ongoing tension between the constitutional acknowledgment of ethnic rights and political limitations on their actual exercise. In the context of weak constitutionalism and the dearth of effective institutions and mechanisms for conflict management (Suny 1989: 504), the disintegration of the Soviet Union was almost a foregone conclusion. Although at the time of these events not a single renowned sovietologist predicted the breakup of the USSR, now, with the privilege of hindsight, it is often qualified as 'inevitable.'

Nowadays, the similar risk of an ethnically induced breakup of the country faces the Ethiopian government. Some see the recent weakening of party discipline in Ethiopia as a welcome transition from 'democratic centralism' to genuine democracy. But it is the increasing assertiveness of ethnic parties that brought about this change. In turn, this assertiveness was exacerbated by the federal government, who recently embarked on a raft of democratic and economic reforms. These ethnic parties had no choice but to find new footing in the changing situation. Their legitimacy and support are drawn from these parties' respective ethnic groups (nations, nationalities and peoples), which serve as loyal electorates. The old status quo established in the mid 1990s is over, and now the parties appeal to ethnic arguments and grievances for the sake of improving their waning popularity and legitimacy.

As a result, the EPRDF's ability to manage ethnic tensions and suppress demands for new ethnically defined autonomous territories dwindled. For instance, at the time of writing (2020), the disintegration of the State of Southern Nations, Nationalities and Peoples (SNNP) is an imminent possibility. In 2018, the Konsos, whose homeland had been part of Segen Zone, were endowed with their own ethnic zone, that is, Konso Zone. In the same year the biethnic Gamo-Gofa Zone was split in two ethnic zones, namely Gamo Zone and Gofa Zone. What is more, in November 2019, a referendum was held on the question whether to exclude Sidama Zone from the SNNP and elevate it to the status of a brand-new regional state. The overwhelming majority of the eligible voters decided in favor of this solution (Ephream Sileshi 2019). This forthcoming new regional State of Sidama will advance the administrative and political position of the Sidamas in the country, thus bringing the number of Ethiopia's regional states to ten. Moreover, in emulation of the Sidamas, at the turn of 2020, about ten other ethnically based zones in the SNNP have submitted demands for separate regional states to the SNNP Regional Council. The extent to which the newly established Prosperity Party will be able to reign in these centrifugal trends will depend on whether the party can uphold internal discipline. Another factor which is going to influence this situation is the outcome of the planned parliamentary elections. These elections might as well bring to power staunchly ethnonationalist parties.

Many of Ethiopia's ethnically based parties now wish to avail themselves of the right to national self-determination, which the Ethiopian Constitution entitles them to. Due to the character of ethnoterritorial federalism, most of collective rights are couched in ethnic (ethnolinguistic) terms. In turn, this fact entails that at times exercising the aforesaid rights may lead to the deepening of existing ethnic cleavages and to opening new ones. The conflictual potential in the unhindered democratic use of the Ethiopian Constitution exposes two problems. First, many of the ethnically underpinned rights in this document are excessively idealistic in character. Second, when these rights were included in the Constitution, perhaps the drafters of the document did not fully predict potential implications, which the exercise of these rights may bring about. Third, the Constitution does not really provide effective constitutional institutions and mechanisms for managing ethnic conflicts. This may endanger the unity of Ethiopia as a state and its citizenry as a whole. The sustainability of the Ethiopian Federation as a state requires stronger constitutionalism, meaning a type of constitutionalism that would rebalance collective (ethnic) rights with individual rights.[14] Such a rebalancing could be achieved, for instance, by stronger respect for the constitutionally protected human rights, including their actual enforcement. At the same time, there is a growing need for developing and bolstering institutions and mechanisms that would at long last ensure the effective management of interethnic relations. Otherwise, if ethnic tensions cannot be addressed, managed and contained in accordance with the law and in an entailed consensual and deliberative manner, a potential for violent conflict will continue to grow.

From Soviet Union to federalism 53

Figure 2.1 Administrative regions and zones of Ethiopia in 2000 (UN Emergencies 2000)

Notes

1 The ADP is a new name, given to the ANDM (Amhara National Democratic Movement) in 2018. The same is true of the ODP (Oromo Democratic Party), whose name changed from OPDO (Oromo People Democratic Organization) in the same year.
2 Influenced by marxist-leninist terminology, the Ethiopian terms *nations, nationalities* and *peoples* (often employed as a tripartite collocation) are used to talk about Ethiopia's over 80 recognized ethnic groups. No legal distinction is made between the three terms. *Nations, nationalities* and *peoples* are defined as identical in their status in Article 39(5) of the Federal Constitution. All these nations, nationalities and peoples are entitled to the same right to national self-determination (Ethiopia – Constitution 1994).
3 The new ethnicity-based decentralized structure of the state was promulgated in Proclamation No. 7/1992, published in the *Negarit Gazeta* (or the official gazette of Ethiopia) on 14 January 1992 (Proclamation No. 7/1992 1992).
4 After the wrapping up of the policy of *korenizatsiia* (nativization, indigenization) at the turn of the 1930s, but especially during World War II, the Kremlin preferred to speak of the 'Soviet *natsiia* (nation)' rather than the Soviet *narod* (people, nation) (cf Sinitsin 2018).

5 In April 1994, the Constitutional Commission (established in 1992 by the Transitional Parliament) submitted a Draft Constitution to the Transitional Parliament and the Council of Representatives (or the Parliament's lower chamber). Following the approval of the Draft Constitution by the Council of Representatives, direct popular elections for a constituent assembly were held in June 1994. The Constituent Assembly approved the final version of the Constitution on 8 December 1994. Finally, the new Constitution came into force after the general parliamentary elections were carried out in May–June 1995.
6 The wording is intentionally euphemistic, to avoid the ideologically unacceptable term *to secede* (отделяться *otdeliat'sia*).
7 Article 49 of the Ethiopian Constitution of 1995 provides the special status of capital city for Addis Ababa, which in practice is equal to that of any of federal Ethiopia's states (Ethiopia – Constitution 1994). Furthermore, in 2004, Dire Dawa became a 'chartered city' (የድሬዳዋ አስተዳደር ቻርተር አዋጅ *yedirēdawa āsitedader chariter āwaj* 'Charter of Dire Dawa Administration'), answerable directly to the federal government (Asnake Kefale 2014).
8 The Amharic term ወረዳ *wereda* means 'district.'
9 Ethiopia conquered the Kingdom of Kaf(f)a in 1897. Wild coffee abounded in this area, from where coffee beans were taken across the Red Sea to the Ottoman Empire. The term *coffee* may stem from this kingdom's name (cf McCann 1995: 174; Shinn and Ofcansky 2013: 245).
10 In 2018, Gamo-Gofa Zone was split into two, that is, Gamo Zone and Gofa Zone.
11 All the nine regional states of the Ethiopian Federation adopted their own regional (state) constitutions. As a result, Ethiopia's current constitutional architecture is composed of one Federal Constitution and the nine regional (state) constitutions. Under the provisions of the 1977 Soviet Constitution, all the country's union republics and autonomous republics were similarly entitled to their own constitutions.
12 However, the EPRDF was dissolved in December 2019. Three out of the four constitutive member parties of the EPRDF (with the notable exception of the TPLF) and all five of the EPRDF's affiliated parties formed the current ruling Prosperity Party. The Prosperity Party is designed as an all-Ethiopian party with regional (*not* ethnic) branches.
13 Since the dissolution of the EPRDF in December 2019, all regions – with the sole exception of Tigray – have been administered by the newly established Prosperity Party. Tigray remains the TPLF's stronghold.
14 During the 1980s and 1990s, this type of 'rebalancing' was an existential need for Belgium, to prevent a looming breakup of this country into two ethnolinguistic nation-states, one for the Flemish and the other for the French-speaking Walloons. The Belgians learned a good lesson from the breakup of federal Czechoslovakia. The conclusion was that dual (dyadic, bipartite) federations are inherently unstable. In light of this diagnosis, politicians decided to transform Belgium into a multidimensional federation of three ethnolinguistic communities (Flemish, French and German) and of three regions, namely the two ethnoterritorial regions of Flanders and Wallonia, alongside the *non*-ethnoterritorial (capital) and bilingual region of Brussels.

Importantly, the borders of these three regions do *not* overlap with the borders of the three communities. Hence, ethnoterritorial and ethnolinguistic cleavages do not fortify each other, because otherwise they would have, if the borders of the communities and regions had overlapped (Third 2020; Wagstaff 1999).

Conclusion

In this study, we offer an initial presentation and analysis of the transfer of two opposed statehood models from Central Europe to Ethiopia during the 20th century. We hope that this contribution to the budding field of the global history of ideas encourages other scholars to probe into our findings more deeply. We are sure that there is much more to discover, given that so many Ethiopians underwent university education in the Soviet Union during the Soviet-Derg period (cf Abye Tassé 2017; Natufe 2011: 330; Patman 1990: 92). On the other hand, this line of inquiry adds to the previously neglected research on the history and practices of the circulation of ideas between the West and the rest of the world, the 'rich North' and the 'poor South' (cf Manifesto 2018; Prashad 2008), or as in our case between Eurasia, where the ethnolinguistic type of nation-state predominates and elsewhere across the globe, where the civic type of nation-state is the norm.

We live in a globalized world, and globalization processes have interlinked all humanity with an increasingly dense network of various connections during the past two centuries. Yet even such seemingly obvious connections as that of the transfer of statehood models between Central Europe and Ethiopia are not studied and commented on, as a matter of course. The observation vantage of the global social sciences and historiography remains relentlessly Eurocentric and focused on the West, almost in the form of navel-gazing. It appears that entrepreneurs and politicians are quicker than their counterparts in academia to take note of globalization and the rapid changes which it generates.

This book's core finding is that the three subsequent political regimes, which have ruled Ethiopia from the late 19th century up to the present – that is, the imperial system, the Soviet-Derg and the TPLF-dominated EPRDF government – have all adopted nation- and state-building strategies modeled on Central European examples. The Ethiopian imperial regime, as inspired by Meiji Japan (and through it, indirectly, by Imperial Germany), pursued

Conclusion 57

assimilationist policies aimed at achieving a unitary, centralized and ethnolinguistically homogenous nation-state. The two subsequent Ethiopian regimes adopted a more accommodating approach to the linguistic and ethnic diversity of the country's inhabitants. The Soviet-Derg drew inspiration from the Soviet Union's model of ethnolinguistic federalism (which, in the first instance, the Bolsheviks had borrowed from Austria-Hungary). However, this regime hardly went further than merely acknowledging Ethiopia's ethnic diversity, which came with the belated and rather tentative introduction of ethnically based decentralization in some parts of the country. In day-to-day practice, the People's Democratic Republic of Ethiopia remained a highly centralized Soviet-style state. The Soviet-Derg did not fail to comply with the main tenets of marxism-leninism, including paying some lip service to the 'nationality policy.' Like the Soviet Union, the meeting of certain demands tabled by Ethiopia's ethnolinguistic groups was to be tactical, specifically for the sake of facilitating society's way toward 'developed socialism.' The ultimate goal was a 'socialist classless society' that – according to marxism-leninism – would transcend people's loyalty to (ethnolinguistic) nationalism (*Fundamentals* 1963: 626–630, 676–678).

The Soviet Union's official ideology of marxism-leninism inspired the TPLF and the corresponding ethnolinguistic Tigrayan national movement. The main attractions of this ideology, especially for the latter, were the vocabulary and means for expressing and giving a political form to the movement's ethnic objectives. The TPLF did not merely borrow such concepts as nation and nationality from marxism-leninism. The party's strategy for coming to terms with Ethiopia's ethnic diversity showed remarkable parallels with the Soviet Union's original 'nationality policy.' Initially, after the removal of the Soviet-Derg in 1991, the *post*-Soviet-Derg government, controlled by the TPLF and the EPRDF, emphasized the importance of ethnicity and identified it as the major cause of continuing oppression in Ethiopian society. This conclusion prompted the EPRDF to develop, support and impose a package of constitutionally guaranteed rights for Ethiopia's 'nations, nationalities and peoples' (recognized ethnic groups). The observance of these rights was quite unprecedented and the last time practiced to such a level only in the *early interwar* Soviet Union. At the turn of the 1930s, the Kremlin began swiftly downgrading such protection, which after World War II was abandoned for the majority of this communist polity's recognized ethnic groups (nationalities). In *post*-Soviet-Derg Ethiopia, this novel accommodating approach to ethnicity, officially enshrined in the 1995 Constitution, was initially backed up with policies that encouraged political mobilization among the population along ethnic (ethnolinguistic) lines. This process was combined with the bureaucratically facilitated social

58 Conclusion

advancement of necessary cadres, who now form the new elites of Ethiopia's 'nations, nationalities and peoples.' The policy is strikingly similar to the interwar Soviet Union's project of indigenization, or *korenizatsiia*. Yet like the Soviet Union, the ruling EPRDF party gradually realized that the constitutionally guaranteed grant of unfettered ethnic rights actually posed two crucial threats. The most important threat was and still is to the unity of the federation as a single polity, while the other threat was to the EPRDF's single-party (i.e. hegemonic) rule over post-1991 Ethiopia.

This realization led to a significant shift in policy. The EPRDF began extolling the unity of state, which entailed a more instrumentalist approach toward the constitutional provisions on ethnolinguistic (ethnic) rights. In this approach, the ruling party was clearly inspired by Vladimir Lenin and Joseph Stalin, who had argued that the offer of extensive ethnic rights (most notably the right to national self-determination) was a temporary measure. The limited exercise of these rights was intended to reduce the salience of ethnicity (ethnolinguistic nationalism) and at the same time gave the government much-needed time to strengthen the integrity of the Soviet state. In other words, the constitutionally guaranteed right to national self-determination was more valued because of its instrumental-cum-ideological role as a tool of all-state integration rather than because it was a goal in itself. Yet as in the Soviet Union, also in Ethiopia, the hard-to-conceal gap between such constitutional entitlements and the actual political practice of mostly *not* acting on them began generating serious societal tensions. Such tensions threatened to get out of control, when it became obvious that the government de facto sought to suppress the unrestricted exercise of these entitlements.

The ruling EPRDF was able to prevent tensions of this type from boiling over by adhering to the marxist-leninist principle of democratic centralism (демократический централизм *demokraticheskii tsentralizm*)[1] and by enforcing strict party discipline. When, despite its best intentions, an ethnic conflict flared up, the EPRDF was at least able to stop it from developing into a direct threat to the state, specifically to its stability and integrity. Yet examples from both Ethiopia and the Soviet Union show that even limited political democratization (known as гласность *glasnost'* 'openness' in Mikhail Gorbachev's original package of reforms in the latter half of the 1980s) in a multiethnic authoritarian (totalitarian) polity may unleash long-suppressed ethnolinguistic grievances and thus create fertile ground for their political exploitation. The opening up of political space for the public at large may be indispensable even at such a cost, because the alternative may be even worse – for instance, a collapse of the economy and governance, which always poses serious threats to peace and stability. However, most cases of ethnic strife from the late Soviet Union and post-1991

Ethiopia prove that ethnoterritorial federalism may not be the optimal solution for striking a maintainable working balance between ethnolinguistic (ethnic) demands and state unity.

First of all, the introduction of ethnoterritorial federalism – be it in the Soviet Union, Ethiopia or other polities – was typically dictated by the exigencies of a given political situation. Alternatives were simply unlikely to garner sufficient political support necessary for holding a given state together. Second, the gap between the constitutional entitlements and their actual suppression contributes to continuing political instability in Ethiopia and actually led to the breakup of the Soviet Union. However, this observation is not an argument for allowing the free and unrestrained exercise of ethnolinguistic entitlements. Constitutionalism alone is insufficient for ensuring that an ethnoterritorial federation becomes a successful and stable state. Any single-minded focus of the crucial constitutional provisions and entitlements on ethnicity is in itself a risk to constitutionalism. Ethnic (ethnolinguistic) rights are collective in their character. Hence, emphasizing rights of this kind may endanger individual rights and therefore threaten the entire state's social cohesion and stability. Respect for ethnic (ethnolinguistic) rights needs to be balanced by measures that protect and ensure state integrity (unity). Collective rights should not allow for trampling individual rights and vice versa. The latter type of rights (i.e. individual rights) bring together citizens of varied ethnic backgrounds, thus creating incentives for interethnic cooperation across the entire state. How can the gap between individual and collective rights be bridged in the context of a highly multiethnic citizenry? For instance, a language policy can be developed, which on the one hand would offer guarantees to users of minority languages and on the other hand would stimulate interethnic communication in the state's official (working) language. A policy of this kind should come with a genuine and fully observed requirement that speakers of the state's official – and thus dominant – language should master ethnic languages of their regions of residence.

This is easier said than done. Many Soviet policies aimed at achieving such an outcome, but most Soviet speakers of other languages than Russian saw these efforts as the de facto or covert form of Russification. Unfortunately, with the privilege of hindsight, we know that they were right. The steep decline in the use of republican and minority languages, as recorded in the 1979 and 1989 Soviet censuses, amply confirmed Soviet non-Russian speakers' suspicions and fears in this regard (Kaiser 1994: 273–281). Hence, the majority of Belarusians nowadays see Belarusian as their 'native language,' but less than 10 percent of Belarus's inhabitants actually speak and write Belarusian in everyday life. On the other hand, Russian speakers almost never acquired other Soviet languages, even if they happened to reside in a union republic, where a language other than Russian was official. In an imperial-like attitude, Russian speakers expected locals ('natives') to understand the state's official language and use it rather than their ethnic ('native') one, when talking to a Russian speaker even in 'their' ethnically non-Russian (union, autonomous) republic.

Whatever the limitations and discontents of ethnoterritorial federalism, as practiced in the Soviet Union or present-day Ethiopia, may be, indisputable advantages of this system should not be forgotten, either. For instance, even if centrifugal trends come to outweigh centripetal ones, ethnoterritorial federalism allows for curbing violence and resultant bloodshed in the situation where a state splits. It is so because in most cases ethnoterritorial federalism prevents open ethnic warfare. Instead ethnopolitical tensions are played out at the level of state administration and through spontaneous street demonstrations. Discussion is more conducive to finding a working compromise than is unbridled violence. State structures and institutions can contain and satisfy administrative and social tensions, while ethnic warfare invariably leaves numerous casualties in its wake. In the latter case, communities are torn apart, the economy is destroyed and a state may be violently broken up, as it happened in the course of such recent bloody ethnic conflicts in the Horn of Africa as the Eritrean War of Independence or the Ethiopian Civil War. Furthermore, none other than ethnoterritorial federalism allowed for the (relatively) bloodless breakup of the Soviet Union (Plokhy 2015; Spruyt 2005: 204–233), though many had originally foreseen an apocalyptic war, if such a scenario would have come true. Indeed, ethnoterritorial federalism did *not* prevent the wars of Yugoslav succession, but the breakup of federal Yugoslavia did differ from that of the Soviet Union. The difference was that Russia (or the legal successor to the USSR) let the other union republics go relatively unhindered. On the other hand, in the case of Yugoslavia, resurgent Serbia aspired to overhaul federal Yugoslavia into a unitary Great Serbian nation-state. Hence, not ethnoterritorial federalism but rather Serbian unitary (ethnolinguistic) nationalism writ large generated the Yugoslav wars (Gordy 1999; Lukic 1994; Pešić 1996).

Another positive aspect of ethnoterritorial federalism is that this form of statehood organization encourages the standardization of indigenous languages. In turn, literatures and cultures are created in such freshly standardized indigenous languages, which nowadays are also employed in the mass media and cyberspace. For instance, without *korenizatsiia* in the interwar Soviet Union, there would not now have been the languages of Belarusian, Kazakh or Tajik. At present, these languages constitute the definition and basis of the respective Belarusian, Kazakh and Tajik nations, which after 1991 were endowed with their own independent nation-states of

Belarus, Kazakhstan and Tajikistan. A limited use of ethnoterritorial federalism in India (signaled by the policy of 'linguistic states' [Ambedkar 1955]) encouraged the standardization and official use of the country's other (mostly regional, i.e. officially dubbed 'scheduled') languages (Languages with Official 2020) than solely the de facto official (and postcolonial) language of English, alongside the national language of Hindi, as prescribed by the Indian Constitution (Constitution of India 1950: Art. 120).

We are bringing the case of India to readers' attention because, nowadays, federal Ethiopia's elites seem to be (perhaps, unconsciously) emulating this model, due to numerous intellectual contacts with Indian scholars and tutors at the country's universities. In post-1991 Ethiopia, the largest group of foreign university staff come from India (Thubauville 2013: 125), which is a good example of the continuation of Afro-Asian cooperation in the spirit of the Non-Aligned Movement (cf Menon 2014). Ethiopia was never a full-fledged colony, but after the short-lived Italian occupation (1936–1941) in the broader context of World War II, Addis Ababa de facto adopted English as the official language.[2] (Ethiopian observers would say that English became the country's 'most important foreign language.') But the role of Amharic as the country's national language was gradually bolstered in the late Ethiopian Empire and then in communist Ethiopia. Under the Soviet-Derg regime, 15 indigenous languages were employed in writing, mainly for the sake of encouraging literacy.[3] Similarly, in freshly independent India, at the turn of the 1950s, in emulation of the Soviet model, many ethnic languages were endowed with a written form for the sake of spreading literacy. Nowadays, in the Ethiopian Federation, all the over 80 indigenous languages are constitutionally recognized as equal. Considerable efforts and financial outlays have also been extended for the standardization and use of non-Amharic indigenous (ethnic) languages in school education and regional (or local) administration. In the former case, such languages are employed mainly in elementary schools, which with time opens a possibility of making them into media of instruction at further levels of education. On the other hand, the use of non-Amharic indigenous languages in administration is amply illustrated, for instance, by five of Ethiopia's nine regional states – that is, by Afar, Tigray, Harari, Oromia and Somali. In these five regional states the locally dominant (titular) languages of Afar, Tigrinya, Harari, Oromo and Somali are in administrative use, alongside Amharic (and de facto English). As in the case of the Soviet Union republics, these regional languages correspond to the regional states' empowered (titular) ethnic groups. Yet the Ethiopian Constitution of 1995 designates Amharic as the sole working language of the federal administration. English is used for international communication and amounts to the preferred medium of education for secondary schools and universities.

One of the main problems of sociopolitical cohesion in such a polyglot, multiethnic and polyconfessional country like Ethiopia is the question of which language should serve as the main medium of interethnic communication *within* the country. The imposition of Amharic (complete with its Ethiopic script) was opposed by other ethnic groups. Russian began to play the role of the Soviet Union's language of interethnic communication only because during the 1930s and 1940s Soviet totalitarianism arbitrarily imposed it on all the communist polity's population. The Kremlin radically curbed the use of republican (titular) languages when the policy of *korenizatsiia* (indigenization) was discontinued at the turn of the 1930s and replaced, in 1938, with Russification in the ideological guise of the process of building classless communism. However, Ethiopia has little taste and no means for instituting totalitarianism. The Soviet-Derg trialed a semblance of Soviet-style totalitarianism, but the attempt was abandoned after 40,000 (or even as many as 100,000) lost their lives in the course of the campaign of the Red Terror (Abbink 1995: 135; Balsvik 2007: 77).

Hence, in all likelihood, in the near future, the majority of Ethiopia's over 80 recognized languages will remain exclusively in oral employment. However, nowadays, orality does not necessarily exclude one from participating in the modern economy, culture, intercontinental communication or cyberspace. Mobile phones, especially smartphones, give speakers of oral (i.e. unwritten or unstandardized) languages opportunities that were previously available exclusively to users of written languages. Enhanced mobile telephony is a great leveler, while intelligent virtual assistants (such as Amazon's Alexa, Apple's Siri or Google Assistant), allow for accessing the web through voice alone, without any written protocol. Yet the danger is that any rapid spread of such devices, solutions and opportunities may negatively impact efforts for improving the overall rate of literacy in Ethiopia and prevent necessary financial outlays for the further standardization of Ethiopia's languages.

Perhaps in fewer than ten of Ethiopia's main languages, books will continue to be more broadly published, or in the official regional languages of Ethiopia's six 'ethnolinguistic' states, as earmarked for single titular ethnic groups. This small group of six languages (i.e. Afar, Amharic, Harari, Oromo, Somali and Tigrinya) will serve as media of instruction in elementary and secondary education, alongside the respective states' regional administration. On the other hand, by 2019, as many as 40 recognized ethnic groups (nations, nationalities and peoples) had been endowed with a variety of autonomous ethnic territorial units in federal Ethiopia (see

Table 5). Should they wish so, this fact – on the basis of the Ethiopian Constitution of 1995 – enables these 40 ethnic groups to develop and use their corresponding 40 languages at least in early elementary education and local administration.

For the time being, the role of Amharic will seemingly remain unchanged, although other languages of numerically large ethnic groups might be elevated to the status of another federal working language, such as Oromo. At 33.8 percent, the plurality of Ethiopia's inhabitants speak Oromo as their first language, in contrast to Amharic, which is spoken by 29.3 percent of Ethiopians (Ethiopia: Languages 2020).[4] In recent years, the status of languages particularly at the federal level has been one area of contestation. In 2020, the federal government adopted a language policy that intends to recognize four languages – Afar, Oromo, Somali and Tigrigna – as working languages of the federal government (Samuel Getachew 2020). Moreover, this policy encourages the teaching of further widespread Ethiopian languages in school, apart from Amharic and schoolchildren's own ethnic languages (Biruki Abidu 2020). This could in the long run help the development of a bilingual or even multilingual society. Already some have appealed for an official decision to recognize English as still-another official language of Ethiopia (Meareg H. 2020).

Another possibility could be the use of English for interethnic communication by educated Ethiopians (cf Sharma 2013). In this respect, future Ethiopia may become similar to present-day Kenya, where indigenous languages are employed in elementary education, while Swahili and English function as languages of secondary education and interethnic communication, apart from being the country's designated official languages (Constitution of Kenya 2010: Art. 7.2). And again, as in the case of Ethiopia's universities, English is the sole medium of education at Kenya's universities (cf Whiteley 1974). The difference, however, is that in Kenya, English is perceived as a colonial language, while in Ethiopia, it is not. In the former country, the semi-indigenous language of Swahili functions as a more neutral medium of communication, unlike Amharic in Ethiopia, where many assess it to have been an instrument of Amhara ethnic domination.

However, from a global perspective, Amharic is a language rather neglected by its own users, although the informal grassroots employment of Amharic does increase in cyberspace. Ethiopian languages such as Amharic, Oromo and Somali are spoken and read by tens of millions. However, *all* the Wikipedias composed in these languages, alongside Tigrinya, include a mere 22,000 articles (List of Wikipedias 2019). In contrast, the sole endangered ('vulnerable') Slavic state official language, Belarusian (*UNESCO Atlas* 2010), is spoken at best by a quarter of Belarus's ten million inhabitants (Haryckaja 2018). However, due to a quarrel on the 'correct' spelling of *Belarusian*, quite uniquely, speakers of this language enjoy *two* Wikipedias, one in classical Belarusian and the other in official Belarusian. These two Wikipedias combined offer their users 291,000 articles (List of Wikipedias 2019), or over ten times more than what is available in this manner to the speakers of Ethiopia's main languages, who number at least 90 million. On top of that, the majority of Somali speakers live in their ethnolinguistic nation-state of Somalia, not in Ethiopia. Hence, the majority of contributors to and readers of the Somali Wikipedia stem from Somalia, not Ethiopia.

Whether the constitutional provisions of Ethiopia's ethnoterritorial federalism will stem the rapid rise in the generalized use of English across the country in favor of the ethnic languages of the 40 ethnic (titular) groups already granted with their own ethnic (autonomous) territorial units remains to be seen. Should the increasing dominance of English continue, Ethiopia's language policy will follow the examples of Kenya and other postcolonial states in sub-Saharan Africa. However, if the titular languages turn out to be preferred in education, administration, the mass media and the economy, then the Ethiopian language policy will take the path of ethnolinguistic (ethnoterritorial) federations and multiethnic states in Eurasia, be it the Soviet Union in the past or China, India and Russia nowadays. The first ('postcolonial') scenario may not be to the liking of Amharic speakers, because it would mean that English would unseat their ethnic language from the elevated position of Ethiopia's once-imperial and sole official (national) language, or now the country's sole working language of the federal administration. Speakers of the titular languages may relish this prospect, but the entailed growing employment of English in most aspects of public life would stymie the further development and standardization of these languages. In the second ('Eurasian') scenario, Amharic speakers may reassert their privileged (dominant, imperial-like) position in Ethiopia's administration, education and culture, as Russian speakers did in the postwar Soviet Union and still do in today's Russian Federation. Otherwise, a more equitable situation may develop, such that the titular languages become dominant in their respective autonomous territories. Then Amharic and English would serve as additional (exoglossic) languages of interethnic communication.

Each scenario comes complete with its own sets of advantages and problems – not unlike the two statehood models successively adopted by Ethiopia during the 20th century, namely that of the centralized homogenous ethnolinguistic nation-state and the other of the ethnoterritorial (ethnolinguistic) federation. While these two models of statehood ultimately originate from 19th century Central Europe, the postcolonial and

Conclusion 65

'Eurasian-style' versions of language politics come from the West. Through colonization, the West imposed the former on the 'rest of the world' – that is, mainly *outside* Eurasia. The other type of language politics arrived to Ethiopia from the 'semi-West of Austria-Hungary, as further developed in the Eurasian communist polity of the Soviet Union on the one hand and in British India and postcolonial India on the other.

During the last 100 years, Ethiopia's government, its elite and its population at large have faced challenges of state, nation and language building that came in forms (models) adopted from outside – that is, from the West (including Central Europe). The correct belief was that adopting such Western models would prevent predatory European powers from colonizing Ethiopia. The West had no choice but to acknowledge Ethiopia as a 'civilized' polity, which thus was not in any need of any 'civilizing mission' from Europe. It is important, however, to know where, when and why these models developed in their original historical, social and political setting, because such a setting has never been and will never be (fully) replicated in Ethiopia. Remembering this original setting and Ethiopia's specific needs and conditions may help policymakers become more aware of the advantages and limitations of the wholesale borrowing of such models from abroad. Also, at times, developing local Ethiopian solutions in response to the country's political, social, cultural, economic and educational needs may be easier and less problematic than borrowing from abroad.

More often than not, borrowings of this type end with the proverbial forcing of a square peg into a round hole. Eventually solutions adapted from abroad may start working and the population at large – however grudgingly – may accept and even wholeheartedly espouse them. But at what cost does this happen? Is it worth paying? The relative economic, political and social success of post-1991 Ethiopia was preceded by devastating wars, foreign occupation, unprecedented famines, political terror, mass repressions, ethnic cleansing, mass killings, a revolution and political upheavals during the short but quite dark 20th century. The gears of Ethiopia's sociopolitical (and at times economic) stage were changed rapidly in 1931, when the model of the centralized ethnolinguistically homogenous state was adopted wholesale; then in 1974, when the revolution led to the introduction of the model of the Soviet-style ethnoterritorial federation; and the final time in 1995, when the latter model began to be actually implemented. Almost three decades of continual readjustment and rebalancing has been needed to smooth out the rough edges of the most recent foreign model, in order to make it Ethiopia's own.

Perhaps the best chance for a stable and prosperous future for all Ethiopians is to stick to the current track, including the by now deeply 'Ethiopianized' model of ethnoterritorial federalism. Dealing with whatever discontents and problems may appear in a piecemeal and consensual manner is better than changing the political gear yet again.[5] This would inevitably lead to tragic upheavals, like those in the not-so-distant past. On the whole, evolutionary change allows for more space and respect for the rights and needs of individuals and ethnic groups than any revolution does. Revolutions always cost innumerable lives, while the former approach limits political violence to verbal barbs, when thorny issues are discussed in a parliament.

Conclusion 67

Table 3.1 Transfer of the two models of statehood from Central Europe to Ethiopia

Unitary, ethnolinguistically homogenous nation-state	Ethnolinguistic federalism	
	With elements of ethnolinguistic federalism	Full ethnolinguistic federalism
German Empire (1871–1945) *Deutsches Reich*	**Austria-Hungary** (1867–1918) *Österreichisch-Ungarische Monarchie* (in German) *Osztrák-Magyar Monarchia* (in Hungarian) (literally 'Austro-Hungarian Monarchy')	
Empire of Japan 大日本帝國 *dai nihon teikoku* (literally 'Great Japanese Empire')		**interwar Soviet Union** Союз Советских Социалистических Республик (СССР) *Soiuz Sovetskikh Sotsialisticheskikh Respublik (SSSR)* Union of Soviet Socialist Republics (USSR)
	postwar Soviet Union USSR	**Communist China** 中华人民共和国 *Zhōnghuá rénmín gònghéguó* (literally, 'China: people's Republic')
Ethiopian Empire	Soviet-Derg Ethiopia	postcommunist Ethiopia
Ethiopian Empire የኢትዮጵያ መንግሥት *ye 'ītiyop 'iya menigišite*	**People's Democratic Republic of Ethiopia** የኢትዮጵያ ሕዝባዊ ዲሞክራሲያዊ ሪፐብሊክ *ye 'ītiyop 'iya ḥizibawī dīmokirasīyawī rīpebilīk*	**Federal Democratic Republic of Ethiopia** የኢትዮጵያ ፌዴራላዊ ዲሞክራሲያዊ ሪፐብሊክ *ye 'ītiyop 'iya fēdēralawī dīmokirasīyawī rīpebilīk*

Table 3.2 Officially recognized ethnic groups in Ethiopia

1 Aari	31 Gedicho	61 Murle
2 Afar	32 Gidole	62 Mursi
3 Agaw-Awi	33 Gof(f)a	63 Nao
4 Agaw-Hamyra	34 Gumuz	64 Nuer
5 Alaba	35 Gurage	65 Nyangatom
6 Amhara	36 Silt'e	66 Oromo
7 Anuak	37 Hadiya	67 Oyda
8 Arbore	38 Hamar	68 Qebena
9 Argobba	39 Harari	69 Qechem
10 Bacha	40 Irob	70 Qewama
11 Basketo	41 Kafa (Kafficho)	71 She
12 Bench	42 Kambaata	72 Shekecho
13 Berta	43 Konta	73 Sheko
14 Bodi	44 Komo	74 Shinasha
15 Brayle	45 Konso	75 Sidama
16 Burji	46 Kontoma	76 Silte
17 Bena	47 Koore	77 Somali
18 Beta Israel	48 Kunama	78 Surma
19 Chara	49 Karo	79 Tigrinya
20 Daasanach	50 Kusumie	80 Tembaro
21 Dawro	51 Kwegu	81 Tsamai
22 Debase (Ale)	52 Male	82 Welayta (Wolayita)
23 Dirashe	53 Mao	83 Werji
24 Dime	54 Mareqo	84 Yem
25 Dizi	55 Mashola	85 Zeyese
26 Donga	56 Mere	86 Zelmam
27 Fedashe	57 Me'en	87 Other Ethiopian national groups
28 Gamo	58 Messengo	
29 Gebato	59 Majang(ir)	
30 Gedeo	60 Mossiye	

Source: (*Summary* 2008: 84–85)

Table 3.3 National autonomous territorial entities in federal Ethiopia (in early 2019)

Autonomous territorial entity	Titular Group(s) (i.e. nation, nationality or people, as empowered by their own autonomous territorial entity)	Official Language & Script (of the autonomous territorial entity)	National (Ethnic) Language & Script (of the Titular Group[s])	Predominant Religion (of the Titular Group or territorial entity)
1 Addis Ababa (አዲስ አበባ *ādīsi ābeba*)	None	Amharic & Ethiopic syllabary	None	Numerous but predominantly Miaphysitic Christianity
2 Afar (Qafār in Afar, ዓፋር *'afar*)	Afars	Afar & Latin alphabet	Afar & Latin alphabet	Islam
a Argobba (አርጎባ *ārigoba*) Special Woreda (ልዩ ወረዳ *liyu wereda*)	Argobbas	Amharic & Ethiopic syllabary	Argobba	Islam
3 Amhara (አማራ *āmara*)	Amharas	Amharic & Ethiopic syllabary	Amharic & Ethiopic syllabary	Miaphysitic Christianity
A Agew Awi (አገው አዊ *āgewi āwī*) Nationality Administration (ብሔረሰብ አስተዳደር *biḫēreseb āsitedaderi*)	Agaws	Amharic & Ethiopic syllabary	Agaw	Miaphysitic Christianity
a Argobba Special Woreda (አርጎባ *ārigoba*)	Argobbas	Amharic & Ethiopic syllabary	Argobba	Islam

(Continued)

Table 3.3 (Continued)

Autonomous territorial entity	Titular Group(s) (i.e. nation, nationality or people, as empowered by their own autonomous territorial entity)	Official Language & Script (of the autonomous territorial entity)	National (Ethnic) Language & Script (of the Titular Group[s])	Predominant Religion (of the Titular Group or territorial entity)
B Kamyr (Agew Himra) Nationality Administration (ካምይር ካሚይሪ [ዋጊብዋሙራ wagib±imira])	Kamyrs	Amharic & Ethiopic syllabary	Kamyr (Xamtanga)	Miaphysitic Christianity
b Kemant Special Woreda (ቅማንት ክ'imaniti)	Kemants	Amharic & Ethiopic syllabary	Amharic	Miaphysitic Christianity
C Oromo Nationality Administration (Oromiyaa in Oromo, ኦሮምያ oromiya)	Oromos	Oromo & Latin alphabet	Oromo & Latin alphabet	Islam
4 Benishangul-Gumuz (ቤንሻንጉል ጉሙዝ bēnishanigul gumuz)	Bertas, Gumuzes, Shinashas, Maos & Komos	Amharic & Ethiopic syllabary	Berta, Gumuz, Shinasha, Mao & Komo	Miaphysitic Christianity & Islam
A Berta Nationality Administration (በርታ berita)	Bertas	Amharic & Ethiopic syllabary	Berta	Islam
B Gumuz Nationality Administration (ጉሙዝ gumuzi)	Gumuzes	Amharic & Ethiopic syllabary	Gumuz (Gumaz)	Nonscriptural ('traditional') religion
C Komo Nationality Administration (የኮሞ yekomo)	Komos	Amharic & Ethiopic syllabary	Komo (Kwama, Gwama)	Nonscriptural ('traditional') religion

Conclusion 71

D Mao Nationality Administration (ማአ *ma'o*)	Maos	Amharic & Ethiopic syllabary	Mao	Nonscriptural ('traditional') religion
E Shinasha Nationality Administration (ሺንሻ *shinisha*)	Shinashas	Amharic & Ethiopic syllabary	Shinasha (Boro)	Mao
5 Dire Dawa (Dirre Dhawaa in Oromo, Diri Dhaba in Somali, ድሬዳዋ *dirēdawa*)	Oromos & Somalis	Amharic & Ethiopic syllabary; Oromo & Latin alphabet; Somali & Latin alphabet	None	Islam
6 Gambela (ጋምቤላ *gambēla*)	Nuers, Anywaas, Majangs, Upos & Komos	Amharic & Ethiopic syllabary	Nuer & Latin alphabet, Anywaa & Ethiopic syllabary	Protestantism
A Anywaa (የአኙዋክ ye 'ānyuwaki) Special Zone (ልዩ ዞን *liyu Zone*)	Anywaas	Amharic & Ethiopic syllabary	Anywaa & Ethiopic syllabary (also Latin alphabet, especially in South Sudan)	Protestantism
<i> Komo (የኮሞ *yekomo*) Nationality Kebele (ብሔረሰብ ቀበሌ *bihēresebi k'ebelē*)	Komos	Amharic & Ethiopic syllabary	Komo (Kwama, Gwama)	Nonscriptural ('traditional') religion
B Majang Special Zone (ማጁንግ *majinig*)	Majangs (Majangirs)	Amharic & Ethiopic syllabary	Majang (Majangir) & Latin alphabet	Protestantism (but also Miaphysitic Christianity)

(*Continued*)

Table 3.3 (Continued)

Autonomous territorial entity	Titular Group(s) (i.e. nation, nationality or people, as empowered by their own autonomous territorial entity)	Official Language & Script (of the autonomous territorial entity)	National (Ethnic) Language & Script (of the Titular Group[s])	Predominant Religion (of the Titular Group or territorial entity)
C Nuer Special Zone (Naath in Nuer, ኑዌር nuwēri)	Nuers	Amharic & Ethiopic syllabary	Nuer & Latin alphabet	Protestantism
<i> Upo Nationality Kebele (ኡፖ opo)	Upos	Amharic & Ethiopic syllabary	Upo (Opuo, Opuuo, Shita, Opo)	Nonscriptural ('traditional') religion
7 Harari (ሐረሪ ḥtāreri)	Hararis	Harari & Ethiopic syllabary, Oromo & Latin alphabet	Harari & Ethiopic syllabary	Islam
8 Oromia (Oromiyaa in Oromo, ኦሮሚያ oromiya)	Oromos	Oromo & Latin alphabet	Oromo & Latin alphabet	Islam, Miaphysitic and Protestant Christianity
9 Somali (Soomaalida in Somali, ሶማሌ somalē)	Somalis	Somali & Latin alphabet	Somali & Latin alphabet	Islam
10 Southern Nations, Nationalities, and Peoples Region (የደቡብ ብሔር ብሔረሰቦችና ሕዝቦች ክልል yedebubi biḥēr biḥłēresebochina hiziboch kilil)	Highly multiethnic	Amharic & Ethiopic syllabary	Highly multilingual	Protestantism (but also Miaphysitic Christianity & Islam)

Conclusion 73

a Ale Special Woreda (አሌ ālē)	Ales	Amharic & Ethiopic syllabary	Ale (Dihina, Gawwada, Worase) & Ethiopic syllabary	Miaphysitic Christianity, Islam
b Amaro Special Woreda (አማሮ āmaro)	Amaros	Amharic & Ethiopic syllabary	Amaro (Badittu, Koore, Koorete, Koyra, Kwera, Nuna)	Protestantism
c Basketo Special Woreda (ባስኬቶ basiketo)	Basketos	Amharic & Ethiopic syllabary	Basketo (Mesketo, Basketo-Dokka)	Protestantism
A Bench-Maji Zone (ቤንች ማጅ bēnich maji)	Benches and other ethnic groups	Amharic & Ethiopic syllabary	Bench (Shenon, Mernon, Gimira)	Protestantism & Nonscriptural ('traditional') religion
d Burji Special Woreda (ቡርጅ buriji)	Burjis	Amharic & Ethiopic syllabary	Burji (Bembala, Daashi)	Protestantism, Miaphysitic Christianity, Islam
B Dawro Zone (ዳውሮ dawiro)	Dawros	Amharic & Ethiopic syllabary	Dawro (Dawragna)	Protestantism & Miaphysitic Christianity
e Dirashe Special Woreda (ድራሼ dirashē)	Dirashes	Amharic & Ethiopic syllabary	Dirashe (Dirasha, Ghidole, Dirayta & Gardulla)	Protestantism, Miaphysitic Christianity & Nonscriptural ('traditional') religion

(*Continued*)

Table 3.3 (Continued)

Autonomous territorial entity	Titular Group(s) (i.e. nation, nationality or people, as empowered by their own autonomous territorial entity)	Official Language & Script (of the autonomous territorial entity)	National (Ethnic) Language & Script (of the Titular Group[s])	Predominant Religion (of the Titular Group or territorial entity)
C Gamo Zone (ጋሞ gamo)	Gamos	Amharic & Ethiopic syllabary	Gamo	Protestantism
D Gedeo Zone (የጌዴኦ yegēdē'o)	Gedeos	Gedeo & Latin alphabet	Gedeo	Protestantism
E Gofa Zone (ጎፋ gofa)	Gofas	Amharic & Ethiopic syllabary	Gofa	Protestantism
F Gurage Zone (ጉራጌ guragē)	Gurages	Amharic & Ethiopic syllabary	Gurage	Islam
G Hadiya Zone (ሀዲያ ādiya)	Hadiyas	Amharic & Ethiopic syllabary	Hadiya (Hadiyya, Hadiyigna, Adiya, Adea, Adiye & Hadia) & Latin alphabet	Protestantism & Miaphysitic Christianity
H Halaba Zone (አላባ ālaba)	Halabas	Amharic & Ethiopic syllabary	Halaba (Alaba, Alaba-K'abeena, Wanbasana)	Islam
I Kafa (Kaffa, Keffa) Zone (ካፋ kafa)	Kafas (Kaffichos)	Kafa & Latin alphabet	Kafa (Kefa, Kafi)	Miaphysitic Christianity
J Kembata Tembaro Zone (ከምባታ ጠምባሮ kemibata t'emibaro)	Kembatas & Tembaros	Amharic & Ethiopic syllabary	Kembata (Kambaata) & Tembaro	Protestantism

Conclusion 75

K Konso Zone (ከንሶ *koniso*)	Konsos	Amharic & Ethiopic syllabary	Konso	Nonscriptural ('traditional') religion
f Konta Special Woreda (ኮንታ *konita*)	Kontas	Amharic & Ethiopic syllabary	Konta	Nonscriptural ('traditional') religion & Miaphysitic Christianity
L Sidama Zone (ሲዳማ *sidama*)	Sidamas	Sidama & Latin alphabet	Sidama (Sidaama, Sidamo)	Protestantism
M Silte Zone (ስልጢ *silit'e*)	Siltes	Amharic & Ethiopic syllabary	Silte (Silt'e, Silti)	Islam
N Sheka Zone (ሽካ *sheka*)	Shekas (Shekos, Shakachos)	Amharic & Ethiopic syllabary	Sheka (Sheko)	Protestantism & Miaphysitic Christianity
O South Omo Zone (ደቡብ ኦሞ ዞን *debub omo zone*)	Highly multiethnic, including Aaris, Males, Daasanaches, Hamars, Bannas, Tsamais & Nyangatoms	Amharic & Ethiopic syllabary	Aari, Male (Maale), Daasanach Marille, Geleba), Hamar (Hamer), Banna (Banya), Tsamai (Ts'amay, S'amai, Tamaha & Bago S'amakk-Ulo), Nyangatom (Donyiro & Idongiro)	Nonscriptural ('traditional') religion & Protestantism

(*Continued*)

Table 3.3 (Continued)

Autonomous territorial entity	Titular Group(s) (i.e. nation, nationality or people, as empowered by their own autonomous territorial entity)	Official Language & Script (of the autonomous territorial entity)	National (Ethnic) Language & Script (of the Titular Group[s])	Predominant Religion (of the Titular Group or territorial entity)
P Wolayita Zone (ወላይታ welayita)	Wolayitas	Wolayita & Latin alphabet	Wolayita (Wolaytta)	Protestantism
g Yem Special Woreda (የም yemi)	Yems	Amharic & Ethiopic syllabary	Yem (Yemsa)	Miaphysitic Christianity
11 Tigray (ትግራይ tagray in Tigrinya, ትግራይ tigiray)	Tigrayans (but also Irobs & Kunamas)	Tigrinya & Ethiopic syllabary	Tigrinya & Ethiopic syllabary	Miaphysitic Christianity
a Irob Woreda (ኢሮብ irob)	Irobs	Tigrinya & Ethiopic syllabary	Irob (Saho)	Miaphysitic Christianity

Significantly, at present in Federal Ethiopia, the following 40 ethnic groups enjoy a form of territorial (or non-territorial) autonomy, namely the (1) Afars, (2) Agaws, (3) Ales, (4) Amaros, (5) Amharas, (6) Anywaas, (7) Argobbas, (8) Basketos, (9) Bertas, (10) Burjis, (11) Dawros, (12) Dirashes, (13) Gamos, (14) Gedeos, (15) Gofas, (16) Gumuzes, (17) Gurages, (18) Hadiyas, (19) Halabas, (20) Hararis, (21) Irobs, (22) Kafas, (23) Kamyrs, (24) Kemants, (25) Komos, (26) Konsos, (27) Kontas, (28) Majangs, (29) Maos, (30) Nuers, (31) Oromos, (32) Shinashas, (33) Sidamas, (34) Siltes, (35) Shekos, (36) Somalis, (37) Tigrayans, (38) Upos (Opos), (39) Wolayitas and (40) Yems. As a result, over 90 percent of the population and about half of the country's recognized ethnic groups (nations, nationalities and peoples) enjoy ethnolinguistically defined territorial (institutional) autonomy, as promised by the 1995 Constitution. In reality, actual provisions (i.e. the use of a given ethnic language in administration, education, publishing, the mass media or the internet) vary. At this moment, it is hard to ascertain how big or small such differences are without someone's conducting dedicated field research on this issue.

Given the multiethnic and polyglot nature of South Omo Zone, in the near future, this will probably become the prime area for establishing territorial autonomies for this zone's numerous ethnic groups (nations, nationalities and peoples). Likewise, any remaining bi-national ethnic (autonomous) zones (and other territories) may split, as has already happened in the case of quite a few.

In line with the tradition of Central Europe's ethnolinguistic nationalism and of the Soviet nationality policy, the ethnonym (name) of the titular group tends to function as the names of this group's language and ethnic (autonomous) territory. What is more, the titular group's auto-ethnonym (self-appellation in the group's own language) is preferred to any variants (in other languages) used in the past.

NB 1: Numerals are employed for distinguishing between Ethiopia's regions (ክልል *kilili*), capital letters for distinguishing between the country's special (enumerated, national) zones (ልዩ ዞን *liyu zone*) and lower case letters for distinguishing between the special (enumerated, national) woredas (ልዩ ወረዳ *liyu wereda*). In addition, the names of the regions are given in bold, while the names of the special woredas are italicized and aligned to the right. Furthermore, in the case of Gambela's constitutionally guaranteed (potential) nationality kebeles (communities, neighborhoods; ብሔረሰብ ቀበሌ *biḫēreseb k'ebelē*), they are displayed like woredas, though such nationality kebeles are numbered with the use of lowercase roman numerals in angle brackets.

78 Conclusion

NB 2: In Benishangul-Gumuz Region, 'nationality administrations' (ብሔረሰብ አስተዳደር *bihēreseb āsitedader*) are equal in rights and purposes to zones, but de facto, zones fulfill some of the legal and constitutional purposes of these aforesaid nationality administrations. Interestingly, to this day, the region's nationality administrations remain *non-territorial* (Muluneh 2017). However, the nationality administrations in Amhara Region are fully operational and *territorial* in their character.

NB 3: In Southern Nations, Nationalities and Peoples Region, the zones (ዞን *zoni*) are not qualified as 'special,' but de facto they were established for these zones' main ethnic groups.

NB 4: As far as possible, the ethnonyms cited are supplied with the regular English '-s' ending, in order to do away with the colonial (imperial) English (Western) tradition of denying this kind of 'European' ('civilized') plural to ('uncivilized') African 'tribes.'

NB 5: An effort was made to provide the names of all the autonomous ethnic territories in these territories' respective ethnic languages, alongside their versions in Ethiopia's federal official language of Amharic. However, we managed to ascertain only a few such names in ethnic languages. More fieldwork is necessary to gather such vital (for this topic) information. Almost all ethnic (autonomous) territories derive their respective names from the ethnonym of a given territory's titular group (main ethnic group).

NB 6: The information gathered in Table 3.3 was collected by Asnake Kefale, Christophe Van der Beken and their students over the course of their research and field trips across Ethiopia. Although the situation may strike western readers as strange, such pieces of information are *not* gathered in a single governmental (official) institution in the Ethiopian capital of Addis Ababa as a matter of course or made accessible to the public at large. In addition, Tomasz Kamusella scoured the internet – in English and in Amharic – for this type of information about Federal Ethiopia's territorial autonomies. Unfortunately, on the internet, even on the official Ethiopian websites, such information is often out of date, while Facebook pages (created by activists and the authorities of this or that autonomous territory) may be unreliable.

Notes

1 Democratic centralism, as developed by Vladimir Lenin in 1917, is a principle which claims that all party members must follow a collective decision – however controversial, immoral or disliked – if a valid vote has led to taking it. In practice, with the use of the delegated votes of the rank-and-file members, a communist

party's leadership could make whatever decision they thought was right. This was sufficient to legitimize and enforce the imposition of such a decision on all the party. In Soviet-style polities, the principle of democratic centralism was extended to running the entire state, because the communist party's structures doubled as the state administration. Often, this principle was nothing more but a license for arbitrary – that is, dictatorial – rule (cf Iroshnikov 1974: 285).

2 A language in de facto official use is one employed for administrative purposes but without any legal provision requiring that.

3 The 15 languages employed as media of instruction during the Soviet-Derg's literacy campaigns were as follows: Amharic (1), Afar (2), Gedeo (3), Hadiyya (4), Kafa (5), Kembata (Kambaata) (6), Kunama (7), Oromo (8), Saho (9), Sidamo (10), Silti (11), Somali (12), Tigrinya (13), Tigre (14) and Wolayta (15) (Klinger 1992: Table 9). The choice of these 15 languages (out of the suggested total of Ethiopia's *about* 80 languages [Klinger 1992: 33]), not fewer or more, curiously correspond to the Soviet Union's 15 constituent union republics and their 15 official languages. The rationality of this choice might be dictated by the Soviet example in this regard.

4 What is more, 6.2 percent of Ethiopians speak Somali (or the official language of the State of Somali), 5.9 percent speak Tigrinya (or the official language of the State of Tigray), 4 percent speak Sidama (or the potential official language of the proposed State of Sidama), 2.2 percent speak Wolayita (or the official language of Wolayita Zone), 2 percent speak Gurage (or the official language of Gurage Zone), 1.7 percent speak Afar (or the official language of the State of Afar), 1.7 percent speak Hadiya (or the official language of Hadiya Zone), 1.5 percent speak Gamo (or the official language of Gamo Zone), 1.3 percent speak Gedeo (or the official language of Gedeo Zone) and 1.1 percent speak Kafa (or the official language of Kafa Zone) (Ethiopia: Languages 2020).

5 Unfortunately, the late 2020 armed confrontation between the PP-led federal government and the TPLF-led Tigray regional government has demonstrated that a consensual approach is not always what transpires. The all-Ethiopia federal and regional elections were scheduled to take place in August 2020, but they were delayed until June 2021, due to the pandemic. However, the TPLF disagreed with this decision and proceeded with the regional elections in the State of Tigray. In light of these events, the federal government deemed the newly elected Tigray regional government as illegitimate, while the latter held the same opinion of the former. One factor that has fueled this conflict is the basic ideological disagreement between the PP and the TPLF. The TPLF seeks more autonomy for the ethnolinguistic regions and the further deepening of Ethiopia's ethnoterritorial federalism, while the governing PP party seems to steer the country toward a more unitary model, in which the common Ethiopian citizenship should take precedence over ethnicity. It is none other than the continuation of the modern Ethiopian quarrel between the two models of statehood, as originally borrowed from Central Europe (cf Tigray Crisis 2020).

Sociopolitical timeline of modern Ethiopia

This timeline is intended for readers with no background knowledge of Ethiopia and the country's history, who consult this book for its main argument about the transfer of the idea of centralized and federal ethnolinguistically defined statehood from Central Europe via Asia to Ethiopia.

1270–1974 **Ethiopian Empire** (መንግሥተ ኢትዮጵያ *menigišite ītiyop'iya*) (Henze 2000: 56)

1789 source of civic nationalism: Declaration of the Rights of Man and of the Citizen (*Déclaration des droits de l'homme et du citoyen*) (Declaration 1789), as adopted in revolutionary France

1813 Source of ethnolinguistic nationalism: Ernst Moritz Arndt's song 'Des deutschen Vaterland' (The German Fatherland) (Arndt 1813), employed as a marching song by Prussian troops in the course of the successful war against Napoleon (1813–1815)

1850 Constitution for the State of Prussia (*Verfassung für den Preußischen Staat*) (Preußische Verfassung 2019)

1513 Latin-Ge'ez psalter was published in Rome; it was the first book published in an Ethiopian language (Gupta 1994: 175)

1855–1868 **Emperor Tewodros II** (ዳግማዊ ዓፄ ቴዎድሮስ *dagimawī 'ats'ē tēwodiros*)
Amharic (known as 'king's language,' that is, ልሳነ ንጉሥ *lisane nigus* in Ge'ez or የንጉሥ ቋንቋ *yeniguši k'wanik'wa* in Amharic) replaced the antiquated liturgical language of Ge'ez as the empire's official language (Girma Awgichew Demeke 2014: 12, 152); the everyday use of Ge'ez (ልሳነ ግዕዝ 'language of the free' in Ge'ez) ceased in the

9th century (Bender, Hailu Fulass and Cowley 1976: 99); but thanks to the 6th-century Ge'ez translation of the Bible (Mikre-Sellassie 2000), this language remains official in the Ethiopian Church to this day

Hence, Tewodros's decision marked the beginning of the separation of state from church

Centralization of the state

1864 in Massawa (today in Eritrea), then under Egyptian rule, the first printed book in Tigrinya was published, a catechism (Gupta 1994: 175)

>1867 unitary Austrian Empire was overhauled into the de facto ethnolinguistic federation of Austria-Hungary

1868 British invasion of Ethiopia followed by internal strife and the collapse of the state structures

>1871 founding and the Constitution of the German Empire (*Die Verfassung des Deutschen Reichs*) (Die Verfassung 1871), which made the country into a unitary ethnolinguistic nation-state

1871–1889 **Emperor Yohannes IV** (ዓፄ ዮሐንስ ፬ኛ '*ats'ē yoḥānis 4nya*)

Reconstruction of the centralized state institutions

1879 printing press was founded in Sanhit (today, Keren in Eritrea), then under Egyptian rule, which produced books in Amharic, Ge'ez and Tigrinya (Gupta 1994: 176)

1886 founding of Addis Ababa (አዲስ አበባ 'new flower,' but since the 1990s, also known as *Finfinne* 'natural spring' in Oromo)

1886 Emperor Yohannes IV imposed a ban on all missionary activities in Ethiopia (Haile Gebriel Dagne 2007: 309)

1888–1892 Great Famine (ክፉ ቀናት *kifu k'enati* 'evil days'); around a third of the country's population perished (Kaplan 1990; Kiros 2006: 15–16)

>1889 Constitution of the Empire of Japan (大日本帝國憲法 *Dai-Nippon Teikoku Kenpō*) (The Constitution 1889) that overhauled the country into a unitary ethnolinguistic nation-state on the model of the German Empire

1889–1913 **Emperor Menelik II** (ዳግማዊ ዓፄ ምኒልክ *dagimawī 'ats'ē minīlik*)

1889–1904 age of military conquests (despite the cost, famine and unprecedented loss of life), because of which Ethiopia was transformed into a multiethnic empire (Podeszwa 2000)

1890 Ethiopia's population: 7.4 million (Ethiopia: Historical 2019)

1891 Addis Ababa became the capital of Ethiopia (Shinn and Ofcansky 2013: 21)

1892 first Amharic-language periodical አእምሮ ā'imiro ('Intellect') published in Addis Ababa; initially in 12 handwritten copies, which has been machine duplicated in 24 copies since 1902, published with the use of a regular printing press beginning in 1914; in 1895, this periodical was followed by the newspaper ሰሜናዊ ኮከብ semēnawī kokebi ('Northern Star') Abdu Mozayen 1976: 505; Gupta 1994: 177)

1895–1899 Western weaponry and Western military technologies introduced to Ethiopia by Russian advisors (Agureev 2011: 35–55, 90–104; Leont'ev 2020)

1895–1896 Italo-Ethiopian War; the first case when a non-Western state defeated a European (Western) colonial power

1896 Battle of Adwa (ዓድዋ 'adiwa in Tigray), Ethiopia defeated the invading Italian army (Jonas 2011)

1896 Emperor Menelik II removed the ban on missionary activity in the country (Haile Gebriel Dagne 2007: 309)

> 1899 Britain extended colonial control over Egypt's Sudan, resulting in a condominium of Anglo-Egyptian Sudan (السودان الإنجليزي المصري as-Sūdān al-Inglīzī al-Maṣrī in Arabic)

1900 Ethiopia's population: 12 million (Ethiopia: Historical 2019)

> 1904–1905 Russo-Japanese War, lauded in the history of decolonization as the first case when a non-Western state defeated a European (Western) colonial power; in fact, this first belongs to Ethiopia, which had defeated Italy in the 1895–1896 Italo-Ethiopian War

1905 in Addis Ababa, missionaries opened the first school for girls in Ethiopia (Haile Gebriel Dagne 2007: 309)

1905–1911 Ethiopia's first significant periodical, *Le Semeur d'Éthiopie* ('Ethiopian Weekly'), was published in French, initially at Harar and since 1908 in Dire Dawa (Pankhurst 2003)

1906 first governmental printing press (Gori 2015: 67)

> 1907 Otto Bauer *The Question of Nationalities and Social Democracyv* (*Die Nationalitätenfrage und die Sozialdemokratie*) (Bauer 1907, 2000), or the main theoretical reflection on ethnolinguistic federalism in Austria-Hungary; Bauer was a leading representative of Austro-marxism, that is, a school of political thought

Sociopolitical timeline of modern Ethiopia 83

1907 first state secondary school, École impériale Menelik (Menelik Imperial School), was founded, and it attracted teachers from Egypt (which then also controlled neighboring Sudan) (Haile Gebriel Dagne 2007: 314–315)

> 1908 Karl Kautsky *Nationalität und Internationalität* (Nationality and Internationalism) (Kautsky 1908), another important Austro-marxist reflection on Austria-Hungary's ethnolinguistic federalism

1908 beginning of the secular ('government') educational system, where French was designated as the medium of education, and Amharic was taught as one of the school subjects (Bowen 1976: 315; Girma Awgichew Demeke 2014: 152)

1908 first Amharic-language novel was published in Rome, namely ልብ ወለድ ታሪክ *libi weled tarīk* ('A Story from My Mind') by Afework Ghebre Jesus (አፈ ወርቅ ገብረ ኢየሱስ *āfe werik gebire īyesus* 1868–1947) (Yonas Admassu 2003)

Previously, all education was provided by church schools and Quranic schools (Islamic madrasas), with Ge'ez and Arabic respectively as their languages of instruction; hence, after 1908, the deepening of the separation of church and state (Haile Gebriel Dagne 2007)

1911 first book published in Addis Ababa, a Ge'ez-language catechism (Gupta 1994: 177)

> 1913 Joseph Stalin's *Marxism and the National Question* (Иосиф Сталин *Марксизм и национальный вопрос* Iosif Stalin *Marksizm i natsionalnyi vopros*) (Stalin 1954 [1913]) drew on the Austro-marxist reflection on Austria-Hungary's ethnolinguistic federalism; this essay became *the* blueprint for the Soviet Union's ethnolinguistic (ethnoterritorial) federalism

1913–1916 **Lij Iyasu** (ልጅ ኢያሱ *liji īyasu*), designated successor (Emperor designate), who, however, was *never* crowned or recognized as Emperor

1913 first commercial printing press founded in Addis Ababa (Gupta 1994: 177)

1916–1930 **Empress Zewditu** (ንግሥት ዘውዲቱ *nigišit zewidītu*) Ras (Duke) Tafari Makonnen (ተፈሪ መኮንን *teferī mekonini*); in 1930, he became Emperor Haile Selassie

1916–1928 regent

1928–1930 king and regent

1920 Britain's East Africa Protectorate (gained in the late 1880s) was transformed into the Colony and Protectorate of Kenya

1920 Ethiopia's population: 14.5 million (Ethiopia: Historical 2019)

1921 books began to be regularly printed in Ethiopia, in Addis Ababa (Abdu Mozayen 1976: 505), mainly thanks to Tafari Makonnen's printing press Berhanena Selam ('Light and Peace' in Ge'ez) (Gupta 1994: 177)

1922 Britain unilaterally ended its protectorate over Egypt, by granting this country limited independence; in addition, this act renamed the Sultanate of Egypt (Arabic: السلطنة المصرية *alsiltanat almisriat*) as the Kingdom of Egypt (المملكة المصرية *almamlakat almisriat* in Arabic)

1923 Ethiopia (under the then internationally preferred name of Abyssinia) became a member state of the League of Nations, as a third non-Western state, after Japan and Siam (Thailand) had co-founded this international organization in 1920 (Iadarola 1975)

1925 main Amharic-language newspaper of Ethiopia's modernizers (Westernizers), ብርሃንና ሰላም (*birihanina šelam* 'Light and Peace'), was established

1926 United States followed the Ethiopian government's wish that this country be known under the preferred name of Ethiopia, instead of the widespread appellation Abyssinia, which persisted in international use until the late 1940s (Tuji Jidda 2009)

1927 Tafari Makonnen's new-style secondary school, where, alongside the still-dominant French, English was introduced as an alternative medium of instruction (Bowen 1976: 318)

1920s secondary school graduates and Ethiopians who were educated abroad constituted a new secular elite, which allowed Emperor Haile Selassie to modernize Ethiopia; Ethiopian historians likened this elite to the Young Turks of the early 20th-century Ottoman Empire: nowadays, in literature, these intellectuals and reformers are collectively known as Young Ethiopians (Balsvik 2007: 13; Bahru Zewde 2002)

1930–1974 **Emperor Haile Selassie** (ንጉሠ ነገሥት ቀዳማዊ ኃይለ ሥላሴ *niguše negešit k'edamawī ḫayile šilasē*)

1930 Ethiopia's population: 16 million (Ethiopia: Historical 2019)

1930 Ethiopia's first Ministry of Education was founded; apart from French and English, Amharic was increasingly employed as a language of education; a system was established of six years of elementary, six years of secondary and four years of university education; and in the absence of universities in Ethiopia, Ethiopian students were sent to colleges and universities in the Middle East (Egypt, Lebanon, Sudan), Europe (Belgium, the United Kingdom, France, Germany, Italy, Spain and Switzerland) and the United States (Bowen 1976: 319–320)

1931 (1923 EC) Constitution (ሕግ መንግሥት *hige menigišit*, literally 'the law of the government, kingdom, state')

'The territory of Ethiopia . . . is subject to the government of His Majesty the Emperor. All the natives of Ethiopia, subjects of the empire, form together the Ethiopian Empire' (Art. 1)

'In the Ethiopian Empire supreme power rests in the hands of the Emperor' (Art. 6)

'All Ethiopian subjects, provided they comply with the conditions laid down by law and the decrees promulgated by the Emperor, may be appointed officers in the army or civil officials, or to any other posts or offices in the service of the State' (Art. 19)

'The nation is bound to pay legal taxes' (Art. 21) (Ethiopian Constitution 1931)

Ergo, Emperor is *above* empire = state = nation = subjects

NB 1: *Not yet* were there any provisions on the official or state language (see the Revised Ethiopian Constitution of 1955)

NB 2: This first Ethiopian Constitution was modeled on the Japanese Imperial Constitution of 1889 (Macleod 2014: 41; Shinn and Ofcansky 2013: 100); the ambition was to overhaul Ethiopia into a unitary ethnolinguistic nation-state on the model of the Japanese Empire (which in turn had borrowed this model of statehood from the German Empire)

1931 radio broadcasting commenced in Ethiopia (Pankhurst 1957)

1932 Heruy Wellde Selasse's (ኀሩይ ወልደ ሥላሴ *hiruy welide šilasē*) influential book ማኅደረ ብርሃን – ሀገረ ጃፓን *mahidere birihan – hāgere japan* (Japan: The Source of Light) was published

1935/1936 about 4,000 students attended the government schools across Ethiopia (Bowen 1976: 320), alongside 5,000 students in the mission schools (Haile Gabriel Dagne 1976: 366); in addition, before the Italian occupation, about 200 Ethiopians had graduated from universities abroad (Balsvik 2007: 15)

1936–1941 **Italian occupation**

The name of Ethiopia was erased from official use, and the country was made into part of the Africa Orientale Italiana (AOI), or Italian East Africa, founded in 1936; the AOI overlaps with today's states of Eritrea, Ethiopia and (most of) Somalia; and the territory of Ethiopia was split among the colonial provinces of Amara, Galla-Sidamo, Harrar, Scioà (Shewa) and Somalia

1936 Amharic was replaced with Italian as the leading official language; likewise, Italian superseded French and English as the medium of secondary education; local languages (Galla [Oromo], Kefa [Kafa], Somali and Tigrinya) were promoted in local administration and elementary education in order to downgrade the previously de facto state language of Amharic to the similar level of a mere local language; and Arabic was made the medium of instruction in all Muslim areas (Bowen 1976: 322)

1936 racial segregation (first trialed by the Italians three years earlier in Eritrea) was introduced across Ethiopia, with secondary and tertiary education reserved for 'higher whiter races' only (Robertson 1988: 48, 51)

1941 by this year, the Italian occupiers had built 7,000 kilometers of roads, thus endowing Ethiopia with a modern transportation network (Whitake 1981: 173)

1941 British and Ethiopian forces defeated the Italians in the Horn of Africa; Addis Ababa was liberated on 6 April 1941 (Spencer 2006: 92); formally, in 1944, Britain recognized the Ethiopian sovereignty in a bilateral treaty; and in the 1947 peace treaty, Italy officially renounced any claims to its former colonies in Africa

1941 Emperor returned to Addis Ababa on 5 May (Spencer 2006: 91); Ethiopia became a client state of the West and after 1949 a member of the anti-Soviet Western bloc when the Cold War commenced (following the Soviet blockade of West Berlin in 1948–1949)

1941 radio broadcasting recommenced with UK assistance, with programs in Amharic, Arabic, English, French and Somali (Abdu Mozayen 1976: 506)

1941 pro-government newspaper አዲስ ዘመን *ādīs zemen* ('New Era') was founded; it is Ethiopia's oldest newspaper that still publishes (Meseret Chekol Reta 2013: 92)

1942 Ethiopian governmental gazette was founded, namely ነጋሪት ጋዜጣ *negarīti gazēt'a* (literally, 'Gazette [that publishes on important] Issues'); the pattern was established that continues to this day, namely to publish all legislation bilingually, in Amharic and in English (Cooper 1976a: 189); and this governmental gazette still continues to publish Ethiopian laws

1942 abolishment of slavery (Hanibal Goitom 2012)

1942 reconstruction of the Ethiopian educational system; however, English was made the sole medium of instruction, in both elementary education and secondary education (Haile Woldemikael 1976: 324; Tesfaye Shewaye and Taylor 1976: 372–373)

1943 ethnically non-Amharic regions resented the reassertion of centralized imperial rule, as assisted by UK forces; the Woyane Uprising (Rebellion) broke out in response; the Tigrayans sought to preserve the ethnolinguistic autonomy for Tigray, as introduced under the Italian occupation; the British forces put down this rebellion (Aaron Tesfaye 2002: 58); and 'Woyane' (also 'Weyane') is the historical Ge'ez term for the Tigrayans, that is, ወያነ *weyane* (Yohannes Woldemariam 2018)

1944 the tradition of allowing missionary activities and schools in non-Christian (and preferably, non-Muslim) areas, on the condition that any preaching and teaching is done through the medium of Amharic, was formalized in a law that explicitly prohibited the use of any other Ethiopian languages for this purpose (Bowen 1976: 315; Cooper 1976a: 189); as a result, the use of Amharic spread to (or rather was imposed on) many southern areas, which Ethiopia had conquered at the turn of the 20th century

1945 Ethiopia joined the United Nations (UN) as one of the 51 founding members; as a member state of the League of Nations, Ethiopia had been officially known under the name of Abyssinia; and hence, 1945 was the turning point in the preferred international use of the name Ethiopia, instead of Abyssinia (Tuji Jidda 2009)

1945 introduced by Arab traders, since the late 18th century, the silver Maria Theresia thaler (first minted in Vienna in 1751) had been Ethiopia's main currency; after the war, with UK assistance, the imperial government collected the thalers; and in the United States, they were melted for the 50-cent silver coin of the Ethiopian Dollar, which became the country's new official currency, known as Birr in Amharic (ብር *biri* 'silver') (Shinn and Ofcansky 2013: 110)

1945 Ethiopia's population: 18.6 million (Ethiopia: Historical 2019)

1946 Ethiopia's first airline, Ethiopian Airlines (የኢትዮጵያ አየር መንገድ *ye'ītiyop'iya āyer meniged*), was founded (Kinfe Abraham 2001: 563)

1948 United Kingdom returned the administration of Ogaden to Ethiopia (Spencer 2006: 199)

1948 Universal Declaration of Human Rights (Universal 1948)

1952 Under the UN's auspices, the United Kingdom handed the former Italian colony of Eritrea over to Ethiopia, on the understanding that Addis Ababa would grant this territory wide-ranging autonomy; as a result, a Federation of Ethiopia and Eritrea (ኢትዮጵያ ኤርትራ ፌዴሬሽን *ītiyop'iya ēritira fēdērēshin*) was proclaimed (Connel and Killion 2011: 249–250)

1953 as a result of the Egyptian Revolution (1952), Egypt gained full independence and was overhauled into an Arab Republic of Egypt (جمهورية مصر العربية *jumhuriat misr alearabia*)

1953 nations are functions of the intensity of in-group communication within a nation-state, conducted in a given language(s) and script(s), as proposed by Karl Deutsch in his monograph *Nationalism and Social Communication* (Deutsch 1953)

1954 first Ethiopian institution of university-level education was founded, namely the University College of Addis Ababa; no language of instruction was designated, but in practice it was English (Cooper 1976a: 189); and the number of graduates grew from 13 in 1954 to 2,054 in 1969 (Haile Woldemikael 1976: 336)

1954 Kebede Mikael's (ከበደ ሚካኤል *kebede mīka'ēl*) influential book ጃፓን እንዴት ሰለጠነች? *japan inidēt selet'enech?* (How Did Japan Modernize Itself?) was published

1955 United Kingdom returned the remaining parts of Ogaden (i.e. Haud and the Reserved Territories) to Ethiopia (Spencer 2006: 282)

1955 this year marked the de facto end of the Eritrean autonomy; the Eritrean law was banned and replaced with the Ethiopian law; Eritrea's languages (Arabic, Tigrinya) were banned and replaced with Amharic; the Ethiopian flag superseded the Eritrean flag; and the Eritrean press and organizations were banned and then replaced by all-Ethiopian counterparts (Redie Bereketeab 2015: 245)

1955 (1948 EC) Revised Ethiopian Constitution (ተሻሻሎ የወጣ የኢትዮጵያ ሕገ መንግሥት *teshashilo yewet'a ye'ītiyop'iya hige menigišit*)

'The official language of the Empire is Amharic' (Art. 125) (Cooper 1976a: 188)

'The Ethiopian Orthodox Church . . . is the Established Church of the Empire and is, as such, supported by the State. The Emperor shall always profess the Ethiopian Orthodox faith. . . .' (Art. 126) (Revised 1955)

NB: Importantly, this Constitution explicitly added an official (national) language to the construction of Ethiopia as a unitary ethnolinguistic nation-state

1955 Revised Constitution of Ethiopia introduced universal suffrage (Revised 1955: Chapter 3)

>   1956 Anglo-Egyptian Sudan was granted independence and became a Republic of Sudan (جمهورية السودان *jumhuriat alsuwdan* in Arabic)

1957 Ethiopia's first five-year plan began (Kinfe Abraham 2001: 563); this developmental instrument was borrowed from the Soviet economic practice of central planning, then quite popular across the developing ('third world') and newly decolonized countries

1958 famine in the province of Tigray, but Addis Ababa declined offers of foreign relief, which led to at least 100,000 victims of starvation and disease (Bahru Zewde 1991: 196)

1958 Amharic replaced English as the medium of instruction in elementary education (Tesfaye Shewaye and Taylor 1976: 373); as a result, the lasting tradition was established that Amharic would be the medium of elementary education (grades one to six), while English that of secondary education (grades seven to 12) (Cooper 1976a: 190; Haile Woldemikael 1976: 325–326); and non-Amharic-speaking children first had to master the Amharic language to enter the educational system at all, which put them at a disadvantage (Cooper 1976b: 294)

1959 Coptic Orthodox Church of Alexandria (Egypt) granted autocephaly (ecclesiastical independence) to the Ethiopian Orthodox Tewahedo (Miaphysitic) Church (የኢትዮጵያ ኦርቶዶክስ ተዋሕዶ ቤተ ክርስቲያን *ye'ītiyop'iya oritodokis tewaḥido bēte kirisitīyan*) (Erlich 2000)

>   1960 British Somaliland Protectorate and the Trust Territory of Somaliland under Italian administration (*Amministrazione fiduciaria italiana della Somalia*) were granted independence and soon afterward united into a Somali Republic (*Jamhuuriyadda Soomaaliyeed* in Somali)

1960 Haile Selassie's overtures to Israel were prompted by the rise of pan-Arab and antimonarchic sentiments in the freshly independent Sudan and across the Middle East in the late 1950s; in return, the

Israelis helped the Emperor foil an attempted coup; and two years later, in 1962, Ethiopia and Israel established diplomatic relations (Spector 2005: 9–10)

1960 failed coup d'état attempt against the Emperor and his government; it broke out because of the frustration with the slow pace of socio-economic progress (modernization); university students demonstrated in support of this coup, which can be seen as the beginning of their politicization as a group (Greenfield 1967: 337–452; Legesse Lemma 1979: 31)

1961 Ethiopia's population: 21 million (Ethiopia: Historical 2019)

1961 University College of Addis Ababa was transformed into Haile Selassie University of Addis Ababa; no language of instruction was specified, but in practice, it was and continues to be English (Cooper 1976a: 189)

1961–1991 Eritrean War of Independence

1962 second five-year plan (Kinfe Abraham 2001: 564)

1962 annexation of Eritrea, made into a mere Ethiopian province, and the dissolution of the Federation of Ethiopia and Eritrea (Connel and Killion 2011: 249–250)

1963–1970 uprising (revolt) of Oromo and Somali Muslims in the southeastern province of Bale (Bali) against Christian (Amharic speaking) settlers and the centralizing state's measures that limited this area's pastoralists' freedom of movement (Tirfe Mammo 1999: 99)

1963 Organization of African Unity (OAU) was founded in Addis Ababa, and the organization's headquarters are in the Ethiopian capital to this day

1964 the Republic of Kenya (*Jamhuri ya Kenya* in Swahili) was proclaimed, terminating the short-lived Dominion of Kenya, into which the United Kingdom's Colony and Protectorate of Kenya had been transformed in 1963

1964 Communist China's Prime Minister, Zhou Enlai, paid a state visit to Ethiopia

1964 Ethiopian–Somali Border War

1965 almost 300,000 students attended the state schools (Haile Woldemikael 1976: 327)

1965 university students demonstrated, demanding 'land to the tiller' (Kinfe Abraham 2001: 565)

Sociopolitical timeline of modern Ethiopia   91

1965–1967 famine in Tigray (Kiros 2006: 17)

1966 university students demonstrated again under the slogan 'Is poverty a crime?' because they were incensed by the desperate situation in the shelter, set up in Shola (ሾላ), at the capital's outskirts, for refugees fleeing the famine in Tigray; to emphasize the situation's urgency, the students dubbed this shelter the 'Shola Concentration Camp' (Bahru Zewde 2014: 139)

> 1967 French Somaliland (*Côte française des Somalis*) renamed as the French Territory of the Afars and the Issas (*Territoire français des Afars et des Issas*)

1968 third five-year plan (Kinfe Abraham 2001: 565)

1968 rebellion in (mainly Amharic speaking) Gojam Province against the centralization of the state (Schwab 1970)

1968 University of Asmara founded (today, in Eritrea) (Klinger 1992: Table 4)

> 1969 marxist-leninist government renamed Somalia the Somali Democratic Republic (*Jamhuuriyadda Dimuqraadiya Soomaaliyeed* in Somali)

1969 Wallelign Mekonnen's (የዋለልኝ መኮንን *yewalelinyi mekonini*) influential essay 'On the Question of Nationalities in Ethiopia' (የብሔሮች ጥያቄ በኢትዮጵያ *yebiḥērochi t'iyak'ē be'ītiyop'iya*) was published in the student magazine *Struggle* (ታገል *tagel*) (yewalelinyi mekonini 1969); it consciously drew on Soviet ethnolinguistic federalism as a model, initially proposed by Joseph Stalin in his 1913 essay; and in turn, Stalin's essay had drawn on Austro-marxist thinkers' ideas developed on the basis of observing Austria-Hungary's ethnolinguistic federalism

1969 after students failed to comply with the imperial order to stop strikes, boycotts and protests, mass repressions and incarcerations of students began (Legesse Lemma 1979: 35)

1969 the president of the Union of Students of Addis Ababa University, Tilahun Gizaw (ጥላሁን ግዛው *ṭəlahun gəzaw* in Tigrinya), was assassinated; this killing and the massacre of around 30 students during his funeral radicalized the student movement (Messay Kebede 2008: 185)

1970 Haile Selassie visited communist China (Kinfe Abraham 2001: 565)

1972 National Academy of the Amharic Language was founded (Getachew Anteneh and Derib Ado 2006: 46; Nigusé Abbebe and Bender 1984)

1972 television broadcasting commenced in Addis Ababa (Abdu Mozayen 1976: 509)

> 1972 adoption of the Latin alphabet for writing Somali, or the national language of independent Somalia (i.e. the ethnolinguistically defined Somali nation-state) (Adam 1983: 33)

1973 foreign lecturers from Western countries constituted over half of the university staff in Ethiopia (Wondwosen Tamrat 2019)

1973 Sephardi Chief Rabbi of Israel, Ovadiah Yosef, officially recognized Ethiopia's Jews, known as the ቤተ እስራኤል *bēte isira'ēli* (Beta Israel 'House of Israel'), as members of the Jewish religion (Judaism) (Spector 2005: 10); the majority of Ethiopian Jews are of Agaw ethnic extraction (Spector 2005: 3)

1973–1974 famine in northern Ethiopia led to at least 200,000 deaths (Kiros 2006: 18)

1974 Ethiopia's population: 26.8 million (Ethiopia: Historical 2019)

1974 only 5 percent of Ethiopians were able to read and write (Gupta 1994)

1974 in print and writing only, the following five Ethiopian languages were employed: Amharic, Harari, Oromo, Tigre and Tigrinya – apart from English employed in administration and education and Arabic and Ge'ez used in religious contexts (Klinger 1992: 43)

1974 not a single publishing house existed in the country, but only 39 printing presses (20 in Addis Ababa, 14 in Asmara, one in Dire Dawa, one in Gondar, one in Harar, one in Jimma and one in Nazaret [Adama]) (Gupta 1994: 180)

1974 Ethiopian Revolution

1974 following the message of Wallelign Mekonnen's 1969 article, university students demanded 'Power to the Peoples' in plural, meaning political empowerment for all Ethiopia's ethnic groups (Balsvik 2007: 44)

1974–1991 **Soviet (Derg, Communist) Ethiopia** (ደርግ *derig* 'committee or council' – that is, 'Soviet')

1974 doctrine of 'Ethiopian socialism' was announced (Selemon Meharenna 1980: 74)

1974 in line with the tenets of the Soviet ideology of marxism-leninism, the Soviet-Derg regime's historiography claimed that in Ethiopia feudalism had come to an end in this year; thus, in the terms of economic and social stages of human development, the country entered the parallel stages of capitalism and nationalism, respectively (Triulzi 1983: 11–118)

1974–1991 Ethiopia became a client (or even member) state of the Soviet bloc

1974–1991 **Ethiopian Civil War** (cf De Waal 1991)

1974–1987 **Provisional Military Government of Socialist Ethiopia** (የጎብረተሰብአዊት ኢትዮጵያ ጊዜያዊ ወታደራዊ መንግሥት *yeḥibiretesebi'āwīti ītiyop'iya gīzēyawī wetaderawī menigišit*)

1974 Chairman Aman Mikael Andom (አማን ሚካኤል አንዶም *āman mīka'ēl ānidom* 1924–1974; ruled 12 September–17 November 1974)

1974–1977 Chairman Tafari Benti (ተፈሪ በንቲ *teferī benitī* 1921–1977)

1977–1987 Chairman Mengistu Haile Mariam (መንግስቱ ኃይለ ማርያም *menigisitu hayile mariyami* 1937–)

1974–1991 Ethiopian Empire was an ideologically Christian polity, whereby default Muslims had fewer rights than Christians did; this situation changed for the better for Muslims under the Soviet-Derg regime, which aimed at treating both confessional groups even-handedly while gradually repressing religion as such, in line with the tenets of marxism-leninism (Abbink 1998: 117; Balsvik 2007: 57–58)

1974–1976 University in Addis Ababa was closed, alongside other higher education institutions across the country; the Soviet-Derg regime ordered the students to join the ዘመቻ *zemecha* (campaign) for spreading literacy and progress across Ethiopia; 52,000 campaigners ran almost 450 campaign posts across the country and convinced six million peasants to join almost 20,000 peasant associations, which became a new basis of Ethiopian agriculture; literacy programs, founded and run by the campaigners, catered to almost 800,000 participants; almost half successfully graduated with the skills of reading and writing; four and a half million basic literacy books were printed and distributed; and literacy was taught in Amharic, Oromo, Somali, Tigrinya and Wolayita, but with the *exclusive* employment of the Ethiopic syllabary only (Balsvik 2007: 59–75; Milkias 1980)

1974–1975 nationalization of all the country's printing presses was executed for the sake of extending full state control over book and press production; this meant the centralization of censorship and propaganda in the hands of the Soviet-Derg regime; the majority of the surviving printing presses were transformed into an Ethiopian Printing Corporation; this state enterprise became the springboard for the country's first publishing houses, namely the Ethiopia Book Centre (የኢትዮጵያ መጽሃፍት ማዕከል *ye'ītiyop'iya mets'ihifit ma'ikel*) and the Kuraz Publishing Agency (ኩራዝ አሳታሚና *kuraz āsatamīna*) (Gupta 1994: 179–180)

1975 nationalization without compensation of arable land, urban land, 'extra houses,' factories and workshops, shops and services; a planned centralized state-owned economy was officially established by 1982 (Keller 1988: 246)

1975 Peasants either voluntarily joined or were forced to join 'peasant associations' (የገበሬ ማህበር *yegeberē mahiberi*) (Kinfe Abraham 2001: 566; shamibeli fik'irešilasē wegideresi 2006EC [2014]: 175), that is, none other than Soviet-style kolkhozes (Russian portmanteau колхоз formed from коллективное хозяйство *kollektivnoe khoziaiistvo* 'collective farm')

1975 National Academy of the Amharic Language was transformed into the Academy of Ethiopian Languages (የኢትዮጵያ ቋንቋዎች አካዳሚ *ye'ītiyop'iya k'wanik'wawochi ākadamī*) (Academy 2019)

1976 Program for the National Democratic Revolution of Ethiopia (NDRE; የኢትዮጵያ ብሔራዊ ዲሞክራሲያዊ አብዮት ፕሮግራም *ye'ītiyop'iya biḫērawī dīmokirasīyawī ābiyot pirogiram*) was adopted in accordance with the marxist-leninist model of parallel economic and social stages of human development (Ottaway 1978); hence, the Soviet-Derg regime also adopted Joseph Stalin's 1913 classical definition of the nation, couched in ethnolinguistic terms (Gilkes 1983: 198–199)

1976 Agricultural Marketing Corporation was founded for an improved management of Ethiopia's centralized state-owned agriculture (Rashid and Asfaw Negassa 2012: 125)

1976 for the sake of literacy campaigns, apart from Amharic (1), 14 additional languages were gradually developed, as written media of education, and employed for this purpose, namely Afar (2), Gedeo (3), Hadiyya (4), Kafa (5), Kembata (Kambaata) (6), Kunama (7), Oromo (8), Saho (9), Sidamo (10), Silti (11), Somali

(12), Tigrinya (13), Tigre (14) and Wolayta (15); work was under way to add three further languages to this repertory (Afar, Anuak and Gumuz) (Klinger 1992: 110), and it was hoped that eventually 40 languages would be employed in education (Klinger 1992: 103); the 15 aforementioned languages of the Soviet-Derg regime's literacy campaigns covered the linguistic needs of 90 percent of the country's population (Getachew Anteneh and Derib Ado 2006: 47; Klinger 1992: Table 9); but all these languages had to be written in the single Ethiopic (i.e. Amharic/Ge'ez) script (syllabary), even if previously or in neighboring countries different scripts had been and continued to be employed for writing and publishing in some of these languages (Getachew Anteneh and Derib Ado 2006: 48; Klinger 1992: 110)

1976 Addis Ababa University and other institutions of higher learning were reopened, marking the end of the *Zemecha* (Campaign) for literacy and progress in Ethiopia; many students, disillusioned by the government and its ideologically driven repressions, staged protests only to be imprisoned and even executed; the regime was especially appalled by students' support for the Oromo, Tigray and Eritrean 'ethnic' liberation movements; and the student opposition to the Soviet-Derg regime came to an end with the draft of male students for the war against Eritrea (Balsvik 2007: 72, 84–86)

1976–1977 Ethiopian Red Terror (ቀይ ሽብር *k'ey shibir*) was visited on competing marxist-leninist groups (De Waal 1991: 101–112), leaving in its wake at least 40,000 victims (Abbink 1995: 135); other sources estimate that 55,000 people lost their lives in Addis Ababa alone and a further 45,000 elsewhere in the country (Balsvik 2007: 76–77)

1977 revolutionary terror in Ethiopia, as known and practiced in the course and wake of both French and Soviet revolutions, was completed – on the Soviet model – with a Gulag-like system of prisons and forced labor camps; this system of incarceration and repression was based mainly on 25,000 kolkhozes ('peasant associations'), each running its own prison (Balsvik 2007: 81)

> 1977 French Territory of the Afars and the Issas gained independence and became the Republic of Djibouti (*République de Djibouti in French* and جمهورية جيبوتي *Jumhūrīyah Jībūtī* in Arabic)

1977 new Soviet Constitution with the right to secession included (Art. 72), that is, the Constitution of the Union of Soviet Socialist Republics (Конституция Союза Советских Социалистических Республик *Konstitutsiia Soiuza Sovetskikh Sotsialisticheskikh Respublik*) (Constitution of the Soviet Union 1977)

1977 in the wake of the Sino-Soviet split (1956–1966), Somalia, as Ethiopia's main competitor in the Horn of Africa, became a client state of communist China; in this year, Somalia terminated the Somali-Soviet Friendship Treaty, and the Soviet advisors were expelled from the country (*Impact* 1978: 163)

1977–1978 Ogaden War, where Somalia (with Chinese aid) attacked Ethiopia (supported by the Soviet Union and Cuba) in an unsuccessful attempt to conquer Ethiopia's Somali-speaking region of Ogaden

1977 Following the Kremlin's advice, Addis Ababa ordered the United States to close its military facilities in Ethiopia; in return, the Soviet-Derg regime received weapons and supplies from the Soviet bloc, including at least 10,000 soldiers from Cuba for fighting the Ogaden War; on the other hand, Washington turned to Somalia as a potential anti-Soviet ally in the Horn of Africa (Henze 2000: 297; Spector 2005: 12)

1977 communist Cuba's leader, Fidel Castro, visited Ethiopia

1977 Soviet-Derg regime criticized communist China as 'reactionary,' due to Beijing's support for Somalia in the Ogaden War; the Soviet Union supported Ethiopia (Kinfe Abraham 2001: 565)

1979 communist East Germany's leader, Erich Honecker, visited Ethiopia

1979 as many as 225 book titles were published in Ethiopia (i.e. in Amharic, in English and in all other Ethiopian languages) (Book Publishing 1996)

1980 like all the Soviet bloc countries, in Ethiopia's schools, the compulsory subject of 'political education' (የፖለቲካ ትምህርት *yepoletīka timihirit*), that is, marxism-leninism, was introduced (Haile Gebriel Dagne 2007: 347; *yepoletīka* 1977EC [1984])

c. 1980 following the Chinese example of establishing the politically motivated 'exact' number of ethnolinguistically defined 'minorities' (Mullaney 2012: 120–133), the Soviet-Derg regime came up with

Sociopolitical timeline of modern Ethiopia 97

the number of 85 (86) such ethnic groups (nationalities) in Ethiopia (Lewis 1983: 20)

1982 Ethiopian–Somali Border War (*Ethiopia's Invasion* 1983)

1983 Ernest Gellner in his monograph on the rise and spread of nationalism in Europe proposes that nations and their nation-states are a product of industrialization (Gellner 1983); the rise of ethnolinguistic nations and their nation-states in the Balkans during the 19th century falsifies this thesis, because industrialization in this region developed only in the first half of the 20th century

1983 Benedict Anderson in his monograph on the global spread of nationalism proposes that people and their groups alone create 'imagined communities' (nations) – in other words- large-scale non-face-to-face human groups with the internationally recognized right to statehood (Anderson 1983)

1983 Eric Hobsbawm and Terence Ranger coedited the volume *Invented Traditions* (Hobsbawm and Ranger 1983); the contributors drew on cases from Europe, Africa and India to illustrate the thesis that nations and national histories are constructs, artifacts of human decisions and imagination

1983 foreign lecturers from the Soviet bloc countries constituted over a third (c. 360) of Ethiopia's university-level staff, who amounted to almost 1,000 (Balsvik 2007: 88; Wondwosen Tamrat 2019)

1983 by this year, the Soviet-Derg regime had indemnified almost all foreign companies for their losses sustained over the course of the nationalization without compensation, as unrolled in the wake of the 1974 Revolution; the regime realized that the further development of Ethiopia depended on foreign investment, because aid offered by the Soviet bloc was insufficient in this regard (Keller 1988: 247)

1983–1985 Ethiopian Famine was partly induced and prolonged by Soviet-Derg policies; this tragic famine affected mainly Tigray and Wello (De Waal 1991: 133–156), resulting in at least 500,000 victims of starvation and disease (De Waal 1991: 175)

1984 founding of the Workers' Party of Ethiopia (WPE) (የኢትዮጵያ ሠራተኞች ፓርቲ [ኢሠፓ] *ye 'ītiyop 'iya šeratenyoch paritī [īšepa]*)

1984–1985 Soviet-Derg regime, faced with the challenges of the famine and war, embarked on mass campaigns of villagization

(በመንደር ማሰባሰብ *bemenideri masebasebi* 'village collecting') and resettlement (ሰፈራ *sefera*), quite similar in scope and character to the Soviet policies of the collectivization of agriculture and Russification; nomadic and pastoralist communities in the east were settled in government-designated villages in order to end their traditional way of life and prevent them from helping certain guerila factions (Eritrean, Oromo or Somali guerillas) or from being attacked by such guerillas; the resettlement of 0.6 million mainly Amharic-speaking peasants from the north to the multiethnic south alleviated the famine; and what is more, it led to the Amharization of the south and brought the regime's Soviet-style economy to this 'backward' region, including kolkhozes (peasant associations) and kolkhoz-based prisons ('gulag') (Balsvik 2007: 96–97; Pankhurst 1992)

1984 ten-year plan of economic and social development was adopted; it was never completed, due to the fall of the Soviet-Derg regime in 1991 (Keller 1988: 252–253)

1984–1985 numerous Ethiopian Jews, who became a pawn in the Soviet-Derg regime's maneuvers between West and East, fled repressions and the famine to Sudan, from where about 8,000 were airlifted via Brussels to Israel (Spector 2005: 12–13)

1985 Czechoslovak (Czech) historian, Miroslav Hroch's, monograph *Social Preconditions of National Revival in Europe* was published in an English translation; it offers a marxian model of the coalescence of stateless ethnolinguistic nations and their quest for statehood, drawing on examples from Central Europe (Hroch 1985)

1985 Alemaya University of Agriculture was founded on the basis of Alemaya College of Agriculture (established in 1954); at present, the university is known as Haramaya University, its English-language name more closely following the Amharic pronunciation of the name of Lake Alemaya (ሐረማያ *hāremaya*)

1986 for the needs of literacy campaigns, nine periodicals were published in Amharic, three in Oromo, two in Tigrinya, one in Sidamo and one in Wolayta (Klinger 1992: Tables 16 and 17); although literacy campaign materials were produced in 15 languages, most copies of such materials were published in Amharic (26.5 million) and the least in Kunama (50,350) (Klinger 1992: Figure 4)

1986 (1978 EC) the most important reference and ideological tool of the Soviet-Derg period was published, namely the የማርከሲዝም

ለኒኒዝም መዝገበ ቃላት *yemarikisīzim lēnīnīzim mezigebe k'alat* (The Dictionary of marxism-leninism) (*yemarikisīzimi* 1978EC [1986]); this dictionary popularized Joseph Stalin's 1913 ethnolinguistic definition of the nation, as adopted in the Soviet Union and communist China (cf Klinger 1992: 46) and in Ethiopia's Constitution of 1987; the lasting influence of this reference is proven by the fact that it is nowadays one of rather few Amharic-language books scanned and available for online use (si'ili 2020)

1987 (1979 EC) Constitution of Ethiopia closely emulated the Soviet Constitution, including the Soviet model of ethnolinguistic federalism

'The feudal system was overthrown . . . in 1974.' . . . the overall objective is . . . the construction of socialism' (Preamble in The Constitution 1988: 182)

'The Ethiopian state has existed as a multinational state. Its nationalities [Russian *nationalnost'*] and diverse communities have forged a unity through cultural intercourse, migrations, commerce and similar interactions in times of peace as well as in times of war. Therefore, Ethiopia's long history of independence has been the history of the united existence and common struggle of her nationalities. . . . [T]he unity of our country and the equality of nationalities, based on our right to self-determination, is ensured' (Preamble in The Constitution 1988: 181–182)

'The People's Democratic Republic of Ethiopia is a unitary state in which all nationalities live in equality' (Art. 2.1)

'The People's Democratic Republic of Ethiopia shall ensure the equality of nationalities, combat chauvinism and narrow nationalism, and strengthen the unity of the working people of all nationalities' (Art. 2.2)

'The People's Democratic Republic of Ethiopia shall ensure the common advancement of the nationalities, by progressively eliminating the disparity in their economic development, paying particular attention to those in lower stages of development [Russian *narodnost'*]' (Art. 2.3)

'The People's Democratic Republic of Ethiopia shall ensure the realization of regional autonomy' (Art. 2.4)

'The People's Democratic Republic of Ethiopia shall ensure the equality, development and respectability of the languages and the nationalities' (Art. 2.5) (The Constitution 1988: 183)

'The People's Democratic Republic of Ethiopia is a unitary state comprising administrative and autonomous regions' (Art. 59) (The Constitution 1988: 194)

'[I]n the People's Democratic Republic of Ethiopia the working language of the state shall be Amharic' (Art. 116) (The Constitution 1988: 207)

NB 1: The terms *federal, federation* and *secession* are *not* mentioned in the Constitution

NB 2: The term *nationality* (ethnic group) is clearly distinguished from that of *citizenship*

NB 3: In spite of the provisions in Article 2.5, apart from Amharic, no other Ethiopian languages were given any official status or employed in administration (Getachew Anteneh and Derib Ado 2006: 48)

1987 Ethiopia's population: 46 million (Ethiopia: Historical 2019)

1987 in emulation of Mikhail Gorbachev's reforms in the Soviet Union, elements of private entrepreneurship were allowed in the Ethiopian economy (Kinfe Abraham 2001: 568)

1987–1991 **PDRE** (People's Democratic Republic of Ethiopia; የኢትዮጵያ ሕዝባዊ ዲሞክራሲያዊ ሪፐብሊክ *ye 'ītiyop 'iya ḥizibawī dīmokirasīyawī rīpebilīk*)

1987–1991 President Mengistu Haile Mariam

1988 Jimma Institute of Health Sciences founded in Jimma (Jimmaa in Oromo) (Gupta 1994: 174); in 1999, it merged with Jimma College of Agriculture (established in 1952), thus yielding today's Jimma University

> 1989 commencement of the Somali Civil War, which continues to this day

> 1989 fall of communism in Europe, the Soviet bloc and the Soviet Union, which lost the ideology that both defined and legitimized these two political projects

> 1990 at least 385 book titles were published in Ethiopia (Book Publishing 1996)

> 1991 central government of Somalia collapsed, leading to the fragmentation of the Somali nation-state; in the north, the de facto polity, a Republic of Somaliland (*Jamhuuriyadda Somaliland* in Somali), was proclaimed

1991 dissolution of the Warsaw Pact and Comecon (Council for Mutual Economic Assistance), or the military and economic pillars of the Soviet bloc

1991 dissolution of the Soviet Union, or the world's largest and oldest ethnoterritorial (ethnolinguistic) federation

1991–2008 war-induced piecemeal dissolution of another ethnoterritorial (ethnolinguistic) federation, namely communist Yugoslavia

1991 in the previous year, the Soviet-Derg regime attracted the country's Jews to Addis Ababa with the false promise of imminent passage to Israel; subsequently, the regime blackmailed Israel that these Jews might face danger unless Tel Aviv agreed to sell weapons to Ethiopia; in response, in one day and a half, on 24–25 May, the majority of Ethiopia's Jews (almost 15,000) were airlifted to safety in Israel; and hence, not a single Jewish settlement remains in today's Ethiopia (Spector 2005)

1991 **Postcommunist (Federal) Ethiopia**

1991 Ethiopia's population: 55 million (Ethiopia: Historical 2019)

1991 only 240 book titles were published in Ethiopia (in Amharic, English and all the country's other languages) (Book Publishing 1996); curiously, this is the most recent data readily available on book production in Ethiopia

1991 *Transitional Charter* (የኢትዮጵያ የሽግግር ወቅት ቻርተር *ye'ītiyop'iya yeshigigir wek'it chariter*); Transitional Government of Ethiopia (የኢትዮጵያ ሽግግር መንግሥት *ye'ītiyop'iya shigigiri menigišiti*)

1991–1995 Interim President Meles Zenawi Asres (መለስ ዜናዊ አስረስ *melesi zēnawī āsiresi* 1955–2012)

1991 between 1991 and 2009, the Ethiopic script for writing Ge'ez, Amharic and other Ethiosemitic languages was incorporated into Unicode's standard Universal Coded Character Set that underlies the internet (Ethiopic 2019); this achievement allowed for the development of Wikipedias in Ethiopia's languages in the early 21st century

1992 Proclamation No. 7/1992: A Proclamation to Provide for the Establishment of National/Regional Self-Governments (Proclamation No. 7/1992 1992): it was the first move in the postcommunist period to implement the Soviet-Derg regime's hardly realized promise of a Soviet-style ethnolinguistic federalism

1993 dissolution of another ethnoterritorial (ethnolinguistic) federation, namely this time the dual (dyadic, bipartite) communist federation of Czechoslovakia

1993 learning from the Czechoslovak failure, Belgium was transformed into a federation of three ethnolinguistic communities (Flemish, French and German) and three regions, namely the two ethnoterritorial regions of Flanders and Wallonia plus the *non*-ethnoterritorial (capital) and bilingual region of Brussels; importantly, the borders of these three regions do *not* overlap with the borders of the three communities (Third 2020; Wagstaff 1999)

1993 European Communities (EC) were transformed into the European Union (EU)

1993 Eritrean independence referendum; Eritrea became an internationally recognized independent state (Fikrejesus Amhazion 2018)

1994 mainly thanks to the Soviet-Derg literacy campaigns, the rate of illiteracy dropped precipitously from 95 percent in 1974 to 65 percent 20 years later (Gupta 1994)

1994 removal from the Ethiopian educational system of the textbooks and curricula prepared under the Soviet-Derg regime in accordance with the tenets of marxism-leninism (Haile Gebriel Dagne 2007: 349)

1995 in the wake of the Bosnian War (one of the wars of Yugoslav succession), the international community imposed a compromise on this country in the form of an asymmetrical ethnolinguistic (ethnoterritorial) federation; Bosnia Herzegovina consists of three federal entities, namely the unitary ethnolinguistic nation-state-like Republika Srpska (for Serbs), the binational Federation of Bosnia and Herzegovina (for Bosniaks and Croats) and the *non*-national Brčko District, shared by the two former entities; the Federation of Bosnia and Herzegovina is territorial in its character, comprising ten Swiss-like cantons that, among other things, decide on their official languages; and only self-declared Bosniaks, Croats and Serbs are eligible for elected posts – hence, this arrangement disenfranchises Bosnian citizens of other ethnicities (especially Jews and Roma) (Belloni 2009; Caplan 2000)

1995 (1987 EC) Constitution of Ethiopia overhauled this postcommunist country into a Soviet-style ethnolinguistic federation (Semahagn Gashu Abebe 2014)

> 'We, the Nations, Nationalities and Peoples of Ethiopia' (Preamble) 'This Constitution establishes a Federal and Democratic State structure' (Art. 1)
>
> 'The territorial jurisdiction of Ethiopia shall comprise the territory of the members of the Federation' (Art. 2)
>
> '(1) All Ethiopian languages shall enjoy equal state recognition. (2) Amharic shall be the working language of the Federal Government. (3) Members of the Federation may by law determine their respective working languages' (Art. 5)
>
> 'All sovereign power resides in the Nations, Nationalities and Peoples of Ethiopia' (Art. 8.1)
>
> '(1) Every Nation, Nationality and People in Ethiopia has an unconditional right to self-determination, including the right to secession. (2) Every Nation, Nationality and People in Ethiopia has the right to speak, to write and to develop its own language; to express, to develop and to promote its culture; and to preserve its history. (3) Every Nation, Nationality and People in Ethiopia has the right to a full measure of self-government which includes the right to establish institutions of government in the territory that it inhabits and to equitable representation in state and Federal governments. . . . (5) A "Nation, Nationality or People" for the purpose of this Constitution, is a group of people who have or share large measure of a common culture or similar customs, mutual intelligibility of language, belief in a common or related identities, a common psychological make-up, and who inhabit an identifiable, predominantly contiguous territory' (Art. 39)
>
> 'States shall be delimited on the basis of the settlement patterns, language, identity and consent of the peoples concerned' (Art. 46.2)
>
> (Ethiopia – Constitution 1994)
>
> NB 1: The term *autonomy* or *autonomous* is *not* mentioned in the Constitution
>
> NB 2: The term *nationality* (ethnic group) is *not* clearly distinguished from that of *citizenship*, which confusingly is rendered with the word 'nationality' (citizenship); see 'No Ethiopian national shall be deprived of his or her Ethiopian nationality against his or her will' (Art. 33.1 in: Ethiopia – Constitution 1994)

1995 Ethiopia's population: 56.4 million (Ethiopia: Historical 2019)

1995 Federal Democratic Republic of Ethiopia (የኢትዮጵያ ፌዴራላዊ ዲሞክራሲያዊ ሪፐብሊክ *ye'ītiyop'iya fēdēralawī dīmokirasīyawī rīpebilīk*)

1995–2012 Prime Minister Meles Zenawi Asres

2012–2018 Prime Minister Hailemariam Desalegn Boshe (ኃይለማርያም ደሳለኝ ቦሼ *hayilemarīyami desalenyi boshē* 1965–)

2018– Prime Minister Abiy Ahmed Ali (ዐቢይ አሕመድ አሊ *'ābīyi āhimedi ālī* 1976–)

1996–2006 southern Somalia found itself under control of the Islamic Courts Union (*Midowga Maxkamadaha Islaamiga* in Somali)

1997 Academy of Ethiopian Languages was transferred from the Ministry of Culture and Tourism to Addis Ababa University; in 2010, this academy was renamed the Academy of Ethiopian Languages and Cultures (Academy 2019)

1998 in northeastern Somalia, another de facto polity was established, the Puntland State of Somalia (*Dowladda Puntland ee Soomaaliya* in Somali)

1998–2000 Eritrean–Ethiopian War

1998–2001 in North Omo Zone (part of Southern Nations, Nationalities, and Peoples Region), local ethnic languages had been employed as media of instruction in schools since 1993, among others, such as the North Omotic language of Wolayita with two million speakers; the authorities, faced with the prospect of developing teaching materials in the further cognate North Omotic languages of Dawro, Gamo and Gofa, decided to follow the heavy-handed Soviet-style top-down path of language engineering aimed at limiting the number of recognized ethnic groups and their languages; drawing on the experience of such composite (pluricentric) languages as Serbo-Croatian or Norwegian, they proclaimed a merged (composite) language of WoGaGoDa, created on the basis of Wolayita with some additions from Gamo, Gofa and Dawro; little or no consultations were conducted with the concerned ethnic groups; textbooks written in WoGaGoDa were introduced to schools in 1999, causing Wolayita students, teachers and local communities to protest; the follow-up clashes with the police led to seven deaths, 11 wounded and over 1,000 incarcerated; the ruling EPRDF party relented, and in 2001, North Omo Zone was split into ethnolinguistically defined zones; and Wolayita was reintroduced to education, and beginning in 2004 Dawro, Gamo and Gofa were also introduced to schools as media of instruction in their own right (Bookkeeping 2008; Cochrane and Yeshtila Bekele 2019: 35–37; Data Dea 2005–2006; Guidi 2012; Hirut Woldemariam 2014)

2000 Ethiopia's population: 64 million (Ethiopia: Historical 2019)

2000 two universities and 17 colleges were active in Ethiopia (Thubauville 2013: 124): the subsequent boom in tertiary education left universities and colleges understaffed, necessitating recruitment from abroad, mainly from the United Kingdom, Cuba, India, Nigeria and the Philippines; for instance, the number of Indian lecturers grew from 500 in 2011 to 1,000 in 2013 (Thubauville 2013: 125)

2001 drawing on the experience of the Organization of African Unity (OAU), an African Union (AU) was officially founded in Addis Ababa; the AU's seat is located in the Ethiopian capital

2002 OAU was officially dissolved

c. 2005 in the mid 2000s, in light of the development of the internet as the main basis of Ethiopia's independent mass media, the government commenced its policy of partial or complete shutdowns of the country's internet during periods of political tension and unrest (Deibert 2008: 283; *Ethiopia's Troubled* 2006: 109); otherwise, the internet is regularly shut down in Ethiopia during the time of statewide school examinations, to reduce web-enabled cheating and other irregularities (Abdi Latif Dahir 2017)

2005 Amharic Wikipedia founded, written in the Ethiopic script (List of Wikipedias 2019)

2005 Afar Wikipedia founded, written in the Latin alphabet, but closed in 2008 because of inactivity (List of Wikipedias 2019)

2006 Tigrinya Wikipedia founded, written in the Ethiopic script (List of Wikipedias 2019)

2006–2009 Ethiopian forces intervened in southern Somalia and seized most of the region from the hands of the Islamic Courts Union; in turn, the more radically jihadist group, Al-Shabaab (حركة المقاومة الشعبية في بالد الهجرتين) *harakat almuqawamat alshaebiat fi bilad alhijratayn* 'Popular Resistance Movement in the Land of the Two Migrations'), captured and continues to control some areas in southern Somalia

2007 Oromo Wikipedia founded, written in the Latin alphabet (List of Wikipedias 2019)

2007 Somali Wikipedia founded, written in the Latin alphabet (List of Wikipedias 2019)

2010 Ethiopia's population: 91.5 million (Ethiopia: Historical 2019)

2011 South Sudan gained independence from Sudan and became the Republic of South Sudan (*Jamhuri ya Sudan Kusini* in Swahili)

2012 in southern Somalia a Federal Republic of Somalia (*Jamhuuriyadda Federaalka Soomaaliya* in Somali) was proclaimed

2012 new administrative center of the African Union was inaugurated during the 18th AU summit; the center was constructed and paid by China, as Beijing's gift to Ethiopia and Africa; on the other hand, this gift symbolizes the growing economic and political presence of China in Ethiopia and Africa and the continent's increasing dependence on Beijing (Linyan 2012; Press Release 2012)

2013 31 universities were active in Ethiopia (Thubauville 2013: 124)

2013 Google Translate added Somali to this online service (Google Translate Adds 2013)

2015 Ethiopia's population: 106.5 million (Ethiopia: Historical 2019)

2016 Tel Aviv decided to allow the last remaining 9,000 Ethiopian Jews to leave for Israel by 2020; the community of Ethiopian Jews in Israel already amounted to 135,000 (Hoffman 2016)

2016 Google Translate added Amharic to this online service (Kelman 2016)

2016 although only 5 percent of Ethiopia's exports went to China, as many as one-third of Ethiopia's imports arrived from China (Ethiopia Exports 2019; Ethiopia Imports 2019)

2017 China is the largest foreign investor in Ethiopia, accounting for one-fifth of all the foreign investment that arrived in Ethiopia between 1992 and 2017 (Global Foreign 2018); during this time, foreign direct investment (FDI) flowing to Ethiopia skyrocketed from US$170,000 in 1992 to US$4 billion in 2017 (Foreign Direct 2019)

2018 although access to landline telephones in Ethiopia remains paltry at 1 percent, the access to mobile telephones increased from 13 to 62 percent and to the internet from 0.2 to 17.5 percent between 2011 and 2017 (Telecommunication 2019); smartphone penetration, allowing for the wide use of social media, was inching toward 5 percent (Poushter 2016)

2018 Peace Treaty officially finished the Eritrean–Ethiopian War

2018 Ethiopia's GDP grew exponentially from US$14 million in 1991 to US$80 million in 2018, thus boosting the political legitimacy of the post-1991 regime (Ethiopia: Gross 2019); in the second decade of the 21st century, Ethiopia's economy grew the fastest in the entire world, at the combined rate of 9.5 percent annually (Kisika 2019); this contributed to halving the population living below the poverty line, from 45 percent in 1996 to 23 percent in 2016 (EthioInfo 2020)

2018 violent demonstrations in Southern Nations, Nationalities and Peoples Region appealed for expelling non-Sidamas from Sidama Zone and making this zone into a separate region (state) in its own right; in the wake of these protests, ten people were left dead and 89 wounded; and in addition, almost 3,000 people were displaced (Cochrane and Yeshtila Bekele 2019: 26–27)

2018 also in Southern Nations, Nationalities and Peoples Region but this time in Wolayita Zone, the Wolayita elders proposed to create a separate region (state) for the Omotic peoples, including the zones of Dawro, Gamo and Gofa; in this manner, it would be a WoGaGoDa (Wagagoda) Region, less the single WoGaGoDa (Wagagoda) language once disastrously imposed by the federal government in 1998 (Cochrane and Yeshtila Bekele 2019: 27)

2019 national self-determination referendum was held in Sidama Zone (Southern Nations, Nationalities and Peoples' Region); almost 99 percent of the voters cast their ballots in favor of a stand-alone Sidama region for the Sidamas (Ephream Sileshi 2019)

2019 Prime Minister Abiy Ahmed received a Nobel peace prize (Burke and Henley 2019); he is the first Ethiopian to have received a Nobel prize

2019 in today's Ethiopia 30 million students attend elementary and secondary schools, while the country boasts over nine million students at its universities; nowadays, practically each Ethiopian child attends elementary school, while 35 percent continue education in secondary and other post-elementary (vocational) schools and as many as 8 percent at universities and colleges; the overall literacy rate is about 52 percent (59 percent for men and 44 percent for women), though over 80 percent among the youth, while less than 20 percent among seniors aged 65 and over (Ethiopia: Education 2019); and of all Ethiopians, 70 percent completed elementary education and 18 percent secondary education (EthioInfo 2020)

2019 in present-day Ethiopia, at least the following languages are used in official capacity at different levels of administration and in education, namely Afar, Agaw (Awngi), Amharic, Arabic, Dawro, English, Gamo, Gedeo, Gof(f)a, Gurage (Kistane), Hadiya, Harari, Kafa, Kembata, Kamyr (Xamtanga), Konso, Majang, Nuer, Oromo, Tigrinya, Sidama, Silti, Somali and Wolayita (Getachew Anteneh and Derib Ado 2006: 49–58); however, adding up to 24 in total, these languages in official use cover one-quarter of the country's 'nations, nationalities and peoples'; on the other hand, they are employed by 90 percent of the population; furthermore, users of these languages can opt for other scripts than the Ethiopic one; and they usually choose the Latin alphabet or the Arabic abjad, apart from the Ethiopic writing system

2019 about 170 universities and colleges operate in Ethiopia (List of Universities 2019); out of 30,000 lecturers in the tertiary education sector, foreigners constitute 8 percent (2,400) (Wondwosen Tamrat 2019)

2019 Amharic Wikipedia contains 14,824 articles, the Somali Wikipedia 5,722 articles, the Oromo Wikipedia 786 articles, the Tigrinya Wikipedia 191 articles and the Afar Wikipedia just one article (List of Wikipedias 2019); the vast majority of Ethiopia's users of the internet consult the English-language Wikipedia

2019 ruling EPRDF was transformed into the Prosperity Party (The EPRDF 2019)

2020 apart from Amharic, also Afar, Oromo, Somali and Tigrinya were planned to become working languages of the federal government (Samuel Getachew 2020)

2020 following the assassination of renowned and charismatic Oromo song performer, poet and civil rights activist Hachalu Hundessa (*Hacaaluu Hundeessaa* in Oromo, ሃጫሉ ሁንዴሳ *hāch'alu hunidēsa* in Amharic), violent protests erupted across Oromia (Gardner 2020; Hachalu 2020)

2020 in the wake of these protests, several opposition leaders were arrested, including US-educated mass media mogul and Oromo politician Jawar Mohammed (Jawaar Mahaammad in Oromo, ጃዋር መሃመድ *jawari mehamedi* in Amharic) (Jawar 2020; Marks 2020)

2020 Ethiopia's population: 122.5 million (Ethiopia: Historical 2019)

Sociopolitical timeline of modern Ethiopia 109

2020 federal government, as led by the PP party, militarily intervenes in the State of Tigray or the TPLF's stronghold; the all Ethiopia federal and regional elections were scheduled to take place in August 2020, but they were delayed until June 2021, due to the pandemic; however, the TPLF disagreed with this decision and proceeded with the Tigray regional elections; as a result, the federal government deemed the new Tigray regional government as illegitimate, while the latter held the same opinion of the former. The tensions ultimately gave rise to armed conflict. (Tigray Crisis 2020)

2030 Ethiopia's population (projection): 145 million (Ethiopia Population 2019)

2050 Ethiopia's population (projection): 205 million (Ethiopia Population 2019)

2100 Ethiopia's population (projection): 294 million (Ethiopia Population 2019)

Bibliography

NB: In the Western system of naming, one's name basically consists of the first (given) name and surname. However, in the traditional Ethiopian system of naming, the name is composed of one's given name and patronymic (father's name). As a result, in this study's bibliography and references, the full traditional name of an Ethiopian author is employed. For instance, '(Addis Hiwet 1975)' in references and 'Addis Hiwet 1975' in the bibliography.

Aaron Tesfaye. 2002. *Political Power and Ethnic Federalism: The Struggle for Democracy in Ethiopia*. Lanham, MD: University Press of America.

Abbas H. Gnamo. 2014. *Conquest and Resistance in the Ethiopian Empire, 1880–1974: The Case of the Arsi Oromo*. Leiden: Brill.

Abbink, Jon. 1995. The Impact of Violence: The Ethiopian 'Red Terror' as a Social Phenomenon (pp 129–145). In: Peter Brunelein, ed. *Krieg und Frieden. Ethnologische Perspektiven* (Ser: Kea Sonderband, Vol. 2). Bremen: Kea-ed.

Abbink, Jon. 1998. An Historical-Anthropological Approach to Islam in Ethiopia: Issues of Identity and Politics (pp 109–124). *Journal of African Cultural Studies*. Vol. 11, No. 2.

Abdi Latif Dahir. 2017. Ethiopia Shut Down the Country's Internet to Beat Exam Cheats. *Quartz Africa*. 31 May. https://qz.com/africa/994990/ethiopia-shut-down-the-internet-ahead-of-a-scheduled-countrywide-national-exams/. Accessed: Sept 22, 2020.

Abdu Mozayen. 1976. The Use of Mass Media in Language Teaching (pp 505–519). In: M L Bender, J D Bowen, R L Cooper and C A Ferguson, eds. *Language in Ethiopia* (Ser: Ford Foundation Language Surveys). London: Oxford University Press.

Abye Tassé. 2017. Les élites éthiopiennes formées en URSS et dans les pays du bloc socialiste: une visibilité éphémère? [Ethiopian Elites Trained in the USSR and Socialist Countries: Fading from View?] (pp 289–312). *Cahiers d'études africaines*. Vol. 2, No. 226. www.cairn.info/revue-cahiers-d-etudes-africaines-2017-2-page-289.htm. Accessed: May 11, 2020.

Academy of Ethiopian Languages and Cultures. 2019. *Addis Ababa University*. www.aau.edu.et/aelc/. Accessed: Dec 27, 2019.

Bibliography 111

Adam, Hussein M. 1983. Language, National-Consciousness and Identity – The Somali Experience (pp 31–42). In: I. M. Lewis, ed. *Nationalism and Self Determination in the Horn of Africa*. London: Ithaca Press.

Addis Hiwet. 1975. *From Autocracy to Revolution* (Ser: Occasional Publication/ Review of African Political Economy, Vol. 1). London: Zed Books.

Agureev, Stanislav. 2011. *Efiopiia v otsenke rossiiskogo obshchestvennogo mneniia v kontse XIX – nachale XX vv.* [Ethiopia in the Reflection of Russian Public Opinion at the Turn of the 20th century]. Moscow: RUDN. www.dissercat.com/ content/efiopiya-v-otsenke-rossiiskogo-obshchestvennogo-mneniya-v-kontse-xix-nachale-xx-vv. Accessed: Jan 1, 2020.

Ambedkar, Bhimrao Ramji. 1955. *Thoughts on Linguistic States*. New Delhi: At Author's Expense. www.drbacmahad.org/Speeches/thoughts-on-linguistic-states. pdf. Accessed: Jan 2, 2020.

Amdissa Teshome. 2008. A Review of Education Policy, Strategies and Programs (pp 47–92). In: Taye Assefa, ed. *Digest of Ethiopia's National Policies, Strategies and Programs*. Addis Ababa: Forum for Social Studies (FSS).

Andargachew Tiruneh. 1993. *The Ethiopian Revolution, 1974–1987: A Transformation from an Aristocratic to a Totalitarian Autocracy*. Cambridge: Cambridge University Press.

Anderson, Barbara A. and Silver, Brian D. 1989. Demographic Sources of the Changing Ethnic Composition of the Soviet Union (pp 609–656). *Population and Development Review*. Vol. 15, No. 4.

Anderson, Benedict. 1983. *Imagined Communities: Reflections on the Origin and Spread of Nationalism*. London: Verso.

Arndt, Ernst Moritz. 1813. Des deutschen Vaterland [The German Fatherland]. In: Ernst Moritz Arndt, ed. *Fünf Lieder für deutsche Soldaten*. Berlin: Reimer.

Arriola, Leonardo R. and Lyons, Terrence. 2016. Ethiopia: The 100% Election (pp 76–88). *Journal of Democracy*. Vol. 27, No. 1.

Asnake Kefale. 2013. *Federalism and Ethnic Conflict in Ethiopia: A Comparative Regional Study* (Ser: Routledge Series in Federal Studies). London: Routledge.

Asnake Kefale. 2014. Ethnic Decentralization and the Challenges of Inclusive Governance in Multiethnic Cities: The Case of Dire Dawa, Ethiopia (pp 589–605). *Regional and Federal Studies*. Vol. 24. No. 5.

Assefa Fiseha. 2015. Legislative – Executive Relations in the Ethiopian Parliamentary System: Towards Institutional and Legal Reform (pp 239–270). In: Jaap de Visser, Nico Steytler, Derek Powell and Ebenezer Durojaye, eds. *Constitution-Building in Africa*. Baden-Baden: Nomos.

Augustyniak, Zuzanna. 2012. The Genesis of the Contemporary Ethiopian Legal System (pp 101–115). *Studies of the Department of African Languages and Cultures*. Vol. 46.

Autonomous Administrative Divisions of China. 2019. *Wikipedia*. https:// en.wikipedia.org/wiki/Autonomous_administrative_divisions_of_China. Accessed: Dec 1, 2019.

Bach, Jean-Nicolas. (2011). Abyotawi Democracy: Neither Revolutionary nor Democratic, a Critical Review of EPRDF's Conception of Revolutionary Democracy in Post-1991 Ethiopia (pp 641–663). *Journal of Eastern African Studies*. Vol. 5, No. 4.

Bahru Zewde. 1991. *A History of Modern Ethiopia, 1855–1974*. London: James Currey; Athens, OH: Ohio University Press; and Addis Ababa: Addis Ababa University Press.
Bahru Zewde. 2002. *Pioneers of Change in Ethiopia: The Reformist Intellectuals of the Early Twentieth Century*. Oxford: James Currey, Athens, OH: Ohio University Press, and Addis Ababa: Addis Ababa University.
Bahru Zewde. 2003 [unpublished conference paper]. *Intellectuals and Soldiers: The Socialist Experiment in the Horn of Africa*. Dakar: CODESRIA (Council for the Development of Social Science Research in Africa) 30th Anniversary Conference, Dakar, 8–11 Dec 2003.
Bahru Zewde. 2014. *The Quest for Socialist Utopia: The Ethiopian Student Movement c. 1960–1974*. Addis Ababa: Addis Ababa University Press.
Balsvik, Rani Rønning. 2005. *Haile Selassie's Students: The Intellectual and Social Background to Revolution, 1952–1974*. Addis Ababa: Addis Ababa University.
Balsvik, Rani Rønning. 2007. *The Quest for Expression: State and the University in Ethiopia Under Three Regimes, 1952–2005*. Addis Ababa: Addis Ababa University.
Bauer, Otto. 1907. *Die Nationalitätenfrage und die Sozialdemokratie* (Ser: Marx-Studien, Vol. 2). Vienna: Verlag der Wiener Volksbuchhandlung Ignaz Brand.
Bauer, Otto. 2000. *The Question of Nationalities and Social Democracy* [translated from the Germany by Joseph O'Donnell]. Minneapolis, MN: University of Minnesota Press.
Baxter, Paul. 1983. The Problem *of* the Oromo or the Problem *for* the Oromo? (pp 130–149). In: I. M. Lewis, ed. *Nationalism and Self Determination in the Horn of Africa*. London: Ithaca Press.
Belloni, Roberto. 2009. Bosnia: Dayton Is Dead! Long Live Dayton! (pp 355–375). *Nationalism and Ethnic Politics*. Vol. 15, No. 3–4.
Bender, Marvin L., Hailu Fulass and Cowley, Roger. 1976. Two Ethio-Semitic Languages (99–119). In: M. L. Bender, J. D. Bowen, R. L. Cooper and C. A. Ferguson, eds. *Language in Ethiopia* (Ser: Ford Foundation Language Surveys). London: Oxford University Press.
Benner, Erica. 1995. *Really Existing Nationalisms: A Post-Communist View from Marx and Engels*. Oxford: Clarendon Press.
Bereket Habte Selassie. 1989. *Eritrea and the United Nations and Other Essays*. Trenton, NJ: Red Sea Press.
Berlin, Noah. 1998. Constitutional Conflict with the Japanese Imperial Role: Accession, Yasukuni Shrine, and Obligatory Reformation (pp 383–414). *University of Pennsylvania Journal of Constitutional Law*. Vol. 1, No. 2.
Beza Dessalegn. 2018. Challenges of Ethnic Representation in Ethiopia and the Need for Reform (pp 1–28). *Mizan Law Review*. Vol. 12, No. 1.
Biruki Abidu ብሩክ አብዱ. 2020. አዲሱ የቋንቋ ፖሊሲ ለዘመናት ጥያቄ ምላሽ ይዞ ይሆን? *ādīsu yek'wanik'wa polīsī lezemenat t'iyak'ē milashi yizo yihoni?* [Has the New Language Policy Brought a Solution to the Age-Old Dilemma?]. *Ethiopian Reporter*. 25 Mar. www.ethiopianreporter.com/article/18444. Accessed: Oct 19, 2020.

Bibliography 113

Blagojević, Dušan, ed. 1974. *Nations and Nationalities of Yugoslavia* [translated from the Serbo-Croatian]. Belgrade: Međunarodna politika.

Blank, Stephen. 1994. *The Sorcerer as Apprentice: Stalin as Commissar of Nationalities, 1917–1924*. Westport, CT: Greenwood Press.

Book Production: Number of Titles by UDC Classes: Table IV.5 Africa. 1996. Washington, DC: UNESCO Institute for Statistics. https://web.archive.org/web/20060618094722/www.uis.unesco.org/TEMPLATE/html/CultAndCom/Table_IV_5_Africa.html. Accessed: Jan 4, 2020.

Bookkeeping: Gamo-Gofa-Dawro: Change Request: 2008–080 ISO 639–3 gmo. 2008. *Glottolog*. https://glottolog.org/resource/languoid/id/gamo1244. Accessed: Mar 31, 2020.

Bourguet, Pierre du. 1991. *Sztuka Koptów* [Coptic Art] [translated from the German by Jadwiga Lipińska] (Ser: Kultury Starożytne i Cywilizacje Pozaeuropejskie). Warsaw: Wydawnictwa Artystyczne i Filmowe.

Bowen, J. Donald. 1976. Historical Background of Education in Ethiopia (pp 305–323). In: M. L. Bender, J. D. Bowen, R. L. Cooper and C. A. Ferguson, eds. *Language in Ethiopia* (Ser: Ford Foundation Language Surveys). London: Oxford University Press.

Brass, Paul R. 1990. Language and National Identity in the Soviet Union and India (pp 300–332). In: Paul R. Brass, ed. *The Politics of India Since Independence*. Cambridge: Cambridge University Press.

Brubaker, Rogers. 1994. Nationhood and the National Question in the Soviet Union and Post-Soviet Eurasia: An Institutionalist Account (pp 47–78). *Theory and Society*. Vol. 23, No. 1.

Burke, Jason. 2018. Ethiopia 'Pardons 2,000 Prisoners' Jailed Over Oromo Protests. *The Guardian*. 26 Jan. www.theguardian.com/world/2018/jan/26/ethiopia-pardons-2000-prisoners-jailed-over-oromo-protests. Accessed: Feb 19, 2019.

Burke, Jason and Henley, Jon. 2019. Abiy Ahmed, Ethiopia's Prime Minister, Wins 2019 Nobel Peace Prize. *The Guardian*. 11 Oct. www.theguardian.com/world/2019/oct/11/abiy-ahmed-ethiopian-prime-minister-wins-2019-nobel-peace-prize. Accessed: Nov 30, 2019.

Busari, Stephanie and Elwazer, Schams. 2018. Former Sworn Enemies Ethiopia and Eritrea Have Declared End of War. *CNN: Breaking News*. 9 July. https://edition.cnn.com/2018/07/09/africa/ethiopia-abiy-ahmed-eritrea-war-intl/index.html. Accessed: Feb 19, 2019.

Caplan, Richard. 2000. Assessing the Dayton Accord: The Structural Weaknesses of the General Framework Agreement for Peace in Bosnia and Herzegovina (pp 213–232). *Diplomacy and Statecraft*. Vol. 11, No. 2.

Caulk, R. A. 1972. Religion and the State in Nineteenth Century Ethiopia (pp 23–41). *Journal of Ethiopian Studies*. Vol. 10, No. 1.

Chakrabarty, Banbehari. 1979. *The Stalin Question*. Calcutta: Kathashilpa.

Cherednichenko, V. 1985. *Kontrrevoliutsiia na eksport. Ukrainskii burzhuaznyi natsionalizm v arsenale sovremennogo antikommunizma* [Counter-Revolution for Export: Ukrainian Bourgeois Nationalism in the Arsenal of Modern Anti-Communism]. Kyiv: Izdatel'stvo politicheskiei literatury Ukrainy.

Bibliography

Chinweizu. 1987. *The West and the Rest of Us: White Predators, Black Slavers and the African Elite*. London: Sundoor.

Clapham, Christopher. 1988. *Transformation and Continuity in Revolutionary Ethiopia*. Cambridge: Cambridge University Press.

Clapham, Christopher. 2006. Ethiopian Development: The Politics of Emulation. *Commonwealth and Comparative Politics*. Vol. 44, No. 1.

Clarke, Joseph Calvitt. 2011. *Alliance of the Colored Peoples: Ethiopia and Japan Before World War II*. Woodbridge, Suffolk: James Currey, an Imprint of Boydell & Brewer.

Cochrane, Logan and Yeshtila Bekele. 2019. Politics and Power in Southern Ethiopia: Imposing, Opposing and Calling for Linguistic Unity (pp 26–45). *Language Matters: Studies in the Languages of Africa*. Vol. 50, No. 3.

Connell, Dan and Killion, Tom. 2011. *Historical Dictionary of Eritrea* (Ser: Historical Dictionaries of Africa, Vol. 114). Lanham, MD: Scarecrow Press.

Connor, Walker. 1989. Leninist Nationality Policy: Solution to the 'National Question'? (pp 23–46). *Hungarian Studies Review*. Vol. 16, No. 1–2.

Constitution of India. 1950. *Wikisource*. https://en.wikisource.org/wiki/Constitution_of_India. Accessed: Jan 2, 2020.

Constitution of Kenya. 2010. *Wikisource*. https://en.wikisource.org/wiki/Constitution_of_Kenya_(2010). Accessed: Jan 2, 2020.

The Constitution of the People's Democratic Republic of Ethiopia. 1987. https://chilot.files.wordpress.com/2011/04/1987-ethiopian-constitution1.pdf. Accessed: Feb 20, 2019.

The Constitution of the People's Democratic Republic of Ethiopia (pp 181–208). 1988. *Review of Socialist Law*. Vol. 14, No. 2.

Constitution of the Soviet Union (1977, Unamended). 1977. *Wikisource*. https://en.wikisource.org/wiki/Constitution_of_the_Soviet_Union_(1977,_Unamended). Accessed: Dec 31, 2019.

Cooper, Robert L. 1976a. Government Language Policy (pp 187–190). In: M. L. Bender, J. D. Bowen, R. L. Cooper and C. A. Ferguson, eds. *Language in Ethiopia* (Ser: Ford Foundation Language Surveys). London: Oxford University Press.

Cooper, Robert L. 1976b. The Spread of Amharic (pp 289–303). In: M. L. Bender, J. D. Bowen, R. L. Cooper and C. A. Ferguson, eds. *Language in Ethiopia* (Ser: Ford Foundation Language Surveys). London: Oxford University Press.

Corazza, M. Torcini. 2002. State and Religion in the Constitution and Politics of Ethiopia (pp 351–395). *European Journal for Church and State Research – Revue Européenne des relations Églises-État*. Vol. 9.

Current Local Date and Time in Ethiopia. 2019. https://time.et/. Accessed: Dec 22, 2019.

Dainihonteikokukenpō 大日本帝國憲法 [Constitution of Japan's Great Empire]. 1889. *Wikisource*. https://ja.wikisource.org/wiki/大日本帝國憲法#第一章_天皇. Accessed: Feb 20, 2019.

Bibliography 115

Data Dea. 2005–2006. Enduring Issues in State-Society Relations in Ethiopia: A Case Study of the WoGaGoDa Conflict in Wolaita, Southern Ethiopia (pp 141–159). *International Journal of Ethiopian Studies*. Vol. 2, No. 1/2.

De Waal, Alexander. 1991. *Evil Days: Thirty Years of War and Famine in Ethiopia*. New York: Human Rights Watch.

Declaration of the Rights of Man and of the Citizen. 1789. *Wikipedia*. https://en.wikipedia.org/wiki/Declaration_of_the_Rights_of_Man_and_of_the_Citizen. Accessed: Dec 30, 2019.

Deibert, Ronald et al., eds. 2008. *Access Denied: The Practice and Policy of Global Internet Filtering*. Cambridge, MA: MIT Press.

Demographics of Ethiopia: Ethnic Groups. 2019. *Wikipedia*. https://en.wikipedia.org/wiki/Demographics_of_Ethiopia#Ethnic_groups. Accessed: Feb 17, 2019.

Demographics of Russia. 2019. *Wikipedia*. https://en.wikipedia.org/wiki/Demographics_of_Russia. Accessed: Feb 17, 2019.

Deutsch, Karl. 1953. *Nationalism and Social Communication*. Cambridge, MA: MIT Press.

Die Japanische Verfassung vom 11. Februar 1889 (Meiji-Verfassung) [The Japanese Constitution of 11 February 1889 (Meiji Constitution)]. 1940. https://web.archive.org/web/20070519022111/www.cx.unibe.ch/~ruetsche/japan/Japan2.htm. Accessed: Feb 20, 2019.

Die Verfassung des Deutschen Reichs [The Constitution of the German Empire]. 1871. www.lwl.org/westfaelische-geschichte/que/normal/que840.pdf. Accessed: Feb 20, 2019.

Don-kun and Gaba, Eric. 2011. Map of Egypt Under Muhammad Ali Dynasty in English. *Wikimedia Commons*. https://commons.wikimedia.org/wiki/File:Egypt_under_Muhammad_Ali_Dynasty_map_en.png. Accessed: Dec 22, 2019.

Dörrbecker, Maximilian (Chumwa). 2019. The 30 Regions of the People's Democratic Republic of Ethiopia Period, 1987–1991. *Wikipedia*. https://en.wikipedia.org/wiki/Provinces_of_Ethiopia#/media/File:Ethiopia_-_Administrative_regions_1987-1991.png. Accessed: Dec 21, 2019.

Endalk Chala. 2015. Violent Clashes in Ethiopia Over 'Master Plan' to Expand Addis. *The Guardian*. 11 Dec. www.theguardian.com/world/2015/dec/11/ethiopia-protests-master-plan-addis-ababa-students. Accessed: Feb 19, 2019.

Ephream Sileshi. 2019. Breaking: Sidama Becomes Ethiopia's 10th Regional State. *Addis Standard*. 23 Nov. http://archive.wikiwix.com/cache/?url=https%3A%2F%2Faddisstandard.com%2Fbreaking-sidama-becomes-ethiopias-10th-regional-state%2F. Accessed: Apr 4, 2020.

The EPRDF Officially Ends: The Prosperity Party Begins. 2019. *Ezega.com*. 26 Dec. www.ezega.com/News/NewsDetails/7599/The-EPRDF-Officially-Ends-The-Prosperity-Party-Begins. Accessed: Jan 1, 2020.

Eribo, Festus. 2001. *In Search of Greatness: Russia's Communications with Africa and the World*. Westport, CT: Ablex Publishing.

Eritrea: Birth of a Nation. 1993. Asmara: Government of Eritrea. www.dehai.org/conflict/history/birth_of_a_nation.htm. Accessed: Feb 19, 2019.

Bibliography

Erlich, Haggai. 2000. Identity and Church: Ethiopian – Egyptian Dialogue, 1924–59 (pp 23–46). *International Journal of Middle East Studies*. Vol. 32, No. 1.

EthioInfo Dashboard. 2020. www.dataforalldemo.org/dashboard/v1/ethioinfo/ethioinfo#/. Accessed: Jan 4, 2020.

Ethiopia around 1850. 2010. *Wikimedia Commons*. https://commons.wikimedia.org/wiki/File:Ethiopia_Map-1850.jpg. Accessed: Dec 22, 2019.

Ethiopia Arrests Suspects Over Haacaaluu Hundeessaa Killing. 2020. *Al Jazeera*. 10 July. www.aljazeera.com/news/2020/07/ethiopia-arrests-suspects-haacaaluu-hundeessaa-killing-200710160901039.html. Accessed: Sept 20, 2020.

Ethiopia – Constitution. 1994. www.servat.unibe.ch/icl/et00000_.html. Accessed: Feb 20, 2019.

Ethiopia: Education and Literacy. 2019. *UNESCO Institute for Statistics*. http://uis.unesco.org/en/country/et. Accessed: Dec 27, 2019.

Ethiopia Exports by Country. 2019. https://tradingeconomics.com/ethiopia/exports-by-country. Accessed: Dec 29, 2019.

Ethiopia's Troubled Situation: Hearing Before the Subcommittee on Africa, Global Human Rights and International Operations of the Committee on International Relations, House of Representatives, One Hundred Ninth Congress, Second Session. 2006. Serial No. 109–165, 28 Mar. Washington DC: U.S. Government Printing Office.

Ethiopia: Gross Domestic Product (GDP) in Current Prices from 1984 to 2024. 2019. *Statista*. www.statista.com/statistics/455080/gross-domestic-product-gdp-in-ethiopia/. Accessed: Dec 29, 2019.

Ethiopia: Historical Demographical Data of the Whole Country. 2019. www.populstat.info/Africa/ethiopic.htm. Accessed: Feb 17, 2019.

Ethiopia Imports by Country. 2019. https://tradingeconomics.com/ethiopia/imports-by-country. Accessed: Dec 29, 2019.

Ethiopia: Languages. 2020. *The World Factbook*. Washington, DC: Central Intelligence Agency. www.cia.gov/library/publications/the-world-factbook/geos/et.html. Accessed: Apr 7, 2020.

Ethiopia Population. 2019. www.worldometers.info/world-population/ethiopia-population/. Accessed: Feb 17, 2019.

Ethiopia: Population Pyramids of the World from 1950 to 2100. 2019. www.populationpyramid.net/ethiopia/. Accessed: Dec 30, 2019.

Ethiopian Aristocratic and Court Titles: Ras. 2019. *Wikipedia*. https://en.wikipedia.org/wiki/Ethiopian_aristocratic_and_court_titles#Ras. Accessed: Feb 19, 2019.

Ethiopian Calendar Converter. 2019. www.ethcalendar.com/ethiopiancalendar/ethiopian_calendar. Accessed: Dec 22, 2019.

Ethiopian Constitution of 1931. 1931. http://file:///C:/Users/Dom/Downloads/ethiopian-constitution-of-1931.pdf. Accessed: Dec 27, 2019.

Ethiopia's Invasion of Somalia, 1982–83. 1983. Mogadishu: Ministry of Foreign Affairs, Somali Democratic Republic.

Ethiopic (Unicode Block). 2019. *Wikipedia*. https://en.wikipedia.org/wiki/Ethiopic_(Unicode_block). Accessed: Dec 29, 2019.

Fasil Nahum. 1997. *Constitution for a Nation of Nations: The Ethiopian Prospect*. Lawrenceville, NJ: Red Sea Press.

Fikrejesus Amhazion. 2018. A Look Back on Eritrea's Historic 1993 Referendum. *Tesfanews*. 23 Apr. www.tesfanews.net/revisiting-eritrea-historic-1993-referendum/. Accessed: Apr 5, 2020.
Fikru Helebo. 2007. Ethiopian Naming System. *Enset*. 17 Mar. www.enset.org/2007/03/ethiopian-naming-system.html. Accessed: Apr 2, 2020.
Fikru Helebo and Ephrem Madebo. 2009. Racism in Ethiopia. *Enset*. 28 Feb. www.enset.org/2009/02/racism-in-ethiopia.html. Accessed: Feb 19, 2019.
File:Population of Former USSR.PNG. 2014. *Wikimedia Commons*. https://commons.wikimedia.org/wiki/File:Population_of_former_USSR.PNG. Accessed: Dec 30, 2019.
Fitzpatrick, Matthew P. 2015. *Purging the Empire: Mass Expulsions in Germany, 1871–1914*. Oxford: Oxford University Press.
Ford, Peter F. 2009. Christian-Muslim Relations in Ethiopia: A Checkered Past, a Challenging Future (pp 52–70). In: Stephen R. Goodwin, ed. *World Christianity in Muslim Encounter: Essays in Memory of David A. Kerr*. London: Continuum.
Foreign Direct Investment, Net Inflows (BoP, current US$) – Ethiopia. 2019. *World Bank*. https://data.worldbank.org/indicator/BX.KLT.DINV.CD.WD?locations=ET. Accessed: Dec 29, 2019.
Fritsch, Emmanuel. 1999. The Liturgical Year and the Lectionary of the Ethiopian Church: Introduction to the Temporal (pp 71–116). *Warszawskie Studia Teologiczne*. Vol. 12, No. 2. http://pwtw.pl/wp-content/uploads/wst/12-2/Fritsch.pdf. Accessed: Dec 22, 2019.
Gaba, Eric. 2011. *Egypt under Muhammad Ali Dynasty*. https://en.wikipedia.org/wiki/Muhammad_Ali_dynasty#/media/File:Egypt_under_Muhammad_Ali_Dynasty_map_en.png. Accessed: Feb 17, 2019.
Gardner, Tom. 2020. How a Musician's Death Unleashed Violence and Death in Ethiopia. *The Guardian*. 3 Aug. www.theguardian.com/global-development/2020/aug/03/how-a-musicians-death-unleashed-violence-and-death-in-ethiopia. Accessed: Sept 20, 2020.
Gellner, Ernest. 1983. *Nations and Nationalism*. Oxford: Blackwell.
Getachew Anteneh and Derib Ado. 2006. Language Policy in Ethiopia: History and Current Trends (pp 37–61). *Ethiopian Journal of Education and Sciences*. Vol. 2, No. 1. www.ajol.info/index.php/ejesc/article/view/41975/56897. Accessed: Dec 27, 2019.
Ghelawdewos Araia. 1995. *The Political Economy of Transition*. Lanham, MD: University Press of America.
Gilkes, Patrick. 1983. Centralism and the Ethiopian PMAC (pp 195–218) In: I. M. Lewis, ed. *Nationalism and Self Determination in the Horn of Africa*. London: Ithaca Press.
Girma Awgichew Demeke. 2014. *The Origin of Amharic*. Trenton NJ: The Red See Press.
Global Foreign Direct Investment into Ethiopia (1992–2017). 2018. *AsokoInsight*. 19 Mar. https://asokoinsight.com/content/quick-insights/global-fdi-ethiopia. Accessed: Dec 29, 2019.
Google Translate Adds African Languages. 2013. *The Guardian*. 29 Aug. www.theguardian.com/world/2013/aug/29/google-translate-african-languages. Accessed: Dec 27, 2019.

Gordy, Eric D. 1999. *Culture of Power in Serbia: Nationalism and the Destruction of Alternatives*. University Park, PA: Pennsylvania State University Press.

Gori, Alessandro. 2015. Between Manuscripts and Books: Islamic Printing in Ethiopia (pp 65–82). In: Caroline Davies and David Johnson, eds. *The Book in Africa* (Ser: New Directions in Book History). Basingstoke: Palgrave Macmillan.

Greenfield, Richard. 1967. *Ethiopia: A New Political History*. London: Pall Mall Press.

Guidi, Pierre. 2012. Les enfants du Wolaitta n'apprendront pas en wogagoda. Les enjeux linguistiques et politiques d'un conflit scolaire en Éthiopie (1999–2000) [Wolaitta Children Will Not Learn in Wogagoda: Language and Political Issues Raised by an Education Conflict in Ethiopia (1999–2000)] (pp 129–148). *Cahiers de la recherche sur l'éducation et les savoirs*. Vol. 11 (Mélanges et variations). https://journals.openedition.org/cres/2263. Accessed: Mar 31, 2020.

Gupta, Sushma. 1992. Cataloging Ethiopian Personal Names (pp 81–92). *Cataloging & Classification Quarterly*. Vol. 14, No. 2.

Gupta, Sushma. 1994. The Development of Education, Printing and Publishing in Ethiopia (pp 169–180). *The International Information and Library Review*. Vol. 26, No. 3.

Hachalu Hundessa – Ethiopia's Murdered Musician Who Sang for Freedom. 2020. *BBC News*. 2 July. www.bbc.co.uk/news/world-africa-53238206. Accessed: Sept 20, 2020.

Haile Gabriel Dagne. 1976. Non-Government Schools in Ethiopia (pp 339–370). In: M. L. Bender, J. D. Bowen, R. L. Cooper and C. A. Ferguson, eds. *Language in Ethiopia* (Ser: Ford Foundation Language Surveys). London: Oxford University Press.

Haile Gebriel Dagne/ኃይለ ገብርኤል ዳኜ. 2007. ባህልና ትምህርት በኢትዮጵያ *bahilina timihiriti be'ītiyop'iya* [Culture and Education in Ethiopia] *Studies on Education in Ethiopian Tradition*. Addis Ababa: Addis Ababa University Press.

Haile Selassie I. 1970 [1931]. የ 1923 ሕገ መንግሥት *ye 1923 hige menigišiti* [The Constitution of 1923 EC/1931] (pp 767–775). In: Mahteme Selassie Wolde Meskel, ed. ዝክረ ነገር *zikre neger* [Book of Memories]. Addis Ababa: Artistic Printing Press.

Haile Woldemikael. 1976. Government Schools in Ethiopia (pp 324–338). In: M. L. Bender, J. D. Bowen, R. L. Cooper and C. A. Ferguson, eds. *Language in Ethiopia* (Ser: Ford Foundation Language Surveys). London: Oxford University Press.

Halliday, Fred and Molyneux, Maxine. 1981. *The Ethiopian Revolution*. London: NLB.

Hanibal Goitom. 2012. Ethiopian Emperors and Slavery. *Library of Congress: Law Library: Blog*. 31 Jan. https://blogs.loc.gov/law/2012/01/ethiopian-emperors-and-slavery/. Accessed: Dec 28, 2019.

Hao, Shiyuan. 2016. *How the Communist Party of China Manages the Issue of Nationality: An Evolving Topic* [translated from the Chinese by Xiaohua Tong]. Heidelberg: Springer.

Harsch, Ernst. 1978. *The Ethiopian Revolution*. New York: Pathfinder.

Haryckaja, Volha. 2018. *Movy Biełarusi ŭ ličbach i maliunkach*. https://dataviz.by/мовы-беларусі-ў-лічбах-і-малюнках. Accessed: Jan 4, 2020.

Heinrich, Patrick. 2012. *The Making of Monolingual Japan: Language Ideology and Japanese Modernity*. Bristol: Multilingual Matters.
Henze, Paul B. 2000. *Layers of Time: A History of Ethiopia*. London: Hurst.
Henze, Paul B. 2007. *Ethiopia in Mengistu's Final Years* (Vol. 2: Until the Last Bullet). Addis Ababa: Shama Books.
Heruy Wellde Selasse (ኅሩይ ወልደ ሥላሴ *ḥiruyi welide šilasē*). 1924 EC/1932. ማኅደረ ብርሃን – ሀገረ ጃፓን *maḥidere birihani – hāgere japani* [Japan: The Source of Light]. Addis Ababa: Goh Tsebha Printing Press.
Higher Constitutional Congress. 1974 (1966 EC). ከፍተኛው ሕገመንግሥታዊ ጉባዔ፤ የኢትዮጵያ ሕገ መንግሥት ረቂቅ፤ሐምሌ 30፤1966 ዓ.ም *kefitenyaw ḥigemenigišitawī guba'ē፤ ye'ītiyop'iya ḥige menigišiti rek'īk'i፤ḥāmilē 30፤1966 'a.mi* [Ethiopian Constitution: The Draft of 30 July 1966 EC/1974].
Hirobumi, Ito. 1889. The Constitution of the Empire of Japan. In: *Commentaries on the Constitution of the Empire of Japan* [translated by Miyoji Ito]. Tokyo: Igirisuhoritsu. https://history.hanover.edu/texts/1889con.html. Accessed: Dec 10, 2019.
Hirut Woldemariam. 2014. Writing Both Difference and Similarity: Towards a More Unifying and Adequate Orthography for the Newly Written Languages of Ethiopia: The Case of Wolaitta, Gamo, Gofa and Dawuro (pp 44–53). *Journal of Languages and Cultures*. Vol. 5. No. 3.
Hobsbawm, Eric J. and Ranger, Terence, eds. 1983. *The Invention of Tradition*. Cambridge: Cambridge University Press.
Hoffman, Gil Stern Stern. 2016. Coalition Crisis Averted: 9000 Ethiopian Immigrants to be Brought to Israel Over 5 Years. *The Jerusalem Post*. 7 Apr. www.jpost.com/Israel-News/Politics-And-Diplomacy/Coalition-crisis-averted-9000-Ethiopian-immigrants-to-be-brought-to-Israel-over-5-years-450594. Accessed: Mar 31, 2020.
Hohhot Conference Program. 2014. *Studylib*. https://studylib.net/doc/6642721/hohhot-conference-program. Accessed: Dec 21, 2019.
Horie, Hideichi. 1952. Revolution and Reform in Meiji Restoration (pp 23–34). *Kyoto University Economic Review*. Vol. 22, No. 1.
Hroch, Miroslav. 1985. *Social Preconditions of National Revival in Europe: A Comparative Analysis of the Social Composition of Patriotic Groups among the Smaller European Nations* (translated from the German by Ben Fowkes). Cambridge: Cambridge University Press.
Iadarola, Antoinette. 1975. Ethiopia's Admission into the League of Nations: An Assessment of Motives (pp 601–622). *The International Journal of African Historical Studies*. Vol. 8, No. 4.
Impact of Cuban-Soviet Ties in the Western Hemisphere (Tuesday, March 14, 1978). 1978. Washington, DC: House of Representatives, Committee on International Relations, Subcommittee in Inter-American Affairs.
Imperial Government of Ethiopia. 1965 EC/1972 [1955]. የተሻሻለው ሕገ መንግሥት *yeteshashalewi ḥige menigišiti* [The Revised Constitution {of 1948 EC/1955}]. In: *Consolidated Laws of Ethiopia* (Vol. 1). Addis Ababa: Law Faculty, Haile Selassie I University.
Imperial Government of Ethiopia. 1969 [1955]. The 1955 Revised Constitution of Ethiopia. In: Margery Perham, ed. *The Government of Ethiopia*. London: Faber and Faber.

Iroshnikov, Mikhail. 1974. *Predsedatel' Soveta Narodnykh Komissarov Vl. Ul'ianov (Lenin). Ocherki gosudarstvennoy deiatel'nosti v 1917–1918 gg.* [Chairman of the Council of People's Commissars Ulianov (Lenin): Essays on State Activities in 1917–1918]. Leningrad: Nauka.

Ishiyama, John. 2007. Nominations and Party Development in Ethiopia: The Opposition and the 2005 Parliamentary Election (pp 81–105). *African and Asian Studies*. Vol. 6, No. 1–2.

Jawar Mohammed: Top Ethiopia opposition figure 'proud' of terror charge. 2020. BBC News. 21 Sept. www.bbc.co.uk/news/world-africa-54236276. Accessed: Sept 22, 2020.

Johnson, Lonnie R. 2011. *Central Europe: Enemies, Neighbors, Friends*. New York: Oxford University Press.

Jonas, Raymond. 2011. *The Battle of Adwa: African Victory in the Age of Empire*. Cambridge, MA: The Belknap press of Harvard University Press.

Judson, Pieter M. 2017. *The Habsburg Empire: A New History*. Cambridge, MA: Harvard University Press.

Kaiser, Robert J. 1994. *The Geography of Nationalism in Russia and the USSR*. Princeton, NJ: Princeton University Press.

Kamusella, Tomasz. 2016. Are Central Europe, and East and Southeast Asia Alike? The Normative Isomorphism of Language, Nation and State (pp 13–78). In: Kiyoshi Hara and Patrick Heinrich, eds. *Standard Norms in Written Languages: Historical and Comparative Studies Between East and West*. Tokyo: Joshibi University of Art and Design. www.academia.edu/27651466/Are_Central_Europe_and_East_and_Southeast_Asia_Alike_The_Normative_Isomorphism_of_Language_Nation_and_State_Scanned_pp_13-78_._2016. Accessed: Dec 21, 2019.

Kamusella, Tomasz. 2018. Nationalism and National Languages (pp 163–182). In: J. W. Tollefson and M. Pérez-Milans, eds. *The Oxford Handbook of Language Policy and Planning*. Oxford: Oxford University Press.

Kaplan, Steven. 1990. Kifu-Qen: The Great Famine of 1888–1892 and the Beta Israel (Falasha) (pp 67–77). *Paideuma: Mitteilungen zur Kulturkunde*. Vol. 36.

Karpov, Iu. 2017. *Natsional'naia politika sovetskogo gosudarstva na severokavkaskoi periferii v 20–30-e gg. XX vv. Evolutsiia problem i reshenii* [The Nationality Policy of the Soviet State in the North Caucasian Periphery During the 1920–30s: The Development of This Problem and Its Solutions] (Ser: Ethnographica Petropolitana). St Petersburg: Izdatel'stvo Peterburgskoe vostokovedenie.

Kautsky, Karl. 1908. *Nationalität und Internationalität* (Ser: Die Neue Zeit; Ergänzungsheft, Vol. 1). Stuttgart: Singer.

Kazuhiro, Takii. 2014. *Itō Hirobumi – Japan's First Prime Minister and Father of the Meiji Constitution* [translated from the Japanese by Takechi Manabu]. London: Routledge.

Kebede Mikael (ከበደ ሚካኤል *kebede mīka'ēl*). 1946 EC/1954. ጃፓን እንዴት ሰለጠነች? *japani inidēti selet'enechi?* [How Did Japan Modernize Itself?]. Addis Ababa: ብርሃንና ሰላም *birihanina šelam*.

Keller, Edmond J. 1985. State, Party, and Revolution in Ethiopia (pp 1–17). *African Studies Review*. Vol. 28, No. 1.

Keller, Edmond J. 1988. *Revolutionary Ethiopia: From Empire to People's Republic*. Bloomington, IN: Indiana University Press.

Kelman, Sveta. 2016. From Amharic to Xhosa, Introducing Translate in 13 New Languages – Now Over 100 in Total! *Blog Google*. 17 Feb. https://blog.google/products/translate/from-amharic-to-xhosa-introducing/. Accessed: Dec 27, 2019.

Khan, Yoshimitsu. 1997. *Japanese Moral Education Past and Present*. London: Associated University Press.

Kibruyisfa Achamyeleh. 1997. Ethiopia: Population Information Resources. www.un.org/popin/regional/africa/ethiopia/. Accessed: Feb 17, 2019.

Kiflu Tadesse. 1993. *The Generation: The History of the Ethiopian People's Revolutionary Party* (Part 1: From the Early Beginnings to 1975). Silver Spring, MD: The Independent Publishers and K & S Distributors.

Kinfe Abraham. 2001. *Ethiopia from Empire to Federation: A Political, Economic, Diplomatic and Social History of the People and Polity of Ethiopia: From Sheba and Axum to the Present, 1000BC – 2000AD*. Addis Ababa: Ethiopian International Institute for Peace and Development (EIIPD Press) and Horn of Africa Democracy and Development (HADAD) International Lobby.

Kiros, Fasil G. 2006. *Enough with Famines in Ethiopia: A Clarion Call*. Hollywood, CA: Tsehai Publishers.

Kisika, Sam. 2019. Yes, Ethiopia 'the Fastest Growing Economy Globally' – but It's All in the Details. *Africa Check*. 17 Dec. https://africacheck.org/reports/yes-ethiopia-the-fastest-growing-economy-globally-but-its-all-in-the-details/. Accessed: Jan 4, 2020.

Klinger, Anne-Marie. 1992 [PhD dissertation]. *Sprachpolitik und ihre Wiederspiegelung im Bildungswesen Äthiopiens. 1974–1990* [Language Policy and Its Reflection in Ethiopia's Education System, 1974–1990]. Leipzig: Universität Leipzig.

Konstitutsiya, SSSR (1977)/redaktsiya 7 oktyabrya 1977 g. [USSR Constitution (1977)/The Text in the Wording of the Edition of October 7, 1977]. 1977. *Vikiteka*. https://ru.wikisource.org/wiki/Конституция_СССР_(1977)/редакция_7_октября_1977_г. Accessed: Apr 1, 2020.

Kulichenko, Mikhail. 1972. *Natsional'nye otnosheniia v SSSR i tendentsii ikh razvitiia* [National Relations in the USSR and Their Development Trends]. Moscow: Mysl'.

Kuusinen, O. W. 1963. *Fundamentals of Marxism-Leninism: Manual*. Moscow: Foreign Languages Publishing House.

Languages with Official Status in India: List of Scheduled Languages of India. 2020. *Wikipedia*. https://en.wikipedia.org/wiki/Languages_with_official_status_in_India#List_of_scheduled_languages_of_India. Accessed: Jan 2, 2020.

Lawson, Konrad and Wojtych, Tadeusz. 2015. Conference Videos Online – Between Federalism, Autonomy and Centralism. Institute for Transnational and Spatial

History. 9 July. http://standrewstransnational.wp.st-andrews.ac.uk/2015/07/09/conference-videos-online/. Accessed: Dec 21, 2019.

Leenco Lata. 1999. *The Ethiopian State at the Crossroads – Decolonization and Democratization or Disintegration?* Lawrenceville and Asmara: The Red Sea Press.

Legesse Lemma. 1979. The Ethiopian Student Movement 1960–1974: A Challenge to the Monarchy and Imperialism in Ethiopia (pp 31–46). *Northeast African Studies*. Vol. 1, No. 2.

Lemberg, Eugen. 1967–1968. *Nationalismus* [Nationalism]. Reinbek bei Hamburg: E. Rowohlt.

Leont'ev, Nikolai Stepanovich: Pervaia Italo-Efiopskaia voina [Leont'ev, Nikolai Stepanovich: The First Italo-Ethiopian War]. 2020. *Vikipediia*. https://ru.wikipedia.org/wiki/Леонтьев,_Николай_Степанович#Первая_Итало-Эфиопская_война. Accessed: Jan 1, 2020.

Levine, Donald. 1965. Ethiopia: Identity, Authority and Realism (pp 245–282). In: Lucian W. Pye and Sydney Verva, eds. *Political Culture and Political Development*. Princeton, NJ: Princeton University Press.

Levine, Donald Nathan. 1974. *Greater Ethiopia: The Evolution of a Multiethnic Society*. Chicago, IL: University of Chicago Press.

Levine, Donald Nathan. 2007. Ethiopia, Japan, and Jamaica: A Century of Globally Linked Modernizations (pp 41–51). *International Journal of Ethiopian Studies*. Vol. 3, No. 1.

Lewis, I. M. 1983. Introduction (pp 1–22). In: I. M. Lewis, ed. *Nationalism and Self Determination in the Horn of Africa*. London: Ithaca Press.

Linyan, Wang. 2012. New Headquarters Shows Partnership Entering Era of Hope: Ethiopia PM. *China Daily*. 30 Jan. www.chinadaily.com.cn/cndy/2012-01/30/content_14502354.htm. Accessed: Oct 4, 2020.

List of Universities and Colleges in Ethiopia. 2019. *Wikipedia*. https://en.wikipedia.org/wiki/List_of_universities_and_colleges_in_Ethiopia. Accessed: Dec 27, 2019.

List of Wikipedias by Language Group. 2019. *Wikimedia: Meta-Wiki*. https://meta.wikimedia.org/wiki/List_of_Wikipedias_by_language_group. Accessed: Dec 27, 2019.

Lukic, Reneo. 1994. Greater Serbia: A New Reality in the Balkans (pp 49–70). *Nationalities Papers*. Vol. 22, No. 1.

Lyons, Roy. 1978. The USSR, China and the Horn of Africa (pp 5–30). *Review of African Political Economy*. Vol. 5, No. 12.

MacLeod, Erin C. 2014. *Visions of Zion: Ethiopians and Rastafari in the Search for the Promised Land*. New York: New York University Press.

Mahteme Selassie Wolde Meskel. 1970. ዝክረ ነገር *zikre neger* [Book of Memories]. Addis Ababa: Artistic Printing Press.

Manifesto: Networks of Decolonization in Asia and Africa: Afro-Asian Networks Research Collective (pp 176–182). 2018. *Radical History Review*. Vol. 131, May. https://eprints.soas.ac.uk/26420/1/RHR_Manifesto_final_submitted_version_SOAS.pdf. Accessed: May 11, 2020.

Marcus, Harold G. 1975. *The Life and Times of Menelik II: Ethiopia, 1844–1913.* Oxford: Clarendon Press.

Markakis, John. 1974. *Ethiopia: Anatomy of a Traditional Polity.* Addis Ababa: Oxford University Press.

Markakis, John. 2003. Ethnic Conflict in Pre-federal Ethiopia (pp 11–24). In: *Proceedings of the First National Conference on Federalism, Conflict and Peace Building.* Addis Ababa: Ministry of Federal Affairs and GTZ.

Markakis, John and Asmelash Beyene. 1967. Representative Institutions in Ethiopia (pp 193–219). *Journal of Modern African Studies.* Vol. 5, No. 2.

Marks, Simon. 2020. Ethiopian Opposition Leader Appears in Court on Terror Charges. *VOA News.* 21 Sept. www.voanews.com/africa/ethiopian-opposition-leader-appears-court-terror-charges. Accessed: Sept 22, 2020.

Martin, Terry. 2001. *The Affirmative Action Empire: Nations and Nationalism in the Soviet Union, 1923–1939.* Ithaca, NY: Cornell University Press.

Matsuzato, Kimitaka. 2017. The Rise and Fall of Ethnoterritorial Federalism: A Comparison of the Soviet Union (Russia), China, and India (pp 1047–1069). *Europe-Asia Studies.* Vol. 69, No. 7.

McCann, James C. 1995. *People of the Plow: An Agricultural History of Ethiopia, 1800–1990.* Madison, WI: University of Wisconsin Press.

McGarry, John. 2018. 'Connor's Communist Control Polities': Why Ethno-Federalism Does Not Explain the Break-Up of the Soviet Union, Yugoslavia and Czechoslovakia (pp 535–545). *Nations and Nationalism.* Vol. 24, No. 3.

McGarry, John and O'Leary, Brendan. 2009. Must Pluri-National Federations Fail? (pp 5–25). *Ethnopolitics.* Vol. 8, No. 1.

Meareg, H. 2020. Time to Make English a Working Language of Ethiopia's Federal Government. *Ethiopia Insight.* 12 Oct. www.ethiopia-insight.com/2020/10/12/time-to-make-english-a-working-language-of-ethiopias-federal-government/. Accessed: Oct 21, 2020.

Menon, Dilip. 2014. Bandung Is Back: Afro-Asian Affinities (pp 241–245). *Radical History Review.* No. 119.

Meseret Chekol Reta. 2013. *The Quest for Press Freedom: One Hundred Years of History of the Media in Ethiopia.* Lanham, MD: University Press of America.

Messay Kebede. 2003a. Eurocentrism and Ethiopian Historiography: Deconstructing Semitization (pp 1–19). *International Journal of Ethiopian Studies.* Vol. 1, No. 1.

Messay Kebede. 2003b. From Marxism-Leninism to Ethnicity: The Sideslips of Ethiopian Elitism (pp 165–188). *Northeast African Studies.* Vol. 10, No. 2.

Messay Kebede. 2008. *Radicalism and Cultural Dislocation in Ethiopia, 1960–1974.* Rochester, NY: University of Rochester Press.

Mikre-Sellassie, G. A. 2000. The Early Translation of the Bible into Ethiopic/Geez (pp 302–316). *The Bible Translator.* Vol. 51, No. 3.

Milkias, Paulos. 1980. Zemecha: Assessing the Political and Social Foundations of Mass Education in Ethiopia (pp 19–30). *Northeast African Studies.* Vol. 2, No. 1.

Modak, Debnarayan. 2006. *Dynamics of National Question in India: The Communist Approach (1942–64).* Kolkata: Progressive Publishers.

Mojdl, Lubor. 2005. *Etiopie* [Ethiopia]. Prague: Libri.
Monin, Boris. 2013. The Visit of *Rās* Tafari in Europe (1924): Between Hopes of Independence and Colonial Realities (pp 383–389). *Annales d'Éthiopie*. Vol. 28. www.persee.fr/doc/ethio_0066-2127_2013_num_28_1_1547. Accessed: Feb 17, 2019.
Mullaney, Thomas S. 2012. *Coming to Terms with the Nation: Ethnic Classification in Modern China*. Berkeley, CA: University of California Press.
Muluneh, Kassa. 2017. The Paradox of Administration of Nationalities in Post-1991 Ethiopia: The Case of Benishangul-Gumuz Regional State (pp 35–65). *International Journal of Advancements in Research & Technology*. Vol. 6, No. 2. www.ijoart.org/docs/The-Paradox-of-Administration-of-Nationalities-in-Post-1991-Ethiopia-The-Case-of-Benishangul-Gumuz-Regional-State.pdf. Accessed: Feb 26, 2020.
Natufe, O. Igho. 2011. *Soviet Policy in Africa: From Lenin to Brezhnev*. Bloomington, IN: iUniverse Inc.
Nigusé Abbebe and Bender, Lionel M. 1984. The Ethiopian Language Academy: 1943–1974 (pp 1–7). *Northeast African Studies*. Vol. 6, No. 3.
Nish, Ian, ed. 2008. *The Iwakura Mission to America and Europe: A New Assessment*. London: Routledge.
Nyang, Magn. 2009. The Difference Between Being an Ethiopian and Being Habesha. *Sudan Tribune*. 17 Feb. www.sudantribune.com/The-difference-between-being-an,30208. Accessed: Feb 19, 2019.
O'Regan, Kate and Khosala, Madhav. 2014. Equality in Asia (pp 277–315). In: Rosalind Dixon and Tom Ginsburg, eds. *Comparative Constitutional Law in Asia*. Cheltenham: Edward Elgar.
Osmond, Thomas. 2012. Knowledge, Identity and Epistemological Choices: Competing Theoretical Trends in Oromo Studies (pp 189–212). In: Susanne Epple, ed. *Creating and Crossing Boundaries in Ethiopia: Dynamics of Social Categorization and Differentiation*. Münster: Lit.
Ottaway, Marina. 1978. Democracy and New Democracy: The Ideological Debate in the Ethiopian Revolution (pp 19–31). *African Studies Review*. Vol. 21, No. 1.
Pałasz-Rutkowska, Ewa. 2017 [1996]. The 'Unique' Character of the Emperor: The Main Leader of Modern Japan? The Japanese Emperor's Position in the Meiji Constitution (pp 116–128). In: Ian Neary, ed. *Leaders and Leadership in Japan*. London: Taylor & Francis.
Pankhurst, Alula. 1992. *Resettlement and Famine in Ethiopia: The Villagers' Experience*. Manchester: Manchester University Press.
Pankhurst, Richard. 2003. Two Early Periodical Publications 'Djibouti' and 'Le Semeur d'Éthiopie' as Sources for Late 19th Century and Early 20th Century Ethiopian History (pp 231–256). *Annales d'Éthiopie*. Vol. 19. www.persee.fr/doc/ethio_0066-2127_2003_num_19_1_1045. Accessed: Dec 26, 2019.
Pankhurst, Sylvia. 1957. The Initiation of Ethiopia's Wireless Communication (p 2). *Ethiopian Observer*. Vol. 2, No. 1.
Parry, Ken, ed. 1999. *The Blackwell Companion to Eastern Christianity*. Oxford: Blackwell.

Patman, Robert G. 1990. *The Soviet Union in the Horn of Africa: The Diplomacy of Intervention and Disengagement*. Cambridge: Cambridge University Press.

The People's Democracies in Eastern Europe (Some Countries Efforts to Build Socialism). 1981. *Encyclopedia of Anti-Revisionism On-Line: Documents for the Criticism of Revisionism*. www.marxists.org/history/erol/ca.secondwave/ispeoples-demo.htm. Accessed: Dec 22, 2019.

Perham, Margery. 1969. *The Government of Ethiopia*. London: Faber and Faber.

Pešić, Vesna. 1996. *Serbian Nationalism and the Origins of the Yugoslav Crisis* (Ser: Peaceworks, Vol. 8). Washington, DC: United States Institute of Peace.

Phạm, Quỳnh N. and Shilliam, Robbie. 2016. Reviving Bandung (pp 3–20). In: ShilliamQuỳnh N. Phạm and Robbie Shilliam, eds. *Meanings of Bandung: Postcolonial Orders and Decolonial Visions*. London: Rowman & Littlefield International.

Plaut, Martin. 2018. Map of the Expansion of the Ethiopian Empire under Menelik II in 1880's [sic]. *Eritrea Hub*. 2 Feb. https://eritreahub.org/map-expansion-ethiopian-empire-menelik-ii-1880s. Accessed: Feb 17, 2019.

Plokhy, Serhii. 2015. *The Last Empire: The Final Days of the Soviet Union*. London: Oneworld Publications.

Podeszwa, Grażyna. 2000. Wprowadzenie [Introduction] (pp 7–27). In: Aleksander Bułatowicz, ed. *Z wojskami Menelika II. Zapiski z podróży do Etiopii* [In the Company of Menelik II's Armies: The Notes Taken During the Sojourn in Ethiopia] [translated from the Russian into Polish by Grażyna Podeszwa] (Ser: Dzieje Orientu). Warsaw: Dialog.

Poushter, Jacob. 2016. Smartphone Ownership and Internet Usage Continues to Climb in Emerging Economies. *Pew Research Center: Global Attitudes & Trends*. 22 Feb. www.pewresearch.org/global/2016/02/22/smartphone-ownership-and-internet-usage-continues-to-climb-in-emerging-economies/. Accessed: Feb 17, 2020.

Praeg, Bertus. 2006. *Ethiopia and Political Renaissance in Africa*. New York: Nova Science Publishers.

Prashad, Vijay. 2008. *The Darker Nations: A People's History of the Third World*. New York: The New Press.

Press Release No 13 / 18th AU Summit: Inauguration of the New African Union Conference Center. 2012. Addis Ababa: African Union. 28 Jan. https://web.archive.org/web/20120216164902/www.au.int/en/sites/default/files/28%2001%202012_18SUMMIT_PR_INAUGURATION.pdf. Accessed: Oct 4, 2020.

Preußische Verfassung (1848/1850). 2019. *Wikipedia*. https://de.wikipedia.org/wiki/Preußische_Verfassung_(1848/1850). Accessed: Dec 31, 2019.

Proclamation No. 7/1992: A Proclamation to Provide for the Establishment of National/Regional Self-Governments [NB: The text of this proclamation is given in Amharic and English]. 1992. *Negarit Gazeta*. Vol. 51, No. 2, 14 Jan.

Rashid, Shahidur and Asfaw Negassa. 2012. Policies and Performance of Ethiopian Cereal markets (pp 123–158). In: Paul Dorosh and Shahidur Rashid, eds. *Food and Agriculture in Ethiopia: Progress and Policy Challenges*. Philadelphia, PA: University of Pennsylvania Press.

Redie Bereketeab. 2015. Eritrea, a Colonial Creation: A Case of Aborted Decolonisation (pp 235–252). In: Redie Bereketeab, ed. *Self-Determination and Secession in Africa: The Post-Colonial State*. Milton Park, Abingdon, Oxon: Routledge.

Revised Constitution of the Amhara National Regional State, Proclamation 59/2001. 2001. Zikre Hig of the Council of the Amhara National Regional State. 5 Nov. https://chilot.files.wordpress.com/2011/11/zikre-hig-59-19941.pdf. Accessed: Apr 4, 2020.

Robertson, Esmonde. 1988. Race as a Factor in Mussolini's Policy in Africa and Europe (pp 37–58). *Journal of Contemporary History*. Vol. 23, No. 1.

Roeder, Philip G. 1991. Soviet Federalism and Ethnic Mobilization (pp 196–232). *World Politics*. Vol. 43, No. 2.

Russell, John G. 2009. The Other Other: The Black Presence in the Japanese Experience (pp 84–115). In: Michael Weiner, ed. *Japan's Minorities: The Illusion of Homogeneity*. Abingdon: Routledge.

Russia Population. 2019. www.worldometers.info/world-population/russia-population/. Accessed: Feb 17, 2019.

Russian Empire Census. 2019. *Wikipedia*. https://en.wikipedia.org/wiki/Russian_Empire_Census. Accessed: Feb 17, 2019.

Samuel Getachew. 2020. Ethiopia Is Adding Four More Official Languages to Amharic as Political Instability Mounts. *Quartz*. 3 Mar. https://qz.com/africa/1812085/ethiopia-adds-afan-oromo-somali-afar-tigrigna-languages-to-amharic. Accessed: Oct 19, 2020.

Sandner, Philipp. 2016. Anti-Government Protests Growing in Ethiopia. *DW*. 9 Aug. www.dw.com/en/anti-government-protests-growing-in-ethiopia/a-19461345. Accessed: Mar 29, 2020.

Schulze, Hagen. 2010. *The Course of German Nationalism: From Frederick the Great to Bismarck 1763–1867* [translated from the German by Sarah Hanbury-Tenison]. Cambridge: Cambridge University Press.

Schwab, Peter. 1970. Rebellion in Gojam Province, Ethiopia (249–256). *Canadian Journal of African Studies/Revue Canadienne des Études Africaines*. Vol. 4, No. 2.

Schwartzberg, Joseph E. 2009. Factors in the Linguistic Reorganization of Indian States (pp 139–182). In: Asha Sarangi, ed. *Language and Politics in India*. New Delhi: Oxford University Press.

Selçuk, Esenbel. 2011. *Japan, Turkey and the World of Islam: The Writings of Selçuk Esenbel*. Folkstone: Global Oriental.

Selemon Meharenna. 1980 [MA thesis]. *The Ethiopian Way to Socialism: The Role of Politico-Institutional Factors in Modernizing the Ethiopian Political System, 1974–1979*. Rome: Pontificia Universitas Gregoriana, Facultas Scientiarum Socialium.

Semahagn Gashu Abebe. 2014. *The Last Post-Cold War Socialist Federation Ethnicity, Ideology and Democracy in Ethiopia*. Farnham: Ashgate.

Semple, Clara. 2005. *A Silver Legend: The Story of the Maria Theresa Thaler* (Ser: Barzan Studies in Arabic Culture, Vol. 1). Manchester: Barzan.

shamibeli fik'irešilasē wegideresi ሻምበል ፍቅረሥላሴ ወግደርስ. 2006 EC [2014]. እኛና አብዮቱ *inyana ābiyotu* [Us and the Revolution]. Los Angeles, CA: Tsehai Publishers.
Sharma, Gopal. 2013. English in Ethiopia (pp 74–85). *Star Journal*. Vol. 2, No. 1.
Shimelis Bonsa. 2000. *Survey of the Private Press in Ethiopia: 1991–1999*. Addis Ababa: Forum for Social Studies.
Shinn, David H. and Ofcansky, Thomas P. 2013. *Historical Dictionary of Ethiopia*. Lanham, MD: Scarecrow Press.
Shtromas, Alexander. 1978. The Legal Position of Soviet Nationalities and Their Territorial Units According to the 1977 Constitution of the USSR (pp 265–272). *The Russian Review*. Vol. 37, No. 3.
si'ili [picture] ስዕል:MarxDictionary.pdf. 2020. ውክፔዲያ *wikipēdīya* [Wikipedia]. https://am.wikipedia.org/wiki/ስዕል:MarxDictionary.pdf. Accessed: Feb 11, 2020.
Sinitsin, Fedor. 2018. *Sovietskaia natsiia i voina. Natsional'nyi vopros v SSSR, 1933–1945* [The Soviet Nation and the War: The National Question in the USSR, 1933–1945]. Moscow: Tsentrpoligraf.
Slezkine, Yuri. 1994. The USSR as a Communal Apartment, or How a Socialist State Promoted Ethnic Particularism (pp 414–452). *Slavic Review*. Vol. 53, No. 2.
Sluglett, Peter and Currie, Andrew. 2014. *Atlas of Islamic History*. London: Routledge.
Smith, Lahra. 2013. *Making Citizens in Africa: Ethnicity, Gender and National Identity in Ethiopia*. Cambridge: Cambridge University Press.
Spector, Stephen. 2005. *Operation Solomon: The Daring Rescue of the Ethiopian Jews*. New York: Oxford University Press.
Spencer, John H. 2006. *Ethiopia at Bay: A Personal Account of the Haile Selassie Years*. Hollywood, CA: Tsehai Publishers and Distributors.
Spruyt, Hendrik. 2005. *Ending Empire: Contested Sovereignty and Territorial Partition*. Ithaca, NY: Cornell University Press.
Staatsgrundgesetz über die allgemeinen Rechte der Staatsbürger [Basic Law on the General Rights of Citizens]. 1867. www.ris.bka.gv.at/Dokument.wxe?Abfrage=B undesnormen&Dokumentnummer=NOR12000058. Accessed: Feb 19, 2019.
Stalin, Joseph. 1954 [1913]. *Marxism and the National Question*. Moscow: Foreign Languages Publishing House.
Subdivisions of Ethiopia. 2019. *Wikipedia*. https://en.wikipedia.org/wiki/Subdivisions_of_Ethiopia. Accessed: Dec 1, 2019.
Summary and Statistical Report of the 2007 Population and Housing Census Results. 2008. *Addis Ababa: Federal Democratic Republic of Ethiopia: Population Census Commission*. https://web.archive.org/web/20120214221803/www.csa.gov.et/pdf/Cen2007_firstdraft.pdf. Accessed: Dec 21, 2019.
Sundhaußen, Holm. 1973. *Der Einfluß der Herderschen Ideen auf die Nationsbildung bei den Völkern der Habsburger Monarchie* [The Influence of Herder's ideas on Nation Building among the Peoples in the Habsburg Monarchy]. Munich: R. Oldenburg Verlag.
Suny, Ronald Grigor. 1989. Nationalist and Ethnic Unrest in the Soviet Union (pp 503–528). *World Policy Journal*. Vol. 6, No. 3.

Synhaivskii, Serhii. 2016. *Doroha na Asmaru* [The Road to Asmara]. Kyiv: TOV Vydavnytstvo Klio.
Tekeste Negash. 1997. *Eritrea and Ethiopia the Federal Experience*. Uppsala: Nordiska, Afrikainstitutet, and New Brunswick, NJ: Transaction Publishers.
Tekle Hawariat Tekle Mariam. 2006. አቶባዮግራፊ: የህይወት ታሪክ *otobayogirafi: yehiyiweti tarīki* [Autobiography: Life Story]. Addis Ababa: Addis Ababa University Press.
Telecommunication Penetration Rate/Density for Ethio Telecom, Ethiopia, from Fiscal Year 2011 to 2018, by Subscription Type. 2019. *Statista*. www.statista.com/statistics/749655/ethiopia-ethio-telecom-density-penetration/. Accessed: Dec 29, 2019.
Tesfaye Shewaye and Taylor, Charles V. 1976. Language Curricula (pp 380–398). In: M. L. Bender, J. D. Bowen, R. L. Cooper and C. A. Ferguson, eds. *Language in Ethiopia* (Ser: Ford Foundation Language Surveys). London: Oxford University Press.
Teshale Tibebu. 1995. *The Making of Modern Ethiopia 1896–1974*. Lawrenceville, NJ: Red Sea Press.
Third and Fourth State Reforms. 2020. Belgium.be. www.belgium.be/en/about_belgium/country/history/belgium_from_1830/formation_federal_state/third_and_fourth_reform_of_state. Accessed: Oct 4, 2020.
Thrall, Lloyd. 2015. *China's Expanding African Relations: Implications for U.S. National Security*. Santa Monica, CA: RAND Corporation.
Thubauville, Sophia. 2013. Indian Academics in Ethiopia: South – South Migration of Highly Skilled Indians (pp 123–133). *Diaspora Studies*. Vol. 6, No. 2.
Tigray Crisis: Ethiopia Orders Military Response After Army Base Seized. 2020. BBC News. 4 Nov. https://www.bbc.co.uk/news/world-africa-54805088. Accessed: Jan 2, 2021.
Tirfe Mammo. 1999. *The Paradox of Africa's Poverty: The Role of Indigenous Knowledge*. Lawrenceville, NJ and Asmara: Red Sea Press.
Triulzi, Allesandro. 1983. Competing Views of National Identity in Ethiopia (pp 111–128). In: I. M. Lewis, ed. *Nationalism and Self Determination in the Horn of Africa*. London: Ithaca Press.
Tschoegl, Adrian E. 2001. Maria Theresa's Thaler: A Case of International Money (pp 454–464). *Eastern Economic Journal*. Vol. 27, No. 4.
Tsegaye Beru and Junker, Kirk W. 2018. Constitutional Review and Customary Dispute Resolution by the People in the Ethiopian Legal System (pp 1–65). *North Carolina Journal of International Law and Commercial Regulation*. Vol. 43, No. 3.
Tsuzuki, Chushichi and Young, R. Jules, eds. 2009. *Japan Rising: The Iwakura Embassy to the USA and Europe 1871–1873*. Cambridge: Cambridge University Press.
Tubiana, Joseph. 1983. The Linguistic Approach to Self Determination (pp 23–30). In: I. M. Lewis, ed. *Nationalism and Self Determination in the Horn of Africa*. London: Ithaca Press.

Tuji Jidda. 2009. Abyssinia to Ethiopia: From Obfuscation to Confusion. *OPride*. 2 Nov. www.opride.com/2009/11/02/abyssinia-to-ethiopia-from-obfuscation-to-confusion/. Accessed: Apr 5, 2020.
Uibopuu, Henn-Juri. 1979. Soviet Federalism Under the New Soviet Constitution (pp 171–185). *Review of Socialist Law*. Vol. 5, No. 1.
UN Emergencies Unit for Ethiopia – USAID/Ethiopia Map Room. 2000. Map of Regions and Zones in Ethiopia as of April 2000. All Boundaries are Approximate and Unofficial. *Wikimedia Commons*. https://commons.wikimedia.org/wiki/Atlas_of_Ethiopia#/media/File:Ethiopia_zone_region.jpg. Accessed: Dec 21, 2019.
UNESCO Interactive Atlas of the World's Languages in Danger: Belarusian. 2010. www.unesco.org/languages-atlas/index.php. Accessed: Jan 4, 2020.
Universal Declaration of Human Rights. 1948. United Nations. www.un.org/en/universal-declaration-human-rights/. Accessed: Dec 31, 2019.
Van der Beken, Christophe. 2012. *Unity in Diversity – Federalism as a Mechanism to Accommodate Ethnic Diversity: The Case of Ethiopia* (Ser: Recht und Politik in Afrika/Law and Politics in Africa, Vol. 10). Zürich and Münster: Lit Verlag.
Van der Beken, Christophe. 2015. Federalism, Local Government and Minority Protection in Ethiopia. Opportunities and Challenges (pp 150–177). *Journal of African Law*. Vol. 59, No. 1.
Van der Beken, Christophe. 2017. *Completing the Constitutional Architecture: A Comparative Analysis of Sub-National Constitutions in Ethiopia*. Addis Ababa: Addis Ababa University Press.
Van der Beken, Christophe. 2018. *The Challenge of Reform Within Ethiopia's Constitutional Order*. London: Rift Valley Institute.
Vaughan, Sarah. 1994. *The Addis Ababa Transitional Conference of July 1991: Its Origins, History and Significance*. Edinburgh: Centre of African Studies Edinburgh University.
Vestal, Theodore M. 2011. *The Lion of Judah in the New World: Emperor Haile Selassie of Ethiopia and the Shaping of the Americans' Attitudes Toward Africa*. Santa Barbara, CA: Praeger.
Vlastos, Stephen. 1997. Opposition Movements in Early Meiji, 1868–1885 (pp 367–431). In: Marius B. Jansen, ed. *The Emergence of Meiji Japan*. Cambridge: Cambridge University Press. https://sites.fas.harvard.edu/~rijs/crrp/papers/pdf/Vlastos_031909.pdf. Accessed: Nov 7, 2019.
Wagstaff, Peter. 1999. Belgium: A New Federalism (pp 74–87). In: Peter Wagstaff, ed. *Regionalism in the European Union* (Ser: European Studies Series). Exeter: Intellect.
Wallelign Mekonnen (የዋለልኝ መኮንን *yewalelinyi mekonini*). 2015 [1969]. On the Question of Nationalities in Ethiopia. www.scribd.com/document/346557603/Walellign-on-the-Question-of-Nationalities-in-Ethiopia. Accessed: Dec 31, 2019.
Wandruszka, Adam and Urbanitsch, Peter, eds. 1980. *Die Habsburgermonarchie 1848–1918* [The Habsburg Monarchy, 1848–1918] (Vol. 3: Die Völker des Reiches). Vienna: Verlag der Österreichischen Akademie der Wissenschaften.

Welch, David. 2004. Nazi Propaganda and the Volksgemeinschaft: Constructing a People's Community (pp 213–238). *Journal of Contemporary History*. Vol. 39, No. 2.
Whitake, Donald P. 1981. The Economy (pp 143–188). In: Harold D. Nelson and Irving Kaplan, eds. *Ethiopia: A Country Study* (Ser: Area Handbook Series, Vol. 28). Washington, DC: Foreign Area Studies, American University.
Whiteley, Wilfred H., ed. 1974. *Language in Kenya* (Ser: Ford Foundation Language Surveys). Nairobi: Oxford University Press.
Wondwosen Tamrat. 2019. Challenges of Attracting and Retaining Foreign Faculty. *University World News*. 22 June. www.universityworldnews.com/post.php?story=20190620065625869. Accessed: Dec 27, 2019.
Worringer, Renée. 2014. *Ottomans Imagining Japan: East, Middle East, and Non-Western Modernity at the Turn of the Twentieth Century* (Ser: Palgrave Macmillan Transnational History Series). New York: Palgrave Macmillan.
Yared Tibebu. 2019. 'On the Question of Nationalities in Ethiopia' – A Historical Review of Wallelign Mekonnen's Article Half a Century Later. *Ethioexplorer.com*. 17 Nov. https://ethioexplorer.com/on-the-question-of-nationalities-in-ethiopia-a-historical-review-of-wallelign-mekonnens-article-half-a-century-later/. Accessed: Dec 31, 2019.
yemarikisīzimi lēnīnīzimi mezigebe k'alati የማርክሲዝም ሌኒኒዝም መዝገበ ቃላት [The Dictionary of Marxism-Leninism]. 1978 EC [1986]. Addis Ababa: በ ኩራዝ አሳታሚ be kurazi āsatamī.
Yeounsuk, Lee. 2010. *The Ideology of Kokugo: Nationalizing Language in Modern Japan* [translated from the Japanese by Maki Hirano Hubbard]. Honolulu, HI: University of Hawai'i Press.
yepoletīka timihiriti – 6 nya kifili የፖለቲካ ትምህርት – 6 ኛ ክፍል [Political Education – 6th Grade]. 1977 EC [1984]. Addis Ababa. www.librarycat.org/lib/newcrossbooks/item/117597263. Accessed: Mar 29, 2020.
yewalelinyi mekonini የዋለልኝ መኮንን [=Wallelign Mekonnen]. 1969. የብሔሮች ጥያቄ በኢትዮጵያ *yebihērochi t'iyak'ē be 'ītiyop'iya*/On the Question of Nationalities in Ethiopia (pp 4–7). ታገል *tagel*/Struggle. 17 Nov.
Yohannes Woldemariam. 2018. The Unenviable Situation of Tigreans in Ethiopia. LSE Blog. 28 Mar. https://blogs.lse.ac.uk/africaatlse/2018/03/28/the-unenviable-situation-of-tigreans-in-ethiopia/. Accessed: Sept 22, 2020.
Yonas Admassu. 2003. Afäwärq Gäbrä Iyäsus (Vol. 1, pp 122b–124a). In: Siegbert Uhlig et al., eds. *Encyclopaedia Aethiopica*. Wiesbaden: Otto Harrassowitz.
Yordanov, Radoslav A. 2017. *The Soviet Union and the Horn of Africa During the Cold War: Between Ideology and Pragmatism*. Lanham, MD: Lexington Books, an imprint of The Rowman & Littlefield Publishing Group.
Young, John. 1997. *Peasant Revolution in Ethiopia – The Tigray People's Liberation Front, 1975–1991*. Cambridge: Cambridge University Press.
Zemelak Ayele. 2018. EPRDF's 'Menu of Institutional Manipulations' and the 2015 Regional Elections (pp 275–300). *Regional and Federal Studies*. Vol. 28, No. 3.

Zheim. 2010a. Menelik's Campaigns (1879–1889). https://en.wikipedia.org/wiki/Menelik_II#/media/File:Menelik_campaign_map_1_3.jpg. Accessed: Feb 17, 2019.

Zheim. 2010b. Menelik's Campaigns 1889–96. https://en.wikipedia.org/wiki/Menelik_II#/media/File:Menelik_campaign_map_2_3.jpg. Accessed: Feb 17, 2019.

Zheim. 2010c. Menelik's Campaigns 1897–1904. https://en.wikipedia.org/wiki/Menelik_II#/media/File:Menelik_campaign_map_3_3.jpg. Accessed: Feb 17, 2019.

Index

Note: Page numbers in *italics* indicate a figure and page numbers in **bold** indicate a table on the corresponding page. Page numbers followed by 'n' indicate a note.

1931 Constitution of Ethiopia 7, 23, 29, 85; adoption of 25; drafting of 25; Haile Selassie's speech after the signing of 26–27; influence of Japanese experience 25; key objectives 27; Meiji Constitution, differences 27–28; Meiji Constitution, influence of 25, 26, 85; mention of law in 27; monarchy concept in 27, 85; nation-state concept in 27; people concept in 27; reformists and traditionalists, struggle between 23; structure and content 25–26, 27

1955 Constitution of Ethiopia 8, 28, 29, 33, 89; centralized nation-state under emperor's absolutist power 29; Federal Act and Eritrean Constitution, narrowing the gap between 29; monarchy concept in 29; nation-state concept in 29; official (national) language, addition of 88; rights under 29, 33; structure and content 28; universal suffrage, introduction of 89

1977 Soviet Constitution 38–44, 51; autonomy of federated units 48; capitalism 38–39; centripetal objectives 40; communist polity's nationalities unification 38; ethnicity 38–39; ethnically (ethnolinguistically) defined federated units 41; ethnoterritorial federations 42–43; Marxist-Leninist ideology 38–39; right to secession 49; union republics and autonomous republics, entitled own constitutions 54; unity and homogeneity 40; unity of the state and its citizenry 42; whole people 39–40

1987 Constitution of Ethiopia 18; multinational state concept 99; socialism construction in 99; Soviet Bloc model 9–10; Soviet Constitution, emulation of 99; and Soviet model of ethnolinguistic federalism 99

1995 Constitution of Ethiopia 11, 18, 37–38; Amharic, as working language of Federal Government 103; drafting and approval 54n5; ethnically (ethnolinguistically) defined federated units 41; ethnicity 38, 39, 40, 46, 50; ethnoterritorial federations 42–43; Federal and Democratic State structure, establishment of 103; identical right to national self-determination 44; language designations 61–62; national self-determination 46; nations, nationalities and peoples 39; Nations, Nationalities and Peoples of Ethiopia, rights of 103; problems with unhindered democratic use of 52; regional states 43; right to secession 40; territorial (institutional) autonomy 11, 77; unity and homogeneity 40

Abiy Ahmed Ali 12, 50, 104, 107
abroad-educated elites 84
abroad education 84
Abyssinia *see* Ethiopian Empire (Abyssinia)
Academy of Ethiopian Languages 94, 104
Academy of Ethiopian Languages and Cultures 104
Addis Ababa 2, **69**, 78, 88; books publications in 83; first commercial printing press in 83; founding of 81; made as capital of Ethiopia 82; missionary activities 82; special status 54n7
Addis Hiwet 25
administrative regions and zones of Ethiopia 9, 52–53, *53*; Agew Awi Zone 43; Anywaa Zone 46, 71; Dawro Zone 44, 73, 108; Gamo-Gofa Zone 44, 52, 74, 104–105, 108; Gedeo Zone 74, 108; Halaba Zone 44; Kafa Zone 44, 74, 108; Konso Zone 44, 51, 108; Majang Zone 46, 71, 108; North Omo Zone 104–105; Oromia Zone 43; Sidama Zone 43, 52, 75, 108; South Omo Zone 75, 77; Wag Hemra Zone 43; Wolayita Zone 44, 104–105, 108
Adwa, Battle of 4, 82
Afar 11, 41–42, 49, 61, **69**, 108
Afar language 61, 62, 63, 94, 108
Afar Wikipedia 105
affirmative action 32, 45
African Union (AU) 105, 106
Africa Orientale Italiana (AOI) 86
Agaw (Awngi) language 108
Agew Awi Zone 43, **69**
Agricultural Marketing Corporation 94
Alemaya College of Agriculture 98
Alemaya University of Agriculture 98
Ale Special Woreda **73**
Algiers peace treaty 11
Al-Shabaab 105
Amaro Special Woreda 44, **73**
Amhara 2, 11, 41–43, 47, 63, **69**, 78
Amhara Democratic Party (ADP) 37, 46, 53n1
Amharas 2, 4–5, 6, 21n6, 30
Amharic language 30, 61, 63, 88, 92, 108; as medium of instruction 84, 89; missionary preaching and teaching through 87; as official language 80; official status of 100; periodicals 82; replacement of 86; as working language of federal government 103, 108
Amharic Wikipedia 105
Amharization 8, 10, 29–30, 35, 98
Anderson, Benedict 97
Andom, Aman Mikael 93
Anglo-Egyptian Sudan 4, 82, 89
antimonarchic sentiments 89
anti-Soviet Western bloc 86, 96
Anywaa Zone 46, **71**
Arabic abjad 108
Arabic language 83, 92, 108
Arab Republic of Egypt 88
Argobbas 44
Arndt, Ernst Moritz 12
Asnake Kefale 78
Asres, Meles Zenawi 101, 104
Assab 9
assertiveness of ethnic parties 51
assimilation policy 8, 29–30, 35, 57
Austria-Hungary 21n6, 65; ethnolinguistic federalism 15, 81, 82, 83, 91; ethnolinguistic nationalism 13
Austrian Empire 13, 15, 81
Austro-Marxism 82, 83, 91
autonomous regions/territories 17–18, 21n11, 41–44, 77, 87; under 1977 Soviet Constitution 48, 54; under 1995 constitution 11, 77; autonomous okrugs 41, 43; in China 19–20; Eritrea 88; Ethiopian People's Revolutionary Democratic Front (EPRDF) 50, 51–52, 58; in federal Ethiopia **69–76**; under People's Democratic Republic of Ethiopia constitution 9–10; pyramids of **19**; subregional autonomous territorial units 43

Bahru Zewde 23
Basketo Special Woreda 44, **73**
Bauer, Otto 17; and Austro-Marxism 82; *Question of Nationalities and Social Democracy, The* 82
Begemider 1
Belarusian language 59, 60, 63

134 *Index*

Belarusian nation 60
Belgium 7, 54n14, 102
Bench-Maji Zone **73**
Benishangul-Gumuz Region 11, 46, 47, 70, 78
Benti, Tafari 93
Berhanena Selam 84
Berlin Conference (1884–1885) 4
Beta Israel 92
Birr 87
Bolshevik Revolution 35, 36
book publishing 82, 83, 100, 101
Boshe, Hailemariam Desalegn 104
Bosnia and Herzegovina 102
Bosnian War 102
Britain: bilateral treaty with Ethiopia 86; Colony and Protectorate of Kenya 84, 90; East Africa Protectorate 84; end of Woyane Uprising (Rebellion) 87; invasion of Ethiopia 3, 82; protectorate over Egypt, end of 84; renaming of Sultanate of Egypt as Kingdom of Egypt 84; Somaliland Protectorate, independence of 89
Brčko District 102
Burji Special Woreda 44, **73**

capitalism 31, 38–39, 93
Castro, Fidel 96
Central Europe 1, 8, 36, 56, 77; monarchical order re-establishment 13; *Volk* concept 14
centralization, of Ethiopia 2, 4, 9, 29, 30, 36
centralized homogenous ethnolinguistic nation-state 8, 38, 57, 64–65
centralized state-owned economy, establishment of 94
China 10, 18, 20; and Africa 106; and Ethiopia 106; foreign investment by 106; imports and exports to 106; and Soviet system of multitiered autonomous regions 19–20
Chinese Revolution 10
Christian Ethiopia 4
Christianity 5–6, 15
church and state, separation of 81, 83
church schools, language of instruction in 83

civic nationalism 12, 13, 80
civilizing mission 14, 65
class struggle, and national self-determination 35
client state of Soviet Bloc, Ethiopia as 93
client state of West, Ethiopia as 86
Cold War 31, 86
colonialism 4, 6, 14–15, 82
Comecon (Council for Mutual Economic Assistance) 101
communism 9–10, 18, 36–37, 39, 46–47, 100
Communist Party of the Russian Soviet Federative Socialist Republic 46
Communist Party of the Soviet Union (CPSU) 46–47, 48, 49; centralized decision making 48; right to secession 49; weakening of 50–51
Congress of Vienna 13
Constitution of the Union of Soviet Socialist Republics 96
Coptic Orthodox Church of Alexandria (Egypt) 89
Croats 102
currency 87
Czechoslovakia, dissolution of 102

Dagestan 43
Dawro 104–105, 108
Dawro Zone 44, **73**, 108
decentralization, ethnicity-based 9, 11, 18, 37, 57
Declaration of the Rights of Man and of the Citizen 80
Decree 1 of 1942 30
democracy 11, 28, 31, 51
democratic centralism, 48, 49, 50, 51, 58, 77n1
'*Des deutschen Vaterland*' (Arndt's song) 80
Deutsch, Karl 88
Dictionary of Marxism-Leninism 99
Dirashe Special Woreda 44, **73**
Dire Dawa 9, 11, 54n7, **71**, 82
Draft Constitution of 1974 33

École impériale Menelik (Menelik Imperial School) 83
education: in abroad 56, 85; students, attendance in schools 85, 90

educational system 17, 89, 102; beginning of secular (government) system 83; establishment of 85; and Haile Selassie 23–24; language of instruction 44, 61–62, 63, 64, 83; political education, as compulsory subject 96–97; reconstruction of 87; secular 26, 83; shut down of internet during examinations 105

Egypt 3–4

Egyptian Revolution (1952) 88

English language 61, 63, 64, 108; as alternative medium of instruction 85; as medium of instruction 86; use in administration and education 92

Eritrea 3, 9–12, 22n12, 28, 88, 90; autonomy, end of 88; flag replacement 88; independence referendum 102; language replacements 88; law replacements 88; press and organizations 88; war with Ethiopia 11, 104, 106; *see also* Federation of Ethiopia and Eritrea

Eritrea-Ethiopia Federation Act 28

Eritrean Constitution 28

Eritrean Liberation Front (ELF) 10

Eritrean People's Liberation Front (EPLF) 10

Eritrean War of Independence 60, 90

Ethiopia Book Centre 94

Ethiopian Airlines, founding of 87

Ethiopian Civil War 10, 37, 60, 93

Ethiopian Empire (Abyssinia) 5, 20n2, 27, 29, **67**, 80, 87; Christian polity 93; and Ottoman Empire, compared 21n6

Ethiopian governmental gazette 87

Ethiopian institution of university-level education 88

Ethiopian intellectuals, influence of Japan on 24–25

Ethiopian Jews 92, 98, 106

Ethiopian Orthodox Church 89

Ethiopian Orthodox Tewahedo (Miaphysitic) Church 89

Ethiopian People's Revolutionary Democratic Front (EPRDF) 10, 11, 32, 37, 46; and 1995 Ethiopian Constitution 49; coalition of ethnically based parties 47, 49; and Communist Party of the Soviet Union (CPSU), compared 46–47; defeat of Soviet-Derg 37; dissolving of 54n12; and ethnically defined autonomous territories 51–52; Marxist-Leninist ideology 49; and TPLF 56; transformation of 108; view on constitutional grant of territorial autonomy 50, 58; view on right to establish new ethnically based territorial units 49–50; view on unity of state 58

Ethiopian People's Revolutionary Party (EPRP) 36, 37

Ethiopian Printing Corporation 94

Ethiopian Revolution 92

Ethiopian socialism, doctrine of 92

Ethiopian–Somali Border War 90, 97

Ethiopian sovereignty, recognition of 86

Ethiopian Student Movement (ESM) 30–31, 35

Ethiopic scripts 95, 101, 105

ethnically (ethnolinguistically) defined autonomous territorial units *see* autonomous regions/territories

ethnically defined union republics 19

ethnic demands 50–52

ethnic diversity 38, 39, 40, 46

ethnicity-based parties, right to national self-determination 52

ethnic Russians 5, 6

ethnolinguistically defined liberation movements 36–37

ethnolinguistic autonomy 87

ethnolinguistic diversity 6–7, 11

ethnolinguistic federalism: Austria-Hungary 15, 81, 82, 83, 91; Soviet 18, 57, 91, 101

ethnolinguistic nationalism 8, 12–13, 14

ethnolinguistic rights 59

ethnonyms 77, 78

ethnoterritorial (ethnolinguistic) federation 42–43, 46, 51–52, 59, 64–66; advantages 60; and constitutionalism 59; discontents 59–60

ethnoterritorial units, ownership of 44–48

136 Index

Eurasia 56, 65
European Communities (EC) 102
European Union (EU) 102

famines 92, 97
Federal Democratic Republic of Ethiopia 11, 39, 104
Federal Republic of Somalia 106
Federation of Bosnia and Herzegovina 102
Federation of Ethiopia and Eritrea 10, 11–12, 49, 88; administrative organization of 18; dissolution of 90; indigenization (nationality) policy 47; sustainability 52
Fetha Negast 23
feudalism, end of 93
five-year plan: first 89; second 90; third 91
forced labor camps 95
foreign investment 97; by China 106; rise of 106
foreign lecturers 97, 106, 108
France 12
French language, as medium of instruction 85
French nationalism 12, 13
French Revolutionary War 12
French Territory of Afars and the Issas 91, 95

Gambela 11, 18, 20, 42, 46, **71**
Gamo 104–105, 108
Gamo-Gofa Zone 44, 52, **74**, 108
Gamo Zone 108
GDP growth, in Ethiopia 107
Gedeo Zone **74**, 108
Ge'ez language 2, 3, 80, 83, 92
Gellner, Ernest 97
German Confederation 13
German Empire 13, 14, 81
German nationalism 12–13, 14
Germany, ethnolinguistic nationalism 8
Gizaw, Tilahun, assassination of 91
globalization 56
Gofa Zone 104–105, 108; *see also* Gamo-Gofa Zone
Gojjam Province 1, 91
Google Translate: addition of Amharic 106; addition of Somali 106

Gorbachev, Mikhail 100
governmental printing press, Ethiopia 82
Greater German Empire 13
Great Famine 81
Großdeutsche (Greater Germany) 13
Gurage (Kistane) 108

Habesha 20n2
Habsburg Monarchy 15
Hachalu Hundessa 50
Hadiya **74**, 108
Hadiya Zone **74**
Haile Selassie, Emperor 7, 10, 23, 83, 84; centralization policy 30; failure of coup against 90; and Israel 89–90; and learnings from Japan 24–25; and modernization 84; ratification of Federation Act 28; reformist 23; secondary school system 23–24, 84; service as regent 23–24; support to modern (Western-style) education expansion 23–24; visit to communist China 91
Haile Selassie University of Addis Ababa 90
Halaba Zone 44, **74**
Haramaya University 98
Harar 4, 82
Harari 11, **72**, 108
Harari language 92
Higher Constitutional Congress, Draft Constitution of 33
Hindi language 61
Hitler, Adolf 13
Hobsbawm, Eric 97
Holy Roman Empire 12, 13
Honecker, Erich 96
How Did Japan Modernize Itself? (book) 88
Hroch, Miroslav 98
human rights 28, 52
Hundessa, Hachalu 108

imagined communities (nations) 97
imperial system 56
imports and exports 106
India 18, 61
Indian lecturers 105
indigenization policy 32, 46, 47

Index   137

industrialization 97
inhabitants 4–6, 8, 20–21n4
internet, in Ethiopia: access to 106; as basis of independent mass media 105; internet users and language preference 108; partial or complete shutdowns policy 105
interwar Soviet Union 17, 20, 51, 57–58, **67**; ethnic diversity 39; ethnic federalization 11, 51; *korenizatsiia* policy 46, 58, 60
Invented Traditions 97
Islam, early expansion of 2
Islamic Courts Union 104, 105
Israel 89–90; Ethiopian Jews in 106; and Soviet-Derg regime 101
Italian East Africa 86
Italian occupation 86; Arabic as medium of instruction in Muslim areas 86; end of 86; erasure of name of Ethiopia from official use 86; Italian language use 86; local languages, promotion in administration and secondary education 86; modern transportation network 86; racial segregation 86
Italo-Ethiopian War 82
Italy: Battle of Adwa 4; Ethiopia's 1896 victory over 15
Iyasu, Lij 83

Japan 4, 7, 84; neologism 14; victory over the Russian Empire 24
Japanese Empire 7, 85
Japanese Imperial Constitution of 1889 *see* Meiji Constitution (1889)
Japanizers 24–25
Jesus, Afework Ghebre 83
Jimma College of Agriculture 100
Jimma Institute of Health Sciences 100
Jughashvili, Ioseb Besarionis dze 22n14

Kafa Zone 44, **74**, 108
Kamusella, Tomasz 78
Kamyr (Xamtanga) **70**, 108
Kautsky, Karl 17; and Austro-Marxism 83; *Nationalität und Internationalität* 83
Kebede Mikael 24, 88
Kebra Negast 23

Kemants 44
Kemant Special Woreda **70**
Kembata **74**, 108
Kenya 63
Kingdom of Kaf(f)a 54n9
Kleindeutschland ('Little Germany') 13
kolkhozes (peasant associations) 94, 98
Konsos 51–52
Konso Zone 44, 51, **75**, 108
Konta Special Woreda 44, **75**
korenizatsiia 17, 32, 45, 46, 54n4, 60, 62
Kulturnation 14
Kuraz Publishing Agency 94

landline telephones, access to 106
land reform 28
languages 9, 13, 15, 59–62, 78n3, 92; administration and educational system 44; employed as media of instruction during the Soviet-Derg's literacy campaigns 78n2; federal government usage 108; main languages 62; orality 62; policy 63; regional languages 61; standardization of indigenous languages 60; used in official capacity 108–109; *see also specific languages*
Latin alphabet 108
Latin-Ge'ez psalter (book) 80
League of Nations (LN) 7, 84
leftism 32–33
Lenin, Vladimir 15, 21n9, 35, 36, 49, 58, 77n1
Le Semeur d'Éthiopie ('Ethiopian Weekly') 82
Liberia 4
'Light and Peace' (newspaper) 24, 84
literacy campaign materials 98
literacy campaigns 94
literacy rate 93, 107

Mahdist War 4
Majang Zone 46, **71**, 108
Makonnen, Tafari 7
Maria Theresia thaler 87
Marx, Karl 15
Marxism and the National Question 17, 83

Marxism-Leninism 8, 31, 37, 51, 57, 93–96
Marxist-Leninist parties 35–36
Massawa 81
Meiji Constitution (1889) 8, 14, 25, 81, 85
Meiji Japan 14, 24, 56
MEISON (All-Ethiopia Socialist Movement) 36, 37
Mekonnen, Wallelign 91, 92
Menelik II, Emperor 4, 81; campaigns, 1889–1896 5; campaigns, 1897–1904 6; removal of ban on missionary activity 82
Mengistu Haile Mariam 9, 93, 100
Mensheviks 36
Miaphysitic Christians/Miaphysitism 5, 8, 21n7
military conquests 81
Ministry of Education, establishment of 85
minorities 96
missionary activities and schools 87; in Addis Ababa 82; civilizing mission 14, 65; and Menelik II, Emperor 82; preaching and teaching through Amharic language 87; and Yohannes IV, Emperor 81
mobile telephones, access to 106
Mohammed, Jawar 108
Muslim polities 2
Muslims 5, 6, 93
Muttersprache 14

Napoleonic War 12, 80
narod 17, 18, 38
narodnost' 17, 18
National Academy of the Amharic Language 92,
National Democratic Revolution of Ethiopia (NDRE) 8, 94
national histories 97
Nationalism and Social Communication (monograph) 88
Nationalität 15
nationalities 15, 18, 21n10; *see also specific ethnic groups*
nationality policy: Ethiopian 43, 46, 47, 57; Soviet 8, 21n10, 37–38, 46, 57, 77
nationalization process 94

national self-determination 8–9, 18, 107; under 1995 Constitution of Ethiopia 44, 46; constitutionally guaranteed right 58; and ethnicity-based parties 52; right to 35, 44, 52
national unity 31–32
nations 88, 97; ethnolinguistic definition of 99; and nationalities, distinction between 36
nations, nationalities and peoples 18, 39, 41–42, 53n2, 57–58
Nations, Nationalities and Peoples of Ethiopia, rights of 103
nation-states 12–13, 56, 97
natsional'nost' 17
Nazi 13
'New Era' (newspaper) 86
newspapers 24, 84, 86
Non-Aligned Movement 61
North Omotic language 104
North Omo Zone 104–105; local ethnic languages 104; protests 104–105
Nuer **72**, 108

October Revolution 36
officially recognized ethnic groups **68**
Ogaden 9, 88
Ogaden War 9, 96
Omotic peoples 108
'On the Question of Nationalities in Ethiopia' (essay) 91
Organization of African Unity (OAU) 90, 105
Oromia 11, 12, 47, 108
Oromia Zone 43, **72**
Oromo 63, 108
Oromo Democratic Party (ODP) 37, 46, 47
Oromo language 92
Oromo Muslims, uprisings 90
Oromo Wikipedia 105
Orthodox Christians 5
Ottoman Egypt 3, *3*, 12
Ottoman Empire 4; and Ethiopian Empire, compared 21n6; modernization 7
Ottoman Sultan 7

pan-Arabism 89–90
Peace and Democracy Conference (1991) 11

peace treaty (1947) 86
peace treaty (2018) 11, 106
peasant associations 93
People's Democratic Republic of Ethiopia 32, 57, 99, 100
Persia 4
Peter the Great 7
political democratization 58
political education, as compulsory subject in schools 96–97
postcommunist (Federal) Ethiopia 18, 37, 38, 101, 103
post-Soviet-Derg Ethiopia 57
poverty reduction, in Ethiopia 107
'Power to the Peoples' 92
printing presses 92, 94
prisons: Gulag-like system 95; *kolkhoz* based prisons 98
private entrepreneurship 100
Proclamation No. 7/1992 101
Prosperity Party (PP) 50, 52, 54n12, 54n13, 108
provisional military government 93
Prussia 13, 33n2, 80
public schools 24
publishing/publishing houses 82, 83, 94, 95, 100, 101
Puntland State of Somalia 104

Quranic schools (Islamic madrasas), language of instruction in 83

racial segregation, introduction of 86
radio broadcasting 85, 86
Red Terror 62, 95
reformists 24–25
regional states 61; governments and administrative institutions, monopolization of 47; own regional (state) constitutions 54n11
Republic of Djibouti 95
Republic of Kenya 90
Republic of Somaliland 100
Republic of Sudan 89, 106
Republika Srpska 102
revolutionary terror, completion of 95
Russian advisors 82
Russian Empire 4, 5, 7

Russian Federation 6
Russian language 59–60, 64
Russification 62
Russo-Japanese War 82

sacred laws (law codes) 23
Sanhit: books production in 81; printing press 81
secessionism 30, 49
Selasse, Heruy Wellde 85
Sellase, Heruy Welde 24
Semitic-speaking ethnic group of Amharas 2
separate regions (states), proposals for creation of 107
Serate Mengist 23
Serbia 60
Serbs 102
Sheka Zone **75**
Shewa 1, 2
Shola 91
Siam (Thailand) 4, 84
Sidamas 52, 108
Sidama Zone 43, 52, **75**, 108
Silte Zone **75**
Silti **75**, 108
slavery, abolishment of 87
socialism 48, 57, 92
social media usage 106
Social Preconditions of National Revival in Europe (monograph) 98
Somalia 4, 9, 92; as client state of communist China 96; and Ethiopia 96; fragmentation of 100; national language of 92; northeastern Somalia 104; southern Somalia, under control of Islamic Courts Union 104; and Soviet Union 96
Somali Civil War 100
Somali Democratic Republic 91
Somali language 9, 11, 63, 64, 108; adoption of the Latin alphabet for writing 92; as working language of federal government 108
Somali Muslims, uprisings 90
Somali Republic 89
Somali-Soviet Friendship Treaty, termination of 96
Somali Wikipedia 108
Source of Light, The (book) 85

Southern Ethiopian People's Democratic Movement (SEPDM) 37
Southern Nations, Nationalities and Peoples Region 11, 41–44, 47, 51, **72**, 78, 107
southern Somalia, Ethiopia's intervention in 105
southern Tigray 1
South Ethiopian Peoples' Democratic Movement (SEPDM) 46, 47
South Omo Zone **75**, 77
South Sudan 106
Soviet-Derg regime 8–11, 21n8, 21n11, 32–33, 36, 56, 57, 61, 93–94; adoption of Stalin's definition of nation 94; Amharic speaking peasants resettlement 98; Amharization of south 98; campaign for spreading literacy and progress 93; campaigns of villagization and resettlement 97–98; criticism of communist China 96; foreign companies, nationalization of 97; foreign investment, need for 97; and imprisonment and execution of students 95; and Israel 101; Jews, attracted to Addis Ababa 101; literacy campaigns 102; Muslims' rights under 93; nomadic communities settlement 98; pastoralist communities settlement 98; student opposition to 95; weapons and supplies from Soviet Bloc 96
Soviet-Derg Revolution 28
Soviet ethnolinguistic federalism *see* ethnolinguistic federalism
Soviet Union 7, 10, 17, 35, 51, 58–59, 96; affirmative action 45; autonomous okrugs 41, 43; communism 39; dissolution of 101; distribution of state powers 42; economic practice of central planning 89; establishment of ethnoterritorial units 45; ethnic diversity 38; ethnolinguistic (ethnoterritorial) federalism 83; ethnoterritorial empowerment 45; indigenization/nativization policy 45; *korenizatsiia* (indigenization) policy 46, 58; nationality policy 8–9, 57; postwar 9, **19**, 38, 64, **67**; republican communist parties 47; socialism 47; *see also* interwar Soviet Union
Staatnation 14
Stalin, Joseph 17, 21n9, 35, 36, 47, 58, 83, 91, 99
statehood models 1
State of Southern Nations, Nationalities and Peoples (SNNP) 44, 47, 51, 52
'Story from My Mind, A' (novel) 83
Struggle (student magazine) 91
students: activism 30–31; attendance in state schools 85, 90; 'ethnic' liberation movements, support for 95; imprisonment and execution of 95; massacre, during Gizaw funeral 91; opposition to Soviet-Derg regime 95; protests 95, 104–105; in war against Eritrea 95
subregional autonomous territorial units 43
Swahili 63

Teferi Mekonnen *see* Haile Selassie, Emperor
Tekle Hawariat Tekle Mariyam 7, 25, 26, 27
television broadcasting, commencement of 92
ten-year plan of development 98
Terence, Ranger 97
terminology of ethnolinguistic nationalism 12–20, **16**
territorial ethnolinguistic autonomy 17–18, 21n11, 77; *see also* autonomous regions/territories
Tewahedo 21n7
Tewodros II, Emperor 2–3, 80; centralization of state 81; separation of state from church 81
thalers 87
Tigray 9, 11, 47, **76**; ethnolinguistic autonomy for 87; famine in 89, 91, 97
Tigray People's Liberation Front (TPLF) 10, 37, 38, 46, 52, 54n13; and EPRDF 56; Marxism-Leninism ideology 57; and Prosperity Party 50
Tigre language 92

Index   141

Tigrinya 63, **76**, 108
Tigrinya language 92; first printed book in 81; as working language of federal government 108
Tigrinya Wikipedia 105
Tigriyans 4
totalitarianism 62
Transitional Charter 101
Transitional Government of Ethiopia 101
Trust Territory of Somaliland, independence of 89

Uganda 4
unitary ethnolinguistic nation-state, Ethiopia as **67**, 81, 85
United Kingdom: handing over Eritrea to Ethiopia 88; and returning of Ogaden administration 88
United Nations (UN) 28; Ethiopia as a founding member 87; Universal Declaration on Human Rights (UDHR) 11, 28, 33, 88
United States: military facilities in Ethiopia 96; and naming of Ethiopia 84; and Somalia 96
universal suffrage 89
university and higher education institutions 95, 105, 106, 108; closure of 93; Indian lecturers 105; politicization of students of 90; recruitment from abroad, need for 105; student's demonstration 90–91, 93
University College of Addis Ababa 88, 90
university-level staff 97
University of Asmara 91
university staff 92
uprisings (revolts) 87, 90, 103, 104–105

Van der Beken, Christophe 78
villagization and resettlement, campaigns of 97–98
Volk 13, 14
Volksstamm 15, 17

Wag Hemra Zone 43
Wallelign Mekonnen 31–32
Warsaw Pact, dissolution of 101
Wello 1, 97
Western Europe 14
Western models, adoption of 7, 65
Western weaponry and military technologies 82
Wikipedia articles, in Ethiopian languages 108
WoGaGoDa (Wagagoda) language 104–105, 107
WoGaGoDa (Wagagoda) Region 107
Wolayita Zone 44, **76**, 104–105, 108
Workers' Party of Ethiopia (WPE) 9, 97
Woyane Uprising (Rebellion) 87

Yem Special Woreda 44, **76**
Yohannes IV, Emperor 3; ban on missionary activities 81; reconstruction of centralized state institutions 81
Yosef, Ovadiah 92
Young Ethiopians 84
Yugoslavia 18, 60; dissolution of 101; succession 60

Zemecha (Campaign) for literacy and progress, end of 95
Zewditu, Empress 7, 83
Zhou Enlai 90

For Product Safety Concerns and Information please contact our EU representative GPSR@taylorandfrancis.com
Taylor & Francis Verlag GmbH, Kaufingerstraße 24, 80331 München, Germany

www.ingramcontent.com/pod-product-compliance
Lightning Source LLC
Chambersburg PA
CBHW051748230426
43670CB00012B/2205